How Can I Be Trusted?

feminist constructions

Series Editors: Hilde Lindemann Nelson and Sara Ruddick

Feminist Constructions publishes accessible books that send feminist ethics in promising new directions. Feminist ethics has excelled at critique, identifying masculinist bias in social practice and in the moral theory that is used to justify that practice. The series continues the work of critique, but its emphasis falls on construction. Moving beyond critique, the series aims to build a positive body of theory that extends feminist moral understandings.

Feminists Doing Ethics
   edited by Peggy DesAutels and Joanne Waugh

Gender Struggles: Practical Approaches to Contemporary Feminism
   edited by Constance L. Mui and Julien S. Murphy

"Sympathy and Solidarity" and Other Essays
   by Sandra Lee Bartky

The Subject of Violence: Arendtean Exercises in Understanding
   by Bat-Ami Bar On

How Can I Be Trusted? A Virtue Theory of Trustworthiness
   by Nancy Nyquist Potter

Moral Contexts
   by Margaret Urban Walker

Recognition, Responsibility, and Rights: Feminist Ethics & Social Theory
   edited by Robin N. Fiore and Hilde Lindemann Nelson

The Philosopher Queen: Feminist Essays on War, Love, and Knowledge
   by Chris Cuomo

The Subject of Care: Feminist Perspectives on Dependency
   by Eva Kittay and Ellen K. Feder

Forthcoming books in the series by:

Anita Allen; Amy Baehr; Maria Lugones; Joan Mason-Grant; Diana Tietjens Meyers; and Robin Schott.

How Can I Be Trusted?

A Virtue Theory of Trustworthiness

Nancy Nyquist Potter

ROWMAN & LITTLEFIELD PUBLISHERS, INC.
Lanham • Boulder • New York • Oxford

ROWMAN & LITTLEFIELD PUBLISHERS, INC.

Published in the United States of America
by Rowman & Littlefield Publishers, Inc.
A Member of the Rowman & Littlefield Publishing Group
4720 Boston Way, Lanham, Maryland 20706
www.rowmanlittlefield.com

12 Hid's Copse Road
Cumnor Hill, Oxford OX2 9JJ, England

British Library Cataloguing in Publication Information Available

Library of Congress Cataloging-in-Publication Data

Potter, Nancy Nyquist, 1954-
How can I be trusted? : a virtue theory of trustworthiness / Nancy Nyquist Potter.
p. cm. – (Feminist constructions)
Includes bibliographical references and index.
ISBN 0-7425-1150-2 (cloth : alk. paper) – ISBN 0-7425-1151-0 (pbk. : alk. paper)
1. Trust. 2. Reliability. I. Title. II. Series.
BJ1500.T78 P68 2002
179'.9—dc21

2002008056

Θ™ The paper used in this publication meets the minimum requirements of American
National Standard for Information Sciences—Permanence of Paper for Printed Library
Materials, ANSI/NISO Z39.48-1992.

Contents

Acknowledgments

Many friends, colleagues, and students have been part of the development of this book, and I thank all who have been willing to share their experiences and think through ideas with me. They have sharpened my thinking and deepened my reflections, making theorizing much richer and more fun than it would otherwise have been.

The writings of Annette Baier and Maria Lugones provided a backbone for this project, and I am indebted to their work. My mother Marian Nyquist has been my lifelong literary companion, sharing the delights of fiction with me and legitimizing fiction as a valuable resource for moral insights. Karen Heegaard, Judy Martin, and Clancy Potter each contributed in important ways to my thinking about trustworthiness, and I am grateful for the many things they have taught me and the ongoing support they have given me for this project. Naomi Scheman's enthusiasm for this work, her keen insights, and marvelous ability to engage in explorations of trust have been absolutely vital to my thinking, and I cannot thank her enough. I remain grateful to Norman Dahl for planting the seed of interest in virtue ethics and for nurturing me along despite the twists and turns my work has taken.

Earlier versions of chapters or portions of chapters have appeared previously in the following journals, and I am grateful to publishers for granting me permission to draw on that material in this book: "Giving Uptake," Social Theory and Practice, vol. 26, no. 3, p. 479-508 (Fall 2000); "Discretionary Power, Lies, and Broken Trust: Justification and Discomfort, " Theoretical Medicine and Bioethics, vol. 17, no. 4, p. 329-352 (1996); "The Severed Head and Existential Dread: The Classroom as Epistemic Community and Student Surviviors of Incest," Hypatia, vol. 10, no. 2, p. 69-92 (1995); and

"Terrorists, Hostages, Victims, and 'The Crisis Team': A 'Who's Who' Puzzle," *Hypatia*, vol. 14, no. 3, p. 126-156 (1999.)

Arthur Caplan, Marilyn Frye, Toni McNaron, Anne Phibbs, and many others commented on early versions of chapters or gave helpful comments at conferences. Eileen John and John Sadler have read portions of this manuscript and provided many insights and good suggestions. Hilde Nelson and Sara Ruddick have been wonderfully diligent, critical, and timely as editors. They have read each chapter in its entirety, commenting, questioning, challenging, and making interesting and helpful connections. This book is greatly improved because of their efforts. Lastly, I want to thank all those in my kinship system who have contributed to my understanding and articulation of trust and trustworthiness, especially Robert Kimball, whose embodiment of good character and moral effort are exemplary.

Introduction

In the work that follows, I offer a theory of trustworthiness that takes into account relations of power. It addresses one of the most central issues in our lives—experiences of trust and distrust—from a philosophical, psychological, sociological, and political perspective. I have set this discussion within virtue theory, for reasons that will begin to emerge as I make these introductory remarks and become clear in subsequent chapters. There are two main reasons why I chose this topic to write about. The first has to do with historical treatments of the subject in the field of philosophy, and the second has to do with a certain vision of what ethics is.

Trust (which I took as my starting point when embarking on this project) is a topic that, until fairly recently, has been largely neglected in moral philosophy. Plato and Aristotle merely mention it, although the virtues of justice and friendship, as both philosophers define them, seem to rely upon background conditions of trust. With some exceptions, such as discussions of trust in God (Aquinas) or trust in governments (Locke, Dunn), the moral significance of trusting relationships has not been directly addressed in philosophical discourse. Furthermore, the infrequent modern philosophical discussions of trust have tended to analyze it in terms of game theory—such as preference schedules or motivations to cooperate (see B. Williams 1988)—or to cast trust in terms of contracts and promises. As Annette Baier states,

> modern moral philosophy has concentrated on the morality of fairly cool relationships between those who are deemed to be roughly equal in power to determine the rules and to instigate sanctions against rule breakers. It is not surprising, then, that the main form of trust that any attention has been given to is trust in governments, and in parties to voluntary agreements to do what they have

agreed to do. The domination of contemporary moral philosophy by the so-called Prisoner's Dilemma problem displays most clearly this obsession with moral relations between minimally trusting, minimally trustworthy adults who are equally powerful. (Baier 1986, 249-52)

Political scientists, sociologists, and thinkers in other disciplines are beginning to contribute more complex and nuanced discussions of the concept of trust as it applies to citizenship and democracy (see Cook 2001; Warren 1999; Sztompka 1999; Seligman 1997). But philosophical treatments of trust that depart from standard fare are still uncommon. Annette Baier, Lorraine Code, and Trudy Govier are notable exceptions to this way of framing philosophical considerations of trust. Each of them has offered important contributions to discussions of trust, and I draw heavily on Baier and Code, in particular, in my own work. At the same time, the practical nature of the subject, the variety of contexts in which trustworthiness needs to be explored, and the insights I have found in writings from other fields have lent this work a multidisciplinary flavor, clustering especially in fields of moral psychology, political theory, and peace and conflict resolution.

Baier explains that trust is taken for granted until it is called into question, which may in part explain its relative absence from much of moral discourse. Of course, not everyone takes trust for granted; as I will argue, how trusting one is, and the ease with which one can assume trust, has much to do with one's sociopolitical situatedness as it intersects with one's narrative history. That the topic of trust is finding a more central place in moral discourse may have something to do with an increasing climate of social distrust that brings to our attention what was formerly overlooked or assumed. In contemporary pluralistic societies, the notion of a shared conception of the good seems to be particularly threatened; the fragmentation of society into communities and identities may, in part, help create pockets of trusting relationships, but paradoxically it may also, in part, fuel distrust through our inability to cope with difference. Increased attention to trust as an interpersonal and social phenomenon may also arise out of some criticisms of modern moral theory, such as a tendency to overvalue impartiality and to devalue personal attachments, family relations, and the ways in which we do and should care about ourselves and others both politically and personally (Blum 1980; Code 1987; Gilligan 1982; Okin 1989; Tronto 1993). Whatever the explanations are for the relative neglect of this topic and the resurgence of interest (and there are likely to be a number of factors involved), it seems clear that philosophical discourse has generally not given enough, or the right kind of, attention to the role that trust plays in our lives. There has been even less emphasis on what it means to be trustworthy to others. Problems of trust, when addressed, tend to take the perspective of the vulnerable (Whom should I trust? When is it reasonable to trust? How can I be sure my trust won't be betrayed?) and to ask with far less frequency how we might live our lives as trustworthy people. The self-examining question "Why don't some people trust me?" is hardly ever asked—at least, it's seldom asked by those in positions of power with regard to the less powerful. Oppressed persons often ask that question in reference to their oppressors, but their voices are also less often found in philosophical literature. In reviewing the literature on this subject and in examining problems in trust in actual communities, I became aware that, when trust is not framed as a pragmatic, game-theoretic problem or a contractual device, it seems to be most often framed from the perspective of the potential victims of betrayal. Both perspectives suggest the deep concern (anxiety, even) that philosophers and nonphilosophers alike have about being betrayed. Those perspectives, although important ones, also carry with them a tendency to shift questions about trust from ones of responsibility-taking to ones of reasonable risk-taking. This project refocuses the subject of trust by making central our responsibility to be trustworthy. The shifting-back of the responsibility—to ask ourselves what we can do to be trustworthy—is a way of moving out of adversarial frameworks where conflicts in trust may evoke defensive reactions. But theorizing about trustworthiness doesn't mean that I depart from questions of trust, because the two concepts are related: trust is the normative concept that provides the counterpoint to this investigation into trustworthiness.

The second reason why I am writing on trustworthiness has to do with what I take to be the project of ethics. Although it can be deeply rewarding, for its own sake, to engage in contemplation or study, and it can be delightful to experience how well one's mind can play with abstract ideas, I hold the view that the purpose of inquiry into ethics is not merely to experience the pleasures of solving moral problems at the theoretical level. As Aristotle says, "the purpose of our examination is not to know what virtue is, but to become good, since otherwise the inquiry would be of no benefit to us" (Aristotle 1985, 1103b26). That discussions of trust have so frequently neglected the question of how we can become trustworthy seems to me an indictment of much of moral inquiry. In both deontological and consequentialist moral theories, rules or principles predominate, and although one might be able to generate dispositions important to rule-following, rules or principles are taken to be the ultimate guides to morality. MacIntyre argues that the emphasis on rules and rule-following is distinctively modern:

> Ronald Dworkin has recently argued that the central doctrine of modern liberalism is the thesis that questions about the good life for man or the needs of human

life are to be regarded from the public standpoint as systematically unsettlable. In arguing thus Dworkin has, I believe, identified a stance characteristic not just of liberalism but of modernity. Rules become the primary concept of the moral life. Qualities of character then generally come to be pursued only because they will lead us to follow the right set of rules. (MacIntyre 1984, 119)

Theories of right action that take following rules or principles to be the path to morality do not adequately address the complex issues involved in trusting others and being trustworthy to them. Rules can tell us how to regard promises and how to act concerning contracts, but trust as a social, moral, psychological, and political component of our lives is much broader than that. This project takes as a starting point that virtue ethics provides a clarity and richness to our thinking about trustworthiness; the wisdom of that path will become clear as my work unfolds.

Furthermore, many modern moral theorists make a distinction between actions that are obligatory (one must do x and it would be wrong not to do x) and actions that are supererogatory (it is morally permissible to do x and it would be good to do x, but it would not be morally wrong not to do x). Virtue ethics typically lacks such a distinction. Rather, it tells us what is involved in being a certain sort of good person, and our responsibility is to keep such dispositional features in mind and strive toward them. Being fully trustworthy requires that we exhibit a disposition to be a certain sort of person, and the features or characteristics of a person who displays full trustworthiness are not "above and beyond" the virtue but integral to it.[1]

Framing moral questions in terms of virtue ethics puts dispositions, and not rules, at the center. This way of framing virtue in general, and trustworthiness in particular, suggests a way of thinking about morality that highlights the self as social and political, as later chapters will detail. Along with modern moral systems that focus on rules and right actions, a certain conception of the self has emerged—the modern democratized self which "has no necessary social content and no necessary social identity" (MacIntyre 1984, 205). This view of the self is an important or integral component of theories of right action, because most of them presuppose and require the impartial and autonomous moral agent. In contrast to that view, numerous writers have argued that the self is situated and inherently social, a view that I hold and will discuss in later chapters. This means that, because we are historical and social selves, we are never simply individuals learning to be good. Individual virtue is integrally bound up with the virtue of the state and its institutions. Aristotle makes this point. Each person, he says, has happiness in proportion to his excellence and wisdom, and the happy state is that which is best and does right actions rightly. But neither individual nor state can do right actions without excellence and wisdom. Therefore, virtues, whether those of the state or of the individual, have the same form and nature (Aristotle 1984, 1323b30). Aristotle goes on to say that some things are a matter of luck for the state but that other things are the responsibility of the legislators to provide:

> And therefore we can only say: may our state be constituted in such a manner as to be blessed with the goods of which fortune disposes (for we acknowledge her power): whereas excellence and goodness in the state are not a matter of chance but the result of knowledge and choice. A city can be excellent only when the citizens who have a share in the government are excellent, and in our state all the citizens share in the government; let us then inquire how a man becomes excellent. For even if we could suppose the citizen body to be excellent, without each of them being so, yet the latter would be better, for in the excellence of each the excellence of all is involved. (1332a27-38)

Aristotle has a truncated and distorted view of *whose* individual virtue it is that is in dynamic relation with institutional structures. But he's certainly right that luck—good or bad—plays a role in virtue. Institutionalized privilege, stratified social systems, economic inequalities, and power imbalances may be a matter of knowledge and choice, but the circumstances we are born into and the opportunities our lives afford are in fortune's hands (see Rawls 1971, 7; Nagel 1979; and Card 1990 for discussions of the relation of luck to moral responsibility). The point I take from Aristotle's passage is that the organization of society can encourage or limit individuals' ability to be moral, as it can enhance or diminish trust. This theory of trustworthiness, then, isn't either a bottom-up one (we extend trust from particular associations to the public domain) or a top-down one (we arrange social institutions properly and proper trust will follow). Ancient Chinese teachings of virtue did emphasize the bottom-up approach (Ta hsueh 1943), and one can find that view lingering today. But I agree with Jean Cohen that trust in government isn't simply a matter of "generalized trust" from individuals to institutions (Cohen 1999, 220). Trust in civil society and in the state are mediated by institutionalized norms, by policies and practices, by collective identities, and by symbolic fields. I would add that not only civil society and the state are so mediated; even intimate relationships bear the marks of institutional norms and social practices. Some of this mediating is good; norms, for example, can provide mechanisms by which entrenched particularist and partialist attitudes are nudged out of dogmatism (221). But norms and practices can also become mechanisms of control. This is why democratic processes at every level of interaction are so crucial to trust: they allow for contestations of the values and practices embodied in our institutions and arrangements. As Cohen writes, "democracy goes with trust and civic initiative or engagement to the degree to which institutions (political and otherwise) exist that are receptive to the influence and/or input of collective actors in an appropriate way" (223). A virtue theoretic approach to trustworthiness fits well with the view that practices and institutions are in dynamic interplay with the individuals whose trust in one another and in complex social systems is sometimes given, sometimes withheld. In today's world, where inequality, exploitation, and multiple oppressions are both everyday and systematic occurrences, distrust is endemic to many people's lives; for others whose lives are relatively insulated by privilege and luck, trust is often assumed or considered to be for the most part unproblematic. Framing questions of trustworthiness in terms of virtue ethics, then, requires that I set this discussion in consideration of diverse people whose lives unfold in the context of social and political structures, institutions, and practices.

Although I draw on Aristotle's writings, I am not claiming the virtue ethic I offer to be Aristotelian. My work is also distinct from Michael Slote's virtue theory of caring that draws on Hume and Hutchinson (2001). Rather than arguing for an agent-based virtue ethics, as Slote does, I argue that being trustworthy is a matter of a *relation between* moral agents and that it doesn't quite make sense, when it comes to this virtue, to talk about "the moral agent" and her motivations as if they are independent of particular trust relations. My work on trustworthiness is its own brand of virtue ethics, with the primary focus on the virtue of trustworthiness rather than virtue theory in general. That said, I will point out that the method of inquiry I follow is, roughly, Aristotelian. After he gives a general account of virtue and introduces the Doctrine of the Mean, Aristotle says that "we must not only state this general account but also apply it to the particular cases" (1985, 1107a28). "Let us take up the virtues again," Aristotle says, "and discuss each singly. Let us say what they are, what sorts of thing they are concerned with, and how they are concerned with them" (1115a5). This is the task I take up regarding the virtue of trustworthiness. Thus I take what look like puzzles in particular cases and examine them to see what the common beliefs are and how one should reason through them to see what this virtue would look like if exhibited in this situation.

The outline of the book is as follows. I first set out an initial theoretical framework, and then I examine particular contexts in which power differentials between and among individuals affect trusting relationships. With each case study, different aspects of trustworthiness will be foregrounded; I identify and clarify the particular issues involved and articulate ways in which various persons can become trustworthy. The concluding chapter offers an extended discussion of one virtue I take to be closely related to trustworthiness and then pulls together the central ideas of the book. In chapter 1, I set out Annette Baier's and H. J. N. Horsburgh's accounts of trust and show how the features of trust lead to a definition of what it means to be trustworthy. To trust someone is to allow him or her the opportunity to care for (in the sense of taking care of) something we value. I discuss epistemological, pragmatic, and moral aspects of trust and show how placing trust in another changes relations of power in that the trusting person becomes vulnerable to another with respect to that valued thing. I discuss failures of trust and betrayals of trust as different kinds of problems in trust. Then I argue that our moral responsibility to cultivate trust leads to the need for us to cultivate a trustworthy character, and I set out a definition of trustworthiness and further features that we must exhibit if we are to be fully trustworthy. These include, for example, that we develop sensitivity to the particularities of others, that we recognize the importance of being trustworthy to the disenfranchised and oppressed, and that we develop other virtues. Finally, this chapter marks a distinction between specific trustworthiness (being trustworthy with respect to some good) and full trustworthiness (the expression of the full virtue), a distinction that I follow up on in the next chapter.

In chapter 2, I highlight the connection between being trustworthy and having discretionary power, a concept of Baier's that I expand on. Mainstream moral theory tends to view lying as justifiable under certain conditions and, if those conditions are satisfied, one who has lied is considered not to have betrayed a trust. A lie that can be justified, then, doesn't call into question the character of the person who lied. But that view neglects problems in trust that can arise in a relationship where a lie has been told. This position frequently arises within the context of medicine, and so I critically examine the notion of a justified lie in light of virtue ethics as I have set it out in chapter 1. This task requires that I critically discuss one of the central concerns for bioethics, that of practitioner discretionary power. I argue that, even when a lie is justified, questions of a practitioner's trustworthiness remain. The conclusion suggests that considerations of practitioner trustworthiness should be moved to a more central place in both theory and practice. This analysis also suggests that some prevalent moral theories may be inadequate in that they insufficiently attend to trustworthiness.

The focus in chapter 3 is on what it means to be trustworthy when one is in what I call a "mid-level" position of power; that is, when one has responsibilities and/or loyalties toward people whom one is serving while at the same time one is accountable (and expected to be trustworthy) to the institution or agency for which one is working. I draw on my experience as a crisis counselor in this chapter and show how various policies and practices within an institution can push us more or less toward trustworthiness. A central component of this chapter involves the unpacking of a dominant ideological framework that underlies the practices of many social service and public service providers. I argue that, in the case I examine, the policies themselves need to be critically assessed. The time to engage in that sort of thing is prior to future urgent and critical situations, as that is the time when crisis counselors are better positioned to reflect on the possibility of their participation in systems of domination and to implement changes. Chapter 4 addresses questions of epistemic responsibility and what is involved in being trustworthy with respect to a particular oppressed group when one is in an institutional role. I take up this question by examining the role of the teacher with respect to student survivors of childhood sexual abuse. Student survivors of childhood sexual abuse are not homogeneous and so teachers would be in error to assume too great a degree of similarity in responses to earlier abuse. However, clinical research identifies some common themes among survivors, and teachers will benefit by becoming aware of the effects on survivors' learning ability in the classroom. To this end, I review and discuss relevant research on survivors' experiences and coping mechanisms and state some of the ways in which difficulties that are a result of childhood abuse can show up in the classroom. I argue that it is part of being a good teacher to create a space in which survivors' experiences can be taken up in a morally and epistemically responsible manner. This claim entails that the teacher cultivate trustworthiness in relation to her students while she attends to the dynamics of knowledge, power, and trust in the classroom. Because teachers usually face diverse student populations with varying relations to power and authority, teachers face a formidable task in trying to be trustworthy in ways that take into account the complex and overlapping oppressions that students bring to the classroom. I discuss some ways that teachers can indicate trustworthiness to oppressed student populations.

In chapter 5, I turn my attention to relations of trust between intimates by considering friends, couples, and lovers. My view is that relations of power virtually always infuse even our most intimate relations, so thinking about what it means to be trustworthy, with its attention to nondomination and nonexploitation, is central to intimacy as well as to civic life. Many of the features of trustworthiness are relevant in intimate contexts as well. In addition, being trustworthy to our intimate friends and lovers involves ways of being that are specific to intimacy. The concept I focus on in chapter 5 is that of connection. I argue that connection is crucial to genuine intimacy and thus to being a trustworthy intimate. In previous chapters, a theme emerges that trustworthiness is part of a family of virtues that require the development of social and civic dispositions and that many of the virtues work together to better develop our character and our relationships. In the last chapter, I link an earlier argument that being trustworthy requires that we attend to injustices and work toward creating a more just society with the claim that being trustworthy requires that one pay attention to others in their particularity. I do this by concentrating on democratic dialogue and interaction. I argue that being trustworthy involves a responsiveness to others' speech acts and silences. This kind of responsiveness is suggested by Austin's notion of "uptake"; I elaborate on that concept and show how giving uptake can enhance trustworthiness and play a role in promoting just and peaceful relations. I conclude this chapter and the book by bringing together the main themes of the theory and drawing out some implications for future theorizing.

There are many contexts in which trust and failures of trust play a central role in our life experiences, and over time I have become more aware and appreciative of the ways in which my own life has been shaped by the fabric of trust. As a friend, as a lover, as a crisis counselor for a large metropolitan agency, as a student and then a teacher in the academy, as a daughter and then a parent, as a sister, and as white woman in a feminist community, I have been part of relationships that have highlighted both the value of trust and trustworthiness and the wrenching anguish of trust gone wrong. But for all the reading, reflection, and experience that have gone into this work, it is necessarily incomplete. While I think that the logical structure of trust does lead to conclusions about the moral responsibility not to exploit the truster's vulnerability, I recognize ways that my perspective and values inform my theorizing. I am committed to the view that ending domination, exploitation, and violence must be a primary goal for social action and that our character is compromised to the extent that we are complicit in maintaining inequalities and practices that breed violence. I readily acknowledge that many more voices must be added before a fuller picture of trustworthiness emerges. This book is as much an invitation to engage in further dialogue as it is a presentation of a theory.

The relative openness of this brand of virtue theory is one of its appeals. Virtue must be particularized; it cannot be universalized; it is relative to situations and persons yet is not wholly subjective. Trustworthiness, too, has some basic features but cannot be specified in ways that fit all situations or would offer guiding principles. A virtue theoretic framework for trustworthiness, therefore—because it emphasizes ways of being that are contextual and grounded in feeling as well as reasoning—provides a solid ground by which we can begin to perceive various harms and vices in the world and to become people who, together, can create a flourishing society with flourishing members.

NOTES

1. Michael Slote sees this as a problem, especially for Aristotelian virtue ethics, and his book *Morals From Motives* (2001) offers a theory of virtue that leaves room for supererogation.

1

A Virtue Theory of Trustworthiness

In Susan Dodd's novel *The Mourner's Bench* (1998), Pamela is a college student with a terrific imagination. Given a writing assignment to present a defense of a position based on personal experience, Pamela writes an impassioned anti-childbearing essay that draws on an elaborate fantasy about experiences with her midwife-grandmother. Later, she is playing the piano when Wim, her professor and the narrator in this passage, asks her where she learned to play.

> "I didn't, yet," she said. "But my grandma got me started."
> "The midwife?"
> "Oh, Lord." She laughed again. "You New England folks do surely hold tight to a tale. I reckon it's the noble suffering you're so fond of." She looked up at me coyly. "I still got you believin' that bull-dinky?"
> "I am a trusting man," I said, then immediately regretted what seemed too candid a remark. "I'm not in the habit of expecting my students to lie to me."
> "Trust's nothing to count on," she said. "A body could hardly pick worse, in fact." (Dodd 1998, 80)

Pamela is right that trust is a risky endeavor. Yet surely she's too cynical; the world would be an impoverished place indeed were everyone to adopt her view as a principle. It's hard to imagine how societies would survive without some degree of trust in political institutions, bartering systems, civic relationships, and kin. Wim comes off as the more likable fellow, even though he may be more trusting than is wise. Being able to trust in others softens us and leaves us open not only to hurt and disappointment but to love and friendship. It makes everyday living easier, too, as we navigate the messy terrain of catching buses and airplanes, working our jobs, reading maps and recipes, talking on the telephone. Being neither too guarded nor too trusting works well for us as a general rule. But Wim is also right that revealing ourselves as trusting souls tells more about us than just that we can be conned. Trust comes harder to those whom life has taught hard lessons. Wim is lucky, and he's had a fairly privileged life. Pamela's experiences growing up as female and poor have taught her to be wary of trusting others. Both of them would do well to find a middle ground between trust and distrust—one that is responsive to context, positionality, and particularity.

Moral knowledge, for us as well as for Wim or Pamela, must be practical and not merely theoretical. I take the central question in morality to be how we are to become morally good persons, so the impulse behind theorizing about trust and trustworthiness is a desire to inquire into and convey ideas about how to become trustworthy and not merely to acquire knowledge of what trustworthiness is. Because trustworthiness is both a characteristic we look for in others and a moral virtue we need to develop in ourselves, a theory of trustworthiness should indicate what is involved in being trustworthy as well as address questions of who should and should not be trusted and what they should be trusted with. In this chapter, I present the framework for a theory of trustworthiness that focuses on the notion of *character*.

Until fairly recently, philosophical discourse has tended to overlook the importance of trust to our personal, political, and institutional relationships. Annette Baier has argued that philosophers, while sometimes including trust as a feature in the moral domain, have tended to emphasize contractual relations and promises (Baier 1986, 249-52). Although contracts and promises are one aspect of the concept of trust, such a narrow focus is not sufficient to give a helpful and adequate account of trust as an operative moral, social, and psychological component of our everyday lives. When we try to determine the trustworthiness of someone, we attempt to "reach a sense of the whole person and his or her integrity and competence"—a claim that highlights the centrality of character to trust (Govier 1991, 18). To the extent that theories of right action do not sufficiently attend to questions about what it takes to be a certain sort of person, such theories would seem to be inadequate to develop a rich account of trustworthiness. Theorizing about trustworthiness requires not only that we examine relations of trust from the perspective of right actions but also that we consider ways in which each of us can enhance proper trust and ease pervasive distrust. I will argue that the best way to do this is to cultivate a trustworthy character.

Not only is the scope of this subject broad, but its field is in constant flux and motion; it is not surprising, therefore, that the concept of trustworthiness eludes straightforward analytic presentation. Phenomenologically, trust is a dynamic relation involving the complex and interwoven perspectives of the truster, the one trusted, the object of one's trust, etc., and philosophical discussions of trust and trustworthiness must be contextualized with regard to these particulars. Furthermore, considerations of when one ought to trust, whom one should trust, and what one is trusting in are integrally bound up with questions of what it means to be trustworthy as people who are variously positioned relative to power and privilege. The complex and contextual nature of this subject, therefore, makes it difficult to separate out the component parts for analysis. Yet I must begin somewhere, so I will start with an initial description of what trust is. In the first sections, I will show how the features of trust lead to a definition of what it means to be trustworthy and that our moral responsibility to cultivate trust leads to the need to cultivate a trustworthy character. The third section sets out the virtue of trustworthiness, drawing on a notion of character virtue. The next section raises questions about the relationship between failures of trust and untrustworthiness, focusing on the role of expectations and inferences in cases of possible betrayal and distrust, and introducing the idea of taking prima facie responsibility for the distrust of others. The last section identifies several additional features of trustworthiness that refine and clarify the initial definition. We are fully trustworthy to the extent that we exhibit these features.

STARTING POINT: DEFINITION AND DESCRIPTION OF TRUST

Annette Baier's illuminating analysis of trust provides a framework within which we can begin to explore problems and possibilities of trusting relations in a more specific context (Baier 1986). Trust, according to Baier, is a cooperative activity in which we engage so that we can assist one another in the care of goods. We trust others when we allow them the opportunity to care for (in the sense of *taking care of*) something we value. We all have to trust others, to some extent, because we cannot, by ourselves, take care of everything that is of value to us. Trust may be unconscious or unwanted; it may not be explicit, but it is possible (though not always easy) to say what, specifically, one is and is not entrusting another with.

We trust in things as well as in people, of course. When we trust in things, we base it on judgments of ascribed pre-given properties of the thing and the trust is, in a sense, a priori. With people, our trust is a posteriori, based on experience (Harre 1999). In both cases, it is persons who are doing the trusting, but the grounds for judgments of trustworthiness differ depending on whether we're talking about trust in persons or in things. While we do sometimes talk about elevators and rain jackets as trustworthy, that is not the kind of trustworthiness I am concerned about. Elevators and rain jackets cannot be trustworthy on moral grounds, and it is the moral aspect of trustworthiness that I am thinking of.

Trust in another involves epistemological and moral dimensions as well as pragmatic ones. When we trust, we hold certain expectations of another. To expect is to look forward to something without anticipating disappointment. When we have expectations of another, we project into the future, making an inference about the sort of person someone is going to be in the future. Trust, then, is a cognitive (epistemological and imaginative) process of envisioning the future and generalizing beyond the present (Luhmannn 1979, 20, 26). It is important to note, however, that trusting another involves more than the epistemological task of being able to infer future character on the basis of past experiences. One can *predict* the behavior of a con artist, for example, but that doesn't indicate his trustworthiness.[1] Baier states that, for one to be trusting rather than merely predicting another, one must believe that the other has good will toward one (Baier 1986, 235). Where trust is concerned, not just any expectations will do—one must expect that the other has good intentions (at least with regard to the cared-about good) and the ability to carry through with what is expected of him or her.

In returning to the initial definition, then, that trust is a cooperative activity that people engage in to assist one another in caring for goods we value, I note that cooperation is an important aspect of trusting relations. But as David Good argues, even cooperation is complicated (Good 1988). As the discussion above suggests, typically trust is not a straightforward matter of one person cooperating with another to facilitate the former's goals or needs, but rather involves explicit and implicit claims about how much or in what ways the other can be counted on to assist one in various ways. An aspect of the cooperative activity, according to Good, is the role one person plays in representing her needs to another and the trust the other places in the former's representation (Good 1988, 33). Thus features of trust such as cooperation in facilitating others' needs and confidence that one's expectations are well-placed are themselves drawing on dynamics of trust and implicate both parties in the potential development of trust at a deeper level than simply the care of some valued good.

Prediction per se isn't a sufficient ground for trust because we can sometimes predict another's bad conduct, her tendency to disappoint us, or even her likelihood of treating us cruelly. Dire predictions needn't be grounded in inferences about the other's bad intentions either. A friend may be very well intentioned but nevertheless untrustworthy when it comes to matters of taste, such as choosing restaurants or movies. Or she may have good will toward me but be someone I wouldn't trust to manage my accounts while I'm on holiday.

We can know one another well enough to predict that no matter how good at heart, some people are going to botch up some things, and we would do better look to others for care of those things. When we trust in others, we predict a positive outcome; for prediction to involve trust, one must have certain beliefs about the other and, depending on what those beliefs refer to in the other, they may involve beliefs about the other's character—a belief that the other has a disposition to be, to some degree, trustworthy. That is to say, there are distinctions in trust between:

- a prediction that one will be well-treated;
- a prediction of being well-treated that is grounded in a belief in the other's good will toward one; and
- a prediction of being well-treated that is grounded in a belief not only in the other's good will toward oneself but in a belief that the other's good will is part of a more general disposition that extends beyond the context of this particular relationship.

While there are different reasons why one might be able to predict a positive outcome in the event that one were to trust another, these may each involve kinds of trust. I say "may" involve trust for the following reason: I might predict that I will be "treated well" by, say, my employer not because of his good will—suppose he's sexist—but because there are legal sanctions against his treating me badly. This doesn't seem to be a case of my trusting him but rather my counting on the sanctions to constrain his otherwise unfair conduct. I don't *trust* the sexist employer, because I think it unlikely that he would take care of something I value and take to be central to my being—my gender identity—in the absence of such sanctions. For a prediction of a positive outcome to be a kind of trust, then, it needs to include certain beliefs about the other's motivations for coming through with regard to the valued good (in the event one were to place within his or her domain the care of that good); we must believe that the other is motivated to take care of something we value, not because one will be punished if one doesn't, but because one in some sense regards the taking-care of that thing to be important, good, or valuable.

Consider another situation. I might predict I will be treated well by someone whom I believe to be committed to certain universal principles, such as that of keeping his word. This does seem to involve a kind of trust, because I believe I can count on this person to apply the principle in my case as well as in the case of others. When we count on someone because we believe he or she is committed to the principle "keep your promises" or "never lie," this is a kind of trust, but it may be an unsatisfactory kind in many contexts, if the motivation (for keeping one's promise or not lying) seems to be that of rule-following. In friendship, for example, I want my friend to keep her word to take care of what I value because she is my friend and not because she feels an obligation to obey a universal principle. As Blum states, "friendship (or, anyway, most genuine friendship) involves a substantial concern for the good of the friend for his own sake, and a disposition to act to foster that good, simply because the other is one's friend" (Blum 1980, 43).

Being moved by a universal principle to "treat others well" doesn't get at what we often look for when evaluating whether or not we can trust someone and what is most central to the virtue of trustworthiness: that is, a disposition that is responsive to others in their particularity and not just an impartial adherence to rules. A Kantian moral agent comes to mind, where her or his feelings toward particular others are not a relevant moral consideration in determining what morality demands.[2] I might reasonably be able to expect to be well-treated by a Kantian moral agent, but it would seem not to have to do with her or his attitudes or feelings toward me or with the particularities of who I am. Although I might be able to trust that a Kantian agent would never lie to me, it would be difficult to trust someone very deeply whose relations with particular others seem to be impersonal and detached and whose principled life seems to lack groundedness and connection with those in her life. An attitude of indifference to particular persons does not foster a great degree of trust even if "right actions" are performed.

The point is that we can predict good treatment on other grounds than an attitude of good will toward us—and predicting good treatment may give one reason to trust—but it is not likely to be trust at a very deep level if the good treatment is based on a commitment to universal principles and accompanied by an indifference to feelings for others or an impersonal and impartial stance. This is not only because "the particularities of context and affiliation cannot and should not be removed from moral reasoning," but that the impartial point of view "masks ways in which the particular perspectives of dominant groups claim universality, and helps justify hierarchical decision-making structures" (Young 1990, 97). The demand for impartiality, Young argues, denies and represses difference through the logic of identity, in which laws of unity conceptualize and organize entities in terms of substance rather than process or relation. Apparently stable categories are generated and systematized under organizing principles, but at the expense of ambiguity, particularity, and difference. In civic life, where impartiality is supposed to be especially relevant, the logic of identity reduces the plurality of subjectivity to a point of view that any and all rational subjects can adopt (chap. 4). The effect of the logic of identity has been to exclude whole groups from consideration as moral agents and from participation in moral and political decision-making. This makes it more difficult for us to take care of things for others and to have our own needs met, undermining trust and re-inforcing distrust. Whom we trust and are trusted by will depend on how well we meet one another's needs and are able to take care of one another's valued goods even when those values differ from ours. To learn about one another's values and needs, and to respond to one another in ways that are mutually flourishing, we must eschew, not embrace, impartiality (106). Trust in government, in institutions, and in the workplace is on shaky ground in-deed if founded on an ideal of impartiality, as the ideal undermines its own claims to justice. Whom we trust, then, should be consistent with a concep-tion of justice that doesn't repress and deny difference. As Young puts it, "a conception of justice which challenges institutionalized domination and op-pression should offer a vision of a heterogeneous public that acknowledges and affirms group differences" (10).

It's not that we should place our trust in people who don't rely on any moral principles or values to guide them. In order to trust someone, we need to have a sense of what is important to her both morally and non-morally, and a person who seems to lack commitment to any values or principles doesn't give us the ability to predict either good or bad treatment. When we want to determine whether or not to trust another with the care of some good we value, we need to know what the other's values, commitments, and loyalties are. This will help us to decide to what extent risk would be involved if we were to count on that person. What can I reasonably expect to happen in the future if I place my trust in this person? How vulnerable would I be? How de-pendable is she with regard to this matter? How deeply committed is she to me, or to values that we share? What conflicting loyalties does she currently face in her life that might affect her ability to come through for me on this is-sue? How self-interested is she and how vulnerable would that leave me in this case? We don't always think through questions this clearly when a po-tential trusting relationship arises. But sometimes what we are entrusting to another matters deeply to us and how these questions would be answered can suggest the reasonableness of trusting in those cases.

In evaluating someone's trustworthiness, then, we need to know that she can be counted on, as a matter of the sort of person she is, to take care of those things with which we are considering entrusting her. Perhaps this is the rea-son Christina, a character in Maria Irene Fornes' play *Fefu and Her Friends,* expresses doubts about Fefu's character. Christina says she knows Fefu tells the truth, and has integrity, but she still senses something dangerous about Fefu's way of being in the world that gives her reasons to distrust Fefu:

> I don't know if she's careful with life...something bigger than the self. I suppose
> I don't mean with life but more with convention. I think she is an adventurer in a

way. Her mind is adventurous. I don't know if there is dishonesty in that. But in adventure there is taking chances and risks, and then one has to, somehow, have less regard or respect for things as they are. That is, regard for a kind of convention, I suppose. I don't like thinking that I am thoughtful of things that have no value. (Fornes 1980, 22)

What seems to be causing Christina such consternation is that she doesn't know where Fefu stands in relation to others—to their commitments, values, feelings. It's not Fefu's commitment to abstract universal moral laws that Christina doubts, but rather her commitment to the norms of a *particular community*: Fefu doesn't seem to value the norms which govern even their own small community of women. There seems to be no solid ground underneath her; instead, to Christina, Fefu is a sort of unbounded, free-floating agent with no commitments, no guidelines, no conventions to answer to.

A prediction of being well-treated that is grounded in a belief in the other's good will toward us as particular persons is stronger than a mere prediction that we will be well-treated and is closer to the trust that is the corollary of trustworthiness. When I trust someone because I believe her to have good will toward me, I have a belief about how I can expect to be treated by her that refers to *me* and that includes both her feelings and actions. When I trust my doctor to give me proper health care, and that trust is grounded in a belief of her good will toward me, I not only trust her to treat me well with regard to fair and ethical medical treatment, but I trust her to be concerned for me as *this* patient that she is caring for and where her good will is personal and particular to me. We trust others more fully when we believe that they have positive feelings toward us not just as members of "humankind" but in our particularity. This is because what we are considering entrusting to another's care matters to us—sometimes greatly—and when we believe that the other cares about us, we have more reason to believe that the taking-care-of will be done well. As Baier suggests, the best reason for believing that someone will care well for what we care about is that that person loves us (Baier 1986, 243).

Even being able to predict a positive outcome based on another's good will toward one does not exhaust the range of proper trust. If we consider a serial killer who loves his mother and treats her well, that example suggests the distinction between (a), a prediction of being well-treated that is grounded in good will toward one and (b), a prediction of being well-treated that is grounded in a belief that the good will toward one is not "out of character" or an aberration of sorts. The son's mother may believe her son has good will toward her and may rightly predict that he will treat her well, but this certainly seems to be a delimited sense of trust—if the mother knows of her son's murderous activities, she would be foolish to consider him trustworthy beyond the scope of their relationship (although it still may make sense to say he is trustworthy *to her*). The point of (b) is to emphasize the importance of the trusted person's more general ways of being and relating in the world. (B), then, suggests that proper trust will often require that we attend not only to another's disposition to be trustworthy toward particular persons or with regard to particular goods but in a more general sense. (The distinction between specific and general trustworthiness will be discussed later in this chapter.) My analysis allows for these distinctions while at the same time it doesn't gloss over the point that being fully trustworthy requires more than "good treatment" or even "good will toward me," and as such, proper trust involves recognizing those distinctions. There is a range of degrees of trust, and a range of dispositions to be trustworthy, and when we trust well, our degree of trust is commensurate with our beliefs about the other's disposition to be trustworthy.

Within trust, there are other important nuances as well. H. J. N. Horsburgh distinguishes between "perfect confidence," where a person has a total absence of doubts as to another's dependability, and "reliance", where a person is uncertain as to whether another will do as she says but trusts anyway to some degree (Horsburgh 1960, 354). Perfect confidence might be specific to a particular task or quality ("I trust that Jane will feed my cats while I am gone," or "I trust that Jane will always return my phone calls as soon as it is convenient") or, much more rarely, perfect confidence might entail trusting absolutely in another's good character. [With regard to (a) above, I might say "I trust her with my life," whereas with regard to (b) above, I might say, "I trust her with my life—and you can, too."] When our trust takes the form of reliance, though, we may doubt in varying degrees; we may be quite sure that the other person will come through, or think it likely, or think it improbable (but place our trust in him or her anyway).[3] It is important to note, however, that if I think it improbable that someone or some institution can be counted on *and* my doubt is based on a concern that the other has an indifferent or malevolent will toward me, then to rely upon that person or institution would be unreasonable.

Trusting another involves an expectation or belief that the trusted person has good intentions with regard to the care of something we value and the ability to carry through with what is expected of him or her. This definition of trust directs us toward an understanding of its *relational* nature: when we trust others, we stand in a particular relation to them with regard to some good which we are entrusting to their care. Furthermore, this relation is one of vulnerability. Trust itself alters power positions (Baier 1986, 240): trusting others involves depending on them, being vulnerable to the possibility of disappointment or betrayal, and risking harm to self. This further feature of trust, in turn, indicates a moral requirement of the one *being trusted*: being worthy of another's trust requires that one takes care to ensure that one does not exploit the potential power that one has to do harm to the trusting person.

Following Baier and Horsburgh, then, I have taken as our starting point that we trust others when we allow them the opportunity to take care of something we value and when we have favorable expectations that they will not disappoint our confidence in them. The degree to which we trust will often depend on the extent to which we believe they have certain dispositions toward us and others (as well as the skills and knowledge specific to various caring activities).

From these remarks, I note that trust involves the following logical features:

1. It is a relational concept, like "is mother of" or "is different from." Linguistically as well as conceptually, it always takes an object: A trusts B.
2. It is typically a three-place predicate: A trusts B to x , where "x" = to act in such a way as to take care of something A values.

The first and second features together generate both the vulnerability and the responsibility inherent in trust. A specific form of trust, stated in (3), seems to be the one about which most current philosophical discussions are focused.

3. A trusts B to do x, where "x" = performing a particular, specified action.

This form is frequently taken to suggest contractual agreements and promises, with an outcome of either a discharging of the duty one has taken on or an exacting of a penalty for breach of contract. Although the contractarian form of trust is important to some formal agreements, it encompasses only one form in a vast domain of trusting relations.

MORAL RESPONSIBILITIES WITH REGARD TO TRUST AND EMERGENCE OF THE THEORY

Problems and possibilities of trusting relations aren't fully addressed by merely knowing what trust is. Trust can be cultivated, but it cannot be demanded of oneself or others (Baier 1986). Secondly, sometimes it is clearly foolhardy to place our trust in someone. Given current societal conditions, where power, privilege, and oppression are realities of our political and social lives, trust is something few of us can afford to offer innocently and unreflectively. It is both morally and intellectually objectionable to trust in the face of strong reasons to suspect betrayal. So it is not the case that morality demands that we trust one another, nor is it the case that trusting people are somehow more virtuous than distrustful people. Those views would certainly be incorrect; the reasonableness of trust depends upon particular contexts, so no such generalization can be drawn.

Nor are we required to accept the trust others place in us. At times it is appropriate to refuse trust—that is, to decline the invitation to be responsible for someone else's placing themselves or some good they care about in a vulnerable state. One might refuse to accept a confidence that a friend is wishing to divulge about her secret affair, for instance, because one wishes to stay free of a net of deception and betrayal. Or one might refuse to accept the responsibility to be entrusted with the care of a friend's aging aunt because one already has many commitments and feels unable to take on another weighty responsibility. These refusals are not failures of trustworthiness, however; in fact, one may *exhibit* trustworthiness by clarifying what one's limits are as well as by caring properly for those goods with which one is entrusted.

However, living moral lives involves us doing our part to cultivate trust where appropriate. An ethic of responsibility and responsiveness to others requires that we do what we can to encourage the development of moral character both in ourselves and others, in our communities of participation and in those with whom we come in contact.

> Moral agents can assist each other in enlarging our capacity for trustworthy and honorable dealing with others—because all moral agents belong to a community whose members are responsive in varying degrees to one another's moral appeals and challenges. (Horsburgh 1960)

When we are trusted or distrusted, we experience the effects. Since trustworthiness is a morally praiseworthy quality, being considered trustworthy builds self-respect and encourages and sustains our trustworthiness (Horsburgh 1960). Knowing one is being trusted may provide the motivation to act morally where one is wavering, as when a teenager, knowing her mother trusts her to refrain from disobeying agreed-upon rules of conduct, decides to comply so that she can feel worthy of her mother's trust. Trust, then, properly placed, develops moral agency. (This isn't always the case, of course; trusting a con artist—or a teenager—in the hopes that he will be motivated to be worthy of that trust might merely provide him the desired latitude for further exploitation. But the entire project of theorizing about trust and trustworthiness rests on the assumption that those engaging in dialogue and discussion on this subject care about morality and have a genuine desire to become morally good persons. Probably very little of this work is relevant to those who are indifferent, callous, or hostile to moral concerns.)

Sometimes the awareness that one is distrusted can provide the necessary impetus for introspection. An employee who realizes she isn't being trusted by her co-workers with shared responsibilities at work might, upon reflection, identify areas where she has consistently let others down or failed to follow through on previous commitments. Others' distrust of her might then motivate her to perform her share of the duties in a way that makes her more worthy of their trust. But distrust of one who is sincere in her efforts to be a trustworthy and dependable person can be disorienting and might cause her to doubt her own perceptions and to distrust herself. Consider, for instance, a teenager whose parents are suspicious and distrustful when she goes out at night; even if she has been forthright about her plans and is not breaking any agreed-upon rules, her identity as a respectable moral subject is undermined by a pervasive parental attitude that expects deceit and betrayal.

Chronic or persistent distrust can be demoralizing, discouraging, and divisive. In groups, it can be contagious. Where various organizations and communities come together with diverse values, interests, and goals, distrust may prevail, impeding cooperation, undermining self-respect, and hindering moral agency (Horsburgh 1960). If we are to effect changes in the current structures of society, we need to avoid or remedy an atmosphere of distrust internal to relationships among and between members of various communities, organizations, committees, institutions, agencies, and so on.

So, while it is not one's moral responsibility to trust others, it is one's responsibility to cultivate proper trust.

My thesis is as follows: one way we can responsibly cultivate trust is to develop a trustworthy character. Developing an appropriately trusting character is relevant as well, but for good reasons, I focus on trustworthiness. The locus of trust is on character because, when differences in privilege and power exist between us, we may be uneasy about what each other cares about: each sees that the other values some things which she or he sees as either incompatible with or hostile to the things *she* or *he* values.[4] Hence, the emphasis is on how willing and able one is to care for those goods others value even when those are not, or do not appear to be, entirely harmonious with the goods one values oneself. However, differences in power and privilege make it more difficult to assess the trustworthiness of others, so it is important to give and receive assurances of our trustworthiness.

Of course, when I talk of willingness to care for others' goods as an indicator for trustworthiness, I do not mean to suggest that a trustworthy person would care for *any* goods of another. If a particular group's good is sacrificial murder in a worship ceremony, considerations of someone's trustworthiness would depend upon whether that person is a member of the cult—in which case one is trustworthy if one *complies* —or a member of various other communities in western society—in which case one is trustworthy if one *objects* to such practices. Trustworthiness is a virtue we have with regard to some thing. It has reference points and perspectivity, and we moral agents who value it as a virtue in ourselves and others are socially situated in various communities within which we move. But groups and communities conflict, so what is trustworthy with regard to one group may be untrustworthy with regard to another.

This observation may seem to imply moral relativism, but rather than focusing attention on debates about universal moral truths and objective standards for morality, I want to reframe these issues in the context of trust and distrust, where diverse moral agents from various communities and groups face conflicts of values, questions of loyalties, and choices about alliances. Reframing the discussion in this way emphasizes our connections with and responsibilities to one another rather than to abstract moral principles. The issue, then, becomes not whether there is some overarching rule or principle which spans all communities and governs the morality of all humankind but rather whether and to what extent diverse and conflicting cultures and communities are able to assist one another in the care of goods in ways which do not either rely upon or result in the exploitation and oppression of some people.

VISION OF THE THEORY: TRUSTWORTHINESS AS A CHARACTER VIRTUE

Whom should we trust and with what shall we trust them? The trivial answer is that we should trust those who are trustworthy with the care of those sorts of things they can be depended upon to care for. But this answer doesn't shed much light on the subject. An understanding of the nature of trust and trustworthiness cannot be gained by merely being able to answer questions of the form, "Ought *A* to trust *B* to do *x* ?" What many of us really want to know—at least some of the time—is not just, Can I trust this person to put up flyers about the meeting next week, but: Could this person still be counted on to be trustworthy if she were backed into a corner? When faced with a conflict of loyalties, would that person still be trustworthy? When the wolf comes knocking at her door, what will she do? If the wolf comes knocking at *my* door, what will she do? What is involved in being trustworthy and how can we determine who is and is not worthy of our trust?

Posing these questions reflects a virtue theoretic conception of morality, which is distinct from either deontological or consequentialist moral theories. In virtue theory, the concept of character is central to morality (see Trianosky 1990; Watson 1990; Slote 2001). The question Aristotle is addressing in the

Nicomachean Ethics, and the question he takes to be fundamentally important to *eudaimonia*, is how we are to become morally good persons. Good persons are those who not only do the right things but who do them from an enduring disposition. These enduring dispositions or states of character he calls virtues.

Virtues are settled states of character that contribute to human flourishing. They are instrumentally good in that they are necessary to living a fully flourishing life, but they are intrinsically good as well (Aristotle 1985, 1097b). They consist in activities that express what is good and noble and that give the agent pleasure (Aristotle 1969). Virtues must be exhibited, not merely possessed (1969, 1098b30-1099a6). To be virtuous, we have to have a tendency to express what is good and fine, using practical reason to decide what to do within a mean that is relative to us. Virtues are distinct from right actions, because we can do the right thing accidentally or inconsistently, and we can do the right thing for the wrong reasons. Virtues, on the other hand, are dispositional; rather than getting it right in a haphazard manner, or only when we are in the mood, when we possess virtues we can be counted on to do the right thing for the reason that doing so will give us pleasure and because we love what is good and fine.

But virtue is not only a matter of being the sort of person who performs right actions but of being the sort of person who has feelings appropriate to a given situation.

> Virtue pursues the mean because it is concerned with feelings and actions, and these admit of excess, deficiency and an intermediate condition. We can be afraid, e.g., or be confident, or have appetites, or get angry, or feel pity, in general have pleasure or pain, both too much and too little, and in both ways not well but (having these feelings) at the right times, about the right things, toward the right people, for the right end, and in the right way, is the intermediate and best condition, and this is proper to virtue. Similarly, actions also admit of excess, deficiency, and the intermediate condition. (Aristotle 1969, 1106b15-25)

As J. O. Urmson reminds us, Aristotle isn't meaning in this passage that virtue has two distinct fields—actions and feelings—but that whenever our actions are displaying our character, we will be manifesting one or more emotions as well. Actions embody emotions, Aristotle seems to be saying (Urmson 1980, 159). Or, as Nancy Sherman puts it, finding the mean requires that we act in a way that is appropriate to the situation, but it equally requires that we respond with the right sort of emotional sensitivity (Sherman 1989, 49). As with actions we perform, emotions are responses that affect both the agent and the observer, and the virtuous person *cares* about these responses; they matter in the way that virtue pursued for its own sake matters.

The virtuous person, then, exhibits actions and feelings within a mean. But the Doctrine of the Mean is neither a mathematical standard nor a mere call for moderation. Aristotle explicitly states that the mean is *relative to us* and, as W. F. R. Hardie puts it, the

> mean must be appropriate to circumstances including facts about the agent himself. The mean is not "one and the same" for all (1106a32). The mathematical terms in which Aristotle chooses to express himself need not, and indeed cannot, be taken very seriously. It is a lecturer's patter. Do not imagine, he is saying, that finding the mean is a matter simply of "splitting the difference" between opposing over-and under-estimates. (Hardie 1980, 135)

Because it is not a simple calculative standard, finding the mean requires that we exercise practical wisdom. As Richard Kraut says, we must consider the consequences that various alternatives would bring about for one's activity as an excellent practical reasoner (Kraut 1989, 332). When I discuss the need to find the mean in given cases, I take it to be a starting point for deliberation that motivates us to concentrate on contextual aspects of a situation while not allowing ourselves to slide into total relativism.

Philippa Foot explains that a person's virtue is assessed not only by his actions, and not only by his intentions, but by his innermost desires as well. "Small reactions of pleasure and displeasure [are] often the surest signs of a man's moral disposition" (Foot 1978, 5). This is why Foot argues that virtues are the expression of a *will* that is good, where "will" is understood to include what is wished for as well as what is aimed at. Virtues engage the will, which is what distinguishes them from other things beneficial to our lives such as good health, and this also is what distinguishes virtues from skills and arts (which express a capacity but do not engage the will.)

Another feature of virtues, according to Foot, is that they are corrective; they motivate us where we are deficient or bolster us where we are inclined to fall short of goodness. Aristotle recognizes that people have natural tendencies toward pleasure and cautions us to ward against it becoming too dominant in our lives. And Foot adds that "there is, for instance, a virtue of industriousness only because idleness is a temptation; and of humility only because men tend to think too well of themselves. Hope is a virtue because despair too is a temptation; it might have been that no one cried that all was lost except where he could really see it to be so, and in this case there would have been no virtue of hope" (Foot 1978, 9). Virtues, then, help us overcome obstacles to living a consistently good life and guard against the tendency to get too caught up in a self-centered world-view with its attendant motives and inclinations. I don't think people are naturally distrustful, though, so trustworthiness doesn't seem to function as a corrective in the way that some other virtues do. Perhaps the safest thing to say is that some virtues are corrective, some—but not all—have a mean, and all are important to living a fully flourishing life.

Virtues involve choice, (most) consist in a mean relative to us, and are
concerned with both action (*praxis*) and feeling (*pathos*). A virtuous person,
then, is one who not only does virtuous things but who does them from an
enduring state of character and in the way a virtuous person would do them
(Aristotle 1985, bk. 2). Linking character with the notion of an enduring disposition does not deny that we are *situated selves*.[5] Aristotle acknowledged
and attended to the situatedness of the members of the polis (but he interpreted differences [in equality, for instance] as detrimental to virtues [such as
friendship]). Furthermore, the essentially social nature of character entails
that, far from being static, it is in dynamic relation to self and other, both as
a developing child and as a mature adult.[6]

Thinking about trust in terms of enduring dispositions, though, does pose
a problem in that it seems to presuppose an essentialist view of subjectivity.
"A conception of multiple, fluid, continually repositioned subjectivity sits uneasily with claims that it is both possible and politically crucial to know people well enough to trust them" (Code 1991, 183). Yet the tension between the
need for trust in society and the recognition that identities are not, in fact, stable and unified should not be dissolved. Instead, we need to "develop creative
strategies for maintaining the tension between them: placing trust where practical deliberation suggests that it is reasonable to place it, with these people,
in these circumstances; recognizing that it may, ultimately, be necessary to revise one's judgment—and that decisions to trust are indeed poised unsteadily
between incompatible beliefs about subjectivity even though trust, to be worthy of the name, needs to be placed firmly and with conviction" (183).

Our socially situated and shaped character is what makes us the sort of
persons we are and gives us the projects and goals we aim at (Aristotle
1985, 1114b22-25). One of those ends is the care of those goods that we
value; hence, issues of trust arise (especially if those goods are social in
the first place, as, for example, in the case of friendship). *A trustworthy
person, I propose, is one who can be counted on, as a matter of the sort
of person he or she is, to take care of those things that others entrust to
one and* (following the Doctrine of the Mean) *whose ways of caring are
neither excessive nor deficient.*[7]

Aristotle himself did not consider trustworthiness to be one of the moral
virtues, but it is not inconsistent with virtue theory, including an Aristotelian
kind, to think that trustworthiness is a virtue of character. Trustworthiness,
on an Aristotelian analysis, is the intermediate condition between extremes
in either direction regarding the care of goods valued by others. An excess of
caring for that with which one was entrusted might be the lack of discretion

as to the limits to what one can reasonably care for or the lack of discretion as to appropriate objects of care. For example, an excess of caring involving a lack of discretion about proper objects with which to be entrusted might be seen when one agrees to keep a confidence that ought to be reported to Child Protection agencies. A deficiency in caring for that with which one was entrusted might be when one cannot be entrusted to properly care for what others value. An example of a deficiency in trustworthiness might be seen in the character of Magnus Pym in John Le Carre's *A Perfect Spy* (1986), who shows little or no moral concern for any of those things that others value and entrust him with. Paraphrasing Aristotle, we can care for that which others value "both too much and too little, and in both ways not well; but [having these feelings] at the right times, about the right things, toward the right people, for the right end, and in the right way, is the intermediate and best condition" (Aristotle 1985, 1106b20).[8]

By framing trusting relations in the context of virtue ethics, I can offer another form of trust as follows:

4. A trusts B to be x sort of person with regard to y , where "x" = (from A's perspective) a positive quality of character or way of performing an action and where "y" = some good that A values.

This way of defining trust reconceptualizes trust as I discussed it in the first section. (4) takes up (3) as it was stated earlier, allowing for trust to involve both tasks and qualities of character, but (4) highlights the integral connection between trust and trustworthiness and emphasizes the pivotal role that character plays. What we have to go on, in this process of assessing the trustworthiness of others and becoming trustworthy moral agents ourselves, is our situated selves, our practices, our dispositions to be the sorts of persons we are and to do the sorts of things we do—our characters.

Participation in a just, equitable, and compassionate civil society requires of each of us the development of a trustworthy character. It is our responsibility to cultivate reasonable trust, then, by becoming trustworthy friends, citizens, fellow workers, lovers, employers, caregivers, educators, etc. But we are, in part, shaped by the social, political, and economic structures which underlie our particular relationships, and hence, questions about what it means to be trustworthy and how we can become trustworthy cannot be answered independently of how the state, institutions, and social relations are organized. I will argue that, because trust and power intersect in ways that often exploit members of some groups, persons with more privilege or power have proportionately more work to do to give assurances which indicate a trustworthy character. This latter claim can be understood in two senses: first, that persons with more privilege bear more of the responsibility to establish trustworthiness; and second, that those with more privilege may initially *be* less trustworthy, because of a disposition to abuse their power.

Power imbalances, I suggest, are a primary generator of problems in trust. Structural differences in power can lead to the development of disenfranchised persons with two general kinds of disposition toward those in power. One kind of disposition is to place unquestioning trust in others in positions of authority or privilege over one. Angela, a college student with low self-esteem who views knowledge as something handed down from experts to novices, says

> I tend to trust more what a professor says than what a student says. I have more faith in the teacher, that what he says is correct and concise. Whereas the student might be giving her opinion; it might not be the right one. The teachers are always more or less right. (Belenky et. al. 1986, 39)

Of course, teachers are not always right—but they are often credited with a degree of authority which may serve to heighten the power they already have in virtue of their institutional roles (a subject to which I return in chapter 4). The trust of a disenfranchised person is not something which privileged people think needs to be earned, in part because they assume their own trustworthiness and in part because trust is sometimes readily given over to them. But unquestioning trust leaves one open to the possibility for further exploitation and is therefore unwise. The inherent vulnerability in trust, coupled with the vulnerability of the too-readily-trusting person, suggests that those who hold positions of authority or are in institutional roles need to be on guard against inadvertently taking advantage of the readily trusting person.

Another kind of disposition—or strategy, even—on the part of the relatively powerless is to *dis*trust those with economic, political, and legal power over them.

Given the exponential vulnerability involved in trusting someone who is in a position of power over one, I assume such an attitude or strategy to be wise as a general attitude or practice: a disposition to distrust allows an already vulnerable person to be on guard against the possibility of further exploitation.[9] A disposition to distrust others based on their membership in groups is learned and, when that distrust is based on repeated experiences of injustice, disrespect, and harm, may be prudent. But a disposition to distrust members of other groups may also be based on stereotypes that prop up social stratification. The distrust of the powerful toward the less powerful is learned, too, but the process is more likely to be one of enculturation into racist, masculinist, classist, and heterosexist ideologies than of exposure to particular experiences of broken trust. People are liable to stereotype others regardless of their positionality, and I'll say more below about the role that stereotyping plays in distrust. My point here is that thinking about learned strategies of distrust in terms not only of individual dispositions but of cultural, material, and ideological forces that influence our dispositions to trust or distrust highlights the importance of shifting questions of trust and distrust to those of trustworthiness. Questions about what it means to be trustworthy can never be answered independently of questions of equality, nondomination, and justice so, although considerations for trustworthiness are contextual, particular, and local, they should not be insular or exclusionary.

The distrust that marginalized people feel toward those with relative power is frequently reinforced by (at least apparent) bonds of trust between and among members of privileged groups. Issues of credibility tend to line up with perceived group memberships and affiliations, so that the judicial system is infected with patterns of trust and distrust that correlate with social stratification. In Louise Erdrich's novel *Love Medicine* (1984), Gerry is a Chippewa who got into a fight "to settle the question with a cowboy of whether a Chippewa was also a nigger." When his trial for an assault charge comes up, Gerry also finds out that

> white people are good witnesses to have on your side, because they have names, addresses, social security numbers, and work phones. Not only did Gerry's friends lack all forms of identification except their band cards, not only did they disappear (out of no malice but simply because Gerry was tried during powwow time) but the few he did manage to get were not interested in looking judge or jury in the eyes. They mumbled into their laps. Gerry's friends, you see, had no confidence in the United States judicial system. They did not seem comfortable in the courtroom, and this increased their unreliability in the eyes of judge and jury. If you trust the authorities, they trust you better back, it seems. It looked that way to Gerry, anyway. (Erdrich 1984, 162)

Trustworthiness with respect to truth-telling and testimony is interwoven with material and symbolic indications of social status, so decisions about whom to believe and whose reports to distrust are bound up in issues of power. White people who believe they are trustworthy because they take themselves to be trustworthy to their fellow human beings may fail to recognize the degree to which their trustworthiness does not extend to people of other colors and, so, is truncated by racialization; for white people, "fellow human beings" is often code for "whites." Relatively privileged men may be able to trust one another in a variety of ways and so mirror to one another a mutual trustworthiness that women do not experience with regard to those men. In corporate or academic settings, men are often surprised to discover that many women have distrustful attitudes toward them and are puzzled about that, given their own assumed trustworthiness. A society that aims to be genuinely and deeply democratic must take on questions of trust and distrust in a way that transforms structural and symbolic relations of power to ones of nondomination and nonexploitation.

If a person in a position of institutional or structural power relative to another wants to be regarded as trustworthy despite being a member of an oppressor class, that privileged person must work harder to overcome the disenfranchised person's disposition to distrust. As Maria Lugones says,

> You [white/anglo women] are asking us [women of color] to make ourselves more vulnerable to you than we already are before we have any reason to trust that you will not take advantage of this vulnerability. So you need to learn to become unintrusive, unimportant, patient to the point of tears, while at the same time open to learning any possible lessons. You will also have to come to terms with the sense of alienation, of not belonging, of having your world thoroughly disrupted, having it criticized and scrutinized from the point of view of those who have been harmed by it, having important concepts central to it dismissed, being viewed with mistrust, being seen as of no consequence except as an object of mistrust. (Lugones and Spelman 1986, 29)

It is our responsibility to cultivate relations of trust, and being trustworthy requires that we assist one another in the care of goods in ways which do not either rely upon or result in the exploitation and oppression of some people. But, because current society is founded upon structural inequalities, many, if not most, of our social, institutional, and interpersonal relationships may be infused with power imbalances—and power imbalances are a primary generator of problems in trust. To cultivate relations of trust that do not rely on or result in exploitation, therefore, will require that we work to overcome institutionally structured and reinforced distrust. As Lugones suggests, part of being trustworthy involves being willing to take prima facie responsibility for the distrust of those to whom one stands in a relation of relative power. (What it means to take prima facie responsibility will be discussed further below and then explored in more detail in later chapters.)

FAILURES OF TRUST

Following the Doctrine of the Mean, one would be untrustworthy if one's ways of caring are excessive or deficient. This definition, however, is only a starting point—it leaves open what counts as the mean, since what is cared for, the scope and limit of ways of caring, and so on, have to be specified in each situation by the parties in particular trust relationships. Later chapters address this aspect of the theory in detail, but in this section I will offer an initial discussion of the complex questions involved in the relationship between failures of trust and untrustworthiness. The question I take up here is whether or not when failures of trust occur, it is reasonable to infer that one party was not worthy of trust.

Failures of trust include betrayals of trust and distrust. A *betrayal* is a failure to do what one was trusted to do or to do what one was trusted to refrain from doing. Of course, it is not always wrong to betray trust; sometimes trust can be misplaced, as when your friend trusts that you will never report her abusive partner. But, as Adrienne Rich so poignantly states, discovering one has been betrayed is, almost without exception, a painful experience.

> When we discover that someone we trusted can be trusted no longer, it forces us to reexamine the universe, to question the whole instinct and concept of trust. For awhile, we are thrust back onto some bleak, jutting ledge, in a dark pierced by sheets of fire, swept by sheets of rain, in a world before kinship, or naming, or tenderness exist; we are brought close to formlessness. (Rich 1979, 192)

The clearest case of betrayal occurs when an explicit assurance was given and then violated, as when someone agrees to be monogamous and then has a sexual relationship with someone other than her avowed partner. Betrayal can also occur when the person one trusts takes on more than she is entrusted with (as when, in addition to feeding my cats and watering my plants, Jane takes it upon herself to read my mail with an eye to paying my bills).[10]

In the first example, it would be reasonable to infer that the person was not worthy of trust with regard to that particular thing. Here, the object of trust and the degree of latitude were explicitly identified and agreed upon by both parties. But many (if not most) of our trust relationships are implicit: we have favorable expectations, we allow ourselves to become vulnerable yet do not *expect* to be hurt, and so (believing it unnecessary to protect ourselves from harm, or perhaps not even being consciously aware of having a trusting attitude) our belief in another's good will goes unstated or understood. Still, when our expectations are unmet, we often feel betrayed. Pam, the lesbian feminist heroine in Barbara Wilson's *The Dog Collar Murders* (1989), feels betrayed by her twin sister Penny when Penny decides to marry. At Penny's wedding reception ("one of the important markers society uses to separate the socially acceptable from the socially unacceptable"), Pam explains to her partner Hadley that her sadness and loss were not just part of the process of accepting her sister's differences from her, but that her sister Penny had chosen to be rewarded for "good" behavior by society in a way that Pam could never be. "It's the principle, Hadley...She should have stuck with me—out of solidarity" (Wilson 1989, 10).

But just because someone *feels* betrayed, does that count as betrayal? Betrayal cannot be purely a subjective experience; the inference from feeling betrayed to really being betrayed may, in fact, be an incorrect one (as when a lover fails to meet you at a rendezvous you arranged by mail and you decide that he betrayed you when in fact he did not receive the letter). Further, one may in actuality be betrayed but not feel betrayed (for example, because one does not know about it—as when a friend relates to a third party something you told her in confidence). In order to count something as a betrayal, we need to know more about the expectations and assumptions involved. Were those expectations known and understood? Should they have been communicated? If your friend expects you to spend your free weekends with her, but you don't know this, has she been betrayed when you call someone else instead?

The role of expectations is central to issues of trust and betrayal. But we cannot do that envisioning well unless we know what is in the present, and because trust is a relation between people, part of what we need to know is what sort of person someone is at present. We are in a position to extrapolate from available evidence and determine the trustworthiness of another by becoming familiar with the sort of person she is. Part of what is involved in trusting another is the expectation that the trusted person has good intentions toward one. The problem is that our expectations of one another intersect with the ways in which power shapes and structures our relationships and our very perceptions.

Part of what is at issue is the way in which expectations are established to begin with. Expectations can be reasonable or unreasonable; what counts as a reasonable expectation of trustworthiness will depend not only upon the parties involved but also on the nature of their relationship, the way in which expectations and assumptions are arrived at, social norms for expectations in similar contexts and situations (as well as the extent to which the parties observe those norms), and whether or not those expectations are agreed upon.

Some people feel betrayed when a friend changes her or his mind about something that had seemed to be an established and stable understanding between them. This last point illustrates a particularly complex aspect of trust and betrayal. It would be unreasonable to count all changes of mind as betrayals. But the expectation of stability in others' values, interests, etc., is a central feature of what makes trust possible; if, in trusting another, we look for dispositions of character, and in particular, a disposition that we can *count on*, then changes of mind about previously understood values and commitments might suggest that that trust was betrayed. Particularly where there are strong political implications of a reversal of interest or values, a change of mind may be experienced as a kind of treason (as, for example, when former President Bill Clinton changed his mind about his commitment to allow Haitian refugees into the United States).

Whether or not it's reasonable to infer that the person whom you trusted was not worthy of your trust (that is, whether or not one has been betrayed in particular situations or by particular persons) will depend upon whether the favorable expectations one held were reasonable ones. Clearly, more dialogue about our expectations is called for. We need to carefully examine both the expectations we hold within communities and those we have of one another: expectations need to be clarified, deliberated upon, and collaboratively mediated between and among members of various communities.

Given the evidence from research studies on reasoning, however, such a suggestion may be rather naïve. As David Good notes, people tend to look for confirming rather than disconfirming evidence, and we tend to exhibit what is called "cognitive inertia"—we reason from a set of beliefs and responses that dominate even when they are useless in producing the desired effects (Good 1988, 39-41). These problems in reasoning suggest that many people may have considerable difficulty when it comes to reasoning about another's trustworthiness: our assessment of another's reputation, as well as the cognitive habits we've built up, are not readily changed even when another's integrity is, from a more objective perspective, on shaky ground (43). One can see why the idea of intellectual virtue is so central to trustworthiness in that it counteracts what may be "natural" tendencies toward cognitive laziness. Good's point is that the confirmation bias, in addition to cognitive inertia, can function to preserve trust even where it should not be preserved. But those reasoning flaws can also work together to sustain distrust where it isn't warranted.

Another type of failure of trust, then (besides betrayal), is that of *distrust*. Our attitudes of trust rely on inferences; we predict the trustworthiness of people on the basis of past experience. Sometimes distrust is entirely appropriate, as when we distrust someone who has betrayed us in the past or who has betrayed others who were entrusted with similar care.[11]

Sometimes we distrust others because we are unwilling to take certain risks or to subject ourselves to further harm; we want to protect ourselves from vulnerability and from what we believe to be the inevitability of getting hurt again. And sometimes retreat is necessary to our survival: when one's ability to trust has been severely damaged, one needs to heal in a community as free from betrayal and threats of betrayal as possible, and communities where strong trusting relationships have developed can provide the necessary moral, psychological, and material safety and encouragement.

Trust is an issue of particular concern to many people because they have been betrayed by those whom they trusted in the past in ways that significantly shape their own dispositions toward trust in the present. Children subjected to systematic abuse by family members, women subjected to acquaintance rape, women of color rendered invisible by white feminists' work, labor workers exploited and deceived by big business, disabled people marginalized in virtually every aspect of the public domain, may find it painfully difficult to trust others. When members of disenfranchised groups learn that such abuses of trust are endorsed by institutions and systematically reinforced by particular groups who participate in and benefit from those institutions, distrust can shift from particular individuals to a more generalized distrust of groups or communities.

Taken as a universal generalization, such distrust seems ill-founded. But group membership is more than membership in a set of similar people: it involves loyalty and partially shapes our identity. Whether or not distrust implies that the distrusted one is not worthy of one's trust will, again, depend on the particulars of the persons involved as well as the projected cared-for good. (Excesses of distrust, of course, would not be appropriate; distrust must be contextualized to "the right people, in the right way, at the right times.") The relationship between distrust and universal generalizations and classes of people will be discussed in a later chapter, but I will reiterate here the claim stated earlier that oppressed and disenfranchised persons' distrust of those in power is prima facie wise and that the burden of responsibility in showing oneself to be trustworthy falls to the person who is in a relative position of power. This view does not imply a necessary connection between "*A* distrusts *B*" and "It is wise that *A* distrusts *B*." *B* may, in fact, turn out to be trustworthy with regard to some good that *A* cares about—but *B* will need to show that.

A failure of trust that is adopted as a strategy may be unstated, it may be informal, or it may be articulated and reinforced by members of a group. When it becomes systematized and supported by institutions, I call it a *practice of distrust* (following Rom Harre 1999, 252.) Practices of distrust involve following sets of articulated rules designed to protect organizations, such as companies, and civil society from the harms that would accrue from breaches of trust. As such, practices of distrust are prophylactic. Harre gives as an example the practice in many stores of giving notice of the conditions under which a personal check will be accepted (252). Security measures at airports are also a practice of distrust, and government wiretapping is arguably another example. Permission to wiretap requires evidence of probable cause, but historians argue that that evidence is sometimes constructed, or at least liberally interpreted, when government has an interest in suppressing groups that threaten the status quo (see Matthiessen 1991; Churchill and Vander Wall 1988.) Practices of distrust need to have external support in the form of funding or legal backing in order to withstand challenges, which is why the majority of them are linked to powerful institutions. While some practices of distrust, like store policies on accepting personal checks, primarily benefit that store's owners, many others are said to be in the public interest. Whether the public actually assents to such measures, though, depends on who "the public" is and how much freedom people believe they have to dissent. After the attacks in the United States on September 11, 2001, practices of distrust were put into place because there had been such a gross failure of trust. A National Public Radio/Kaiser/Kennedy School poll found that the majority of people were willing to cede some of their civil liberties in the interest of curbing terrorism (reported on NPR November 30, 2001). For example, Americans supported giving broader authority to law enforcement to wiretap telephones (69 percent), intercept e-mail (72 percent), examine people's Internet activity (82 percent), and detain suspects for a week without charging them (58 percent). Yet 65 percent of those polled also said that they were concerned that, if granted greater power, that power could be used against innocent people. Nevertheless, these practices of distrust, which are putatively oriented toward distrusting potential terrorists, do indicate a degree of trust in government that apparently overrides an acknowledgement of the potential of government to exploit the public trust with their expanded powers. But the trust people place in government doesn't settle questions about a government's trustworthiness any more than trust in our friends or co-workers is evidence that they are worthy of that trust. We make mistakes in assessing trustworthiness all the time, in our civic as well as in our interpersonal lives. Whether or not the government is viewed as trustworthy to all its citizens in the effort to protect and secure America will depend on how trustworthiness is construed and from what perspectives the question is examined.

The analysis of trustworthiness presented in this chapter raises what looks like a tension in understanding trustworthiness as a virtue. If one can be trustworthy with respect to some people and some goods and yet not be trustworthy with respect to other people and other goods, how is trustworthiness still a virtue in the usual sense of the word? This tension can, I believe, be cleared up by pointing out that trustworthiness has two senses. Trustworthiness, like trust, can be specific with respect to the trusting person, the trusted one, and the valued good entrusted. This is one sense of trustworthiness, then: a person is trustworthy to another with respect to some valued good. But full trustworthiness requires much more than that one be trustworthy in the specific sense. The second sense, then, is that of being fully trustworthy. Being trustworthy in the more general sense involves being the sort of person who can be counted on, given who one is in relation to diverse others, to have the right feelings toward the right sorts of things, to deliberate and make choices, and to act from a trustworthy disposition. General trustworthiness requires that one be nonexploitative and nondominating not only to particular others in specific contexts but that one attend to the myriad ways that local ways of being affect broader power relations. A fully trustworthy person exhibits virtue by being the sort of person who not only fulfills specific trusting responsibilities, but who does so in a way that attends to the various features of the virtue (as set out below). Thus, a trustworthy person may, at times, be required *not* to be trustworthy to certain others in order to exhibit full virtue. The next chapter shows how a claim that a person is a trustworthy person is compatible with a claim that that person is not trustworthy to someone else with respect to some good. The last section of this chapter sets out some of the dispositional qualities that are required for someone to be trustworthy in the general, rather than the specific, sense.

SOME FURTHER REQUIREMENTS OF TRUSTWORTHINESS

In this section, I identify several other features of being a trustworthy person. The importance of each of these features will emerge in the case studies and discussions which are presented in the following chapters. I argue that these features are, in fact, requirements that must be met for a person to be the virtue of trustworthiness.

1. *That we give signs and assurances of our trustworthiness.* Trusting certainly seems risky in the face of doubts as to another's trustworthiness. As Baier states, reasonable trust requires that we have good grounds for believing another to be trustworthy and that we don't have reasons to suspect that another has strong operative motives, interests, affiliations, and loyalties which conflict with ours; distrust is reasonable when those conditions are absent (Baier 1986, 235). But these suggestions should not be taken as a gesture toward necessary and sufficient conditions for proper trust: the most that can be provided are heuristics. Trust is a practice that resembles induction: in trusting others, we always extrapolate from available evidence. In the final analysis, no decisive grounds for reasonable trust can be offered.

This point highlights the vulnerability of uncertainty involved in trusting others. How, given the sociopolitical world in which we live, can we cultivate trust in a way that attends to structural power differences as well as to the inherent vulnerabilities that arise from the practice of trusting relations?

In evaluating the trustworthiness of someone, we need to know that that person can be counted on to take care of those things with which we are considering entrusting her or him. A natural thing to want to know, then, when deciding whether we have reasons to trust someone, is what sorts of things he or she cares about. We may decide that another is trustworthy when we care about the same things, or at least we mutually care about that which we are considering entrusting to the other. We may feel someone is trustworthy when we know that person loves us and for that reason will care for those things we value. Or we may feel someone is trustworthy because we know that one of the things that person values most is being a trustworthy person.

A further feature of trustworthiness, then, is as follows: a trustworthy person is one who is not only dependable at the right times, about the right things, toward the right people, etc., but one who indicates to the trusting others where one stands—not only in relation to us, but in relation to others, to social codes, to political activities and ideals. It is not enough merely to be trustworthy; to be fully virtuous, one must indicate to potential trusting others that one is worthy of their trust. Put another way, one cannot be fully trustworthy if one is not disposed to give assurances of one's trustworthiness.

2. *That we take epistemic responsibility seriously.* The discussion of the first requirement leads to a second one. As members of epistemic and moral communities, there are things we are expected to know (Code 1987, 166-97).[12] That properly trusting others requires epistemic effort might be obvious; we have to at least know enough about a person to make warranted inferences about their good will and their various abilities as we entrust something we value to another's care. But it may be less obvious that being trustworthy also requires epistemic effort. Being trustworthy requires not merely a passive dependability but an active engagement with self and others in knowing and making known one's own interests, values, moral beliefs, and positionality, as well as theirs. To do so may involve engaging in considerable study: how does one's situatedness affect one's relation to social or economic privileges? How do one's particular race and gender, for example, affect relations of trust with diverse others? In what ways do one's values and interests impede trust with some communities and foster it with others? This responsibility is especially important to those who are in positions of institutional and social power relative to some others. The discussion of discretionary power is relevant here, because (as I discuss in chapter 2) institutionally granted discretionary power often intersects with the already-vulnerable trusting person to leave him or her open to misuses or abuses of such power. Thus, the second requirement makes the Aristotelian point that we need to develop both intellectual and moral character in order to be fully virtuous: knowing well and being good are inextricably bound up with practical reason (Aristotle 1985, 1141b9-1142a10, 1144b14-31).

It will be a sign that we have taken seriously both the moral demand of cultivating trust and that of developing trustworthy characters if we actively engage in further reflection and dialogue about our assumptions of ourselves and others, the ways those assumptions underlie trust and distrust, and what we want and can expect from one another. And (returning to the first requirement) it will also be a sign of our trustworthiness if we accept others' gestures of commitment to address these issues. Trusting relations cannot develop when someone persistently rejects all assurances and efforts toward developing a trustworthy character in relation to her or him. Assurances are given of our commitment to the enhancement of trusting relations through developing trustworthiness in ourselves when we continue to challenge and be challenged by one another rather than withdraw and when we make genuine efforts to understand each other's worlds in their historical, social, and cultural contexts.

3. *That we develop sensitivity to the particularities of others.* To become trustworthy, one must attend to trust and distrust on a sociopolitical level. But this is not to suggest that a trustworthy person sees others only as members of various groups. Being trustworthy also involves seeing others in their particularity. Baier says that "when we are trusted, we are relied upon to realize what it is for whose care we have some discretionary power, and *normal people can pick up the cues that indicate the limits of what is entrusted*" (Baier 1986, 236, emphasis mine), but I'm not convinced it is as easy as she makes it appear. Sensing what others are counting on when they place their trust in us, and having a fairly good idea of who they are independent of our needs, projections, stereotypes, and fantasies, calls for moral struggle: clear vision is a result of moral imagination and moral effort (Murdoch 1985, 37). Trustworthiness cannot be found without grasping what it is, *in the trusting person's view*, that one is caring for; and this involves an interactive and imaginative process of gaining some understanding of what the world is like from the perspective of that particular person.

4. *That we respond properly to broken trust.* How we respond, when we are (intentionally or not) complicit in the harms done to others, reflects and shapes our moral character. One *expects* a trustworthy person to care about having broken or disappointed his or her trust, and when the trusted person seems indifferent or callous to harm done to the trusting relation, it speaks ill of his or her character. Being accountable to others involves, in part, making efforts to bridge distrust and heal wounds when relations of trust are broken. When we have disrupted relations of trust (through our use of institutionally granted power and authority, as well as in interpersonal relationships), we ought to do what we can to restore that trust.[13] Part of being trustworthy, then, involves trying to make reparations when we have harmed another. This restorative process, in the form of explanation, apology and, often, critical self-reflection and transformation, allows each person to address the harm and heal the damage.

5. *That we deal with hurt in relationships—both the hurt we inflict on others and the hurt we experience from others—in ways that sustain connection.*

Hurt in relationships doesn't necessarily lead to distrust, and it may not reflect untrustworthiness. It may not be the result of broken trust. Yet we do sometimes hurt those we care about, and our responses to others' hurt reflect our degree of trustworthiness. Part of being trustworthy is taking responsibility for causing hurt, even when we didn't mean to, and changing those character flaws that repeatedly wind up hurting those we love. Likewise, others—even those who love us and mean well—sometimes hurt us, and how we respond to the wounds that others inflict on us says something about our character. Dealing with hurt in relationships in a trustworthy manner involves addressing attendant emotions and material effects of hurt in such a way that, when possible and desirable, quality connection is sustained.

6. *That our institutions and governing bodies be virtuous.* This point is the Aristotelian one that one cannot be fully trustworthy without having the right sorts of institutions. As Aristotle argues, we are political by nature (Aristotle 1984, 1253a2), and how good we are is a matter of how good our institutions are (1985, 1103b3, 1179b31-1180a20; 1984, bk. VII. 7). If part of being a trustworthy person involves cultivating relations of trust and, when trust is broken, doing what we can to restore that trust, then institutional structures must be such that this character virtue can be realized. Institutional structures can promote or impede our being fully trustworthy, and so attention to betrayals of trust and responses to them, and attention to exploitation and vulnerability in terms of socially situated, particular persons, can lead to the recognition for the need to reform social institutions. Part of becoming trustworthy, then, will include that we work to create that fully virtuous state.

7. *That we recognize the importance of being trustworthy to the disenfranchised and oppressed.* Our trustworthiness may particularly come into question when we are faced with conflicts of loyalties and interests. Many of those conflicts take the form of having to decide to whom we most want to be trustworthy. When we can't be trustworthy to both one person and another, how should we decide whom to betray and whose trust we want to remain worthy of? Whom and what we are disposed to betray, when moral dilemmas of this sort arise, says much about our trustworthiness. The nature of trustworthiness is nonexploitative and nondominating. As such, exhibiting this virtue demands that, when we face conflicts with regard to whom to sustain or to break trusting relations, we take as a primary consideration those who are already vulnerable in relation to dominant structures, in general, and to us, in particular. This claim includes, within certain parameters, situations under which we are coerced into colluding with current dominant practices to further exploit trusting disempowered others. To the extent that we allow ourselves to be coerced by dominant structures and ideologies into betraying the trust of someone who is already disenfranchised, we are failing to be trust-

worthy.[14] The point is that a fully trustworthy person will exercise her agency, even under coercion, in a way such that she doesn't decide to retain the trust of members of dominant groups at the sacrifice or neglect of members of nondominant groups who have placed their trust in her.

This requirement represents a departure from much of standard political theory, but it follows from the nature of trustworthiness as nonexploitative and nondominating.[15] Being trustworthy in this way may be particularly difficult: when there are multiple relationships and responsibilities to consider, we may discover that deciding to whom to be trustworthy and whom to betray is much more complex. Since we cannot always anticipate just when coercive situations will develop in which we might be faced with conflicts about whom to betray, a trustworthy person will prepare by developing strategies of resistance.

8. *That we are committed to mutuality in intimate as well as in civic relationships.* There are two reasons why mutuality is crucial to trustworthiness. The first has to do with interactive processes in relations. We need just, responsive democratic interactions in our interpersonal relationships as much as we do in civic life, and in neither domain should they be assumed to be secured or circumscribed. We need to be able to contest perceived power imbalances at every level. To make that possible, each of us needs to be committed to mutual relations in which such contestations are given and received without domination, exploitation of vulnerability, or threat.

The second reason mutuality is crucial to trustworthiness has to do with what it takes to live flourishing lives—not just a few of us but, as much as possible, all of us. We need a number of goods, some material, some psychological, and some spiritual, in order to flourish; how much of these things and what counts as fulfilling them will vary from person to person and culture to culture. We do know, though, that some cooperation is necessary to meet our needs for survival and flourishing and that one form of cooperation is trust. And we know that we cannot be exploitative and dominating and still be trustworthy. Nonmutual relations are untrustworthy ones and so impede flourishing; they drain us of vitality, hope, and dignity as well as depriving millions of people of material goods. Nonmutuality enflames distrust which, in turn, makes it more difficult for each of us to live interdependent lives. Since it is virtually impossible for an individual to be entirely self-sufficient and independent, the loss of trust in others that comes from nonmutual relations is a severe one—one that at the most pragmatic level makes flourishing difficult.

9. *That we work to sustain connection in intimate relationships while neither privatizing nor endangering mutual flourishing.* Trustworthiness in our close relationships has all the features of the virtue already discussed. In

friendship, in lover relationships, and in couples relationships, the closeness can take on a depth that heightens both trust and vulnerability. Intimacy is marked by a quality of connection that gives the intimate ones mutual zest, vitality, and energy. But in order to sustain that manner of interrelating—and in order to make it desirable and safe to do so—we need to be trustworthy in ways that are particular to those relationships. Because the quality of connection in genuine intimacy is life-enhancing and vitalizing, it tends to open us up to others rather than to close us off from them. Being trustworthy in intimacy in the ways that sustain connection allows us to expand our capacity for caring, just, and mutually enlivening relationships beyond primary ones to our social, professional, and political lives in civil society.

10. *That we need also to have other virtues.* It is not surprising that an Aristotelian account of trustworthiness would include the feature that one cannot be fully virtuous without having all the virtues. Although I will not take up an argument for unity of the virtues, I take the Aristotelian line that trustworthiness is part of a family of virtues that require the development of other-regarding or altruistic dispositions and that each of the virtues is necessary for the full expression of the rest. One such requirement, then, that is complementary to trustworthiness is that we have a genuine regard for the good of others.

Being trustworthy involves exhibiting the appropriate responses to others' pleasures and pains, suffering and joy. One cannot be fully trustworthy if one takes no pleasure in others' successes or if one is not disposed to share in the happiness of one's friend or fellow citizen. Likewise, one cannot be fully trustworthy if one has a disposition to ignore or overlook the harm and suffering of others. As Lawrence Blum argues concerning the virtue of compassion, when it is possible for one to relieve another person's suffering without undue demands on her time, energy, and priorities, the compassionate person is disposed to attempt to help. We wouldn't attribute compassion to someone if she sauntered by a fallen elderly man and left him on the sidewalk, Blum notes (Blum 1987, 233-34).

It may seem odd to say that a person doesn't have the virtue of trustworthiness just because he or she lacks compassion. Certainly, one may argue, Alan can be trustworthy to Bill with regard to some x (for example, where x = posting Bill's letter, or returning Bill's borrowed car) without considerations about Alan's disposition toward compassion entering in. But, viewed from an Aristotelian perspective, Alan's dispositions *matter* even when not immediately exhibited: if Alan can be counted on to post the letter or return the car regardless of *whatever* moral problems he confronts on his way (for example, on his way to the post office, Alan sees the elderly man who has fallen on the sidewalk, but he leaves him there on the reasoning that Bill has trusted him to post the letter) Alan has surely failed to find the Mean in this situation.[16]

Callousness toward others indicates that one hasn't developed the proper feelings toward pain and pleasure, the development of which is vital to moral education. Being virtuous, on an Aristotelian account, requires an intermediate condition of both feeling and action, and a person who generally feels little concern for the suffering of others or who is not moved to act to prevent harm and alleviate suffering seems to lack a quality that is vital to virtue (Aristotle 1985, bk. 2). The requirement that we have a genuine regard for the good of others, then, asks of those who desire to become trustworthy that they cultivate feelings and actions that are properly responsive to harms done to others and suffering endured by others, relative to the Mean. It requires of the trustworthy person not only that she be concerned about the possibility that *she* could exploit or harm others through excessive or deficient taking-care in trust and be disposed to nonexploitative caring, but also that she be concerned about the ways in which *others are exploited* or are suffering and that, even when she isn't the *cause* of the exploitation or suffering, she be disposed to do what she can to improve others' conditions of living. Thus, being trustworthy is integrally bound up with other virtues such as thoughtfulness, beneficence, justice, and compassion.

CONCLUSION

This discussion of trustworthiness, like Aristotle's notion of character virtues in general, has a certain circularity to it; one must be trustworthy in order to be properly trusted, but in order to have the virtue of trustworthiness, one must be *entrusted with* the care of some valued good. But the circularity need not bother us, as there are ways to ease ourselves into becoming virtuous: the development of trustworthiness is a dynamic process, as is the cultivation of trust. Trusting relations are part of an interplay of finding our way through the various nuances of assessing trustworthiness, self-disclosing, reasoning well, giving assurances, self-disclosing more when appropriate—listening, responding, reflecting, attending—as trust and trustworthiness spiral outward and flourish. Trustworthiness cannot, in the final analysis, be understood in terms of discrete situations or particular actions but rather in terms of moral agents' practices in relation to one another within the context of our social and political lives.

NOTES

1. The film *House of Games* (1987), screenplay by David Mamet, is a wonderful example of how a "confidence" game relies on trust as more than just a predictor of behavior; the psychologist, fascinated by the con game, trusted the con artist to show her how the con worked without conning her, thus failing to make the inference from his character as a con artist to a future world of conning in which she was included as a victim.

2. Kant says: "The moral imperative must therefore abstract from every object to such an extent that no object has any influence at all on the will. Thus, for example, I ought to endeavor to promote the happiness of others, not as though its realization were any concern of mine (whether by immediate inclination or by any satisfaction indirectly gained through reason), but merely because a maxim which excludes it cannot be comprehended as a universal law in one and the same volition" (Kant 1993, 441; see also 402n).

3. Horsburgh explains that such cases (where we rely upon someone while thinking it improbable that she can be counted on) are only considered a form of trust when the specific reliance is aimed at increasing the trustworthiness of the person. He calls this form of trust "therapeutic," as it is meant to induce the person to act more honorably than she originally intended. This kind of reliance seems like a much weaker form of trust, although it may still be a family resemblance. Even the second form of uncertain reliance seems more like hope than trust.

4. Conversation with Marilyn Frye.

5. Nancy Sherman's book, *The Fabric of Character* (1989), provides a good discussion of this argument.

6. Aristotle's books on friendship (Aristotle 1985, bks. xiii and ix) illustrate this point through a theory of "human beings" (we would say "theory of the self" now) that is at once metaphysical, psychological, and moral. Friendship, which is "most necessary for our lives" (1155a3), is a relation by which we come to see ourselves through our associations with others: "a friend," he says, "is another himself" (1170b7), and this is why it is good to cultivate the virtue of friendship in oneself and others. This intersubjectivity enhances character development. See also 1169b30-1170a4.

7. Again, one doesn't need to care about *any* thing which others value in order to be considered trustworthy. I needn't be worthy of the trust of a local white supremacists' group in order to be trustworthy to my colleagues—and, in fact, if I were thought trustworthy by white supremacists, it would most certainly call into question my trustworthiness for virtually all who know me. Trustworthiness must be contextualized to communities and groups.

8. Note that it also requires virtues of thought: "doing well or badly in action requires both thought and character," 1139a35.

9. Both dispositions may involve excesses of trust or distrust, however. The following section emphasizes the importance of contextualizing trust and distrust.

10. Baier would likely call this an abuse of discretionary power. I discuss this subject in the next chapter.

11. Unless that person has subsequently given reasonable assurances that she has mended her ways.

12. The idea that we ought to be epistemically responsible is in keeping with an Aristotelian view of virtue and responsibility. Aristotle argues that there are those things which I am held responsible for knowing because it is up to me to pay attention to particulars (Aristotle 1985, 1113b30-1114a3).

13. There are, however, situations where it is not necessary (or even wise) to try to restore relations of trust with someone whose trust in one has been shaken. For example, if a young woman's male date rapes her, he may be "trusting her to not tell." But if she does report the rape and then he says to her something like "How can I trust you? You twisted what happened and got me into incredible trouble..." she is not morally required to try to repair the "damage she has done him" with explanations, reasons, apologies, etc.

14. Again, this claim must be understood to have certain parameters.

15. If I am right that this account of the virtue of trustworthiness is consistent with Aristotle's theory of virtue, then the requirement that a virtuous person attend especially to ways in which he or she can avoid exploiting others suggests a flaw in Aristotle's political theory—a not unexpected suggestion.

16. It seems plausible to say that Bill's trust of Alan includes trusting that Alan would keep his full moral vision and use his practical reasoning in taking care of Bill's valued good, including knowing when not to be single-minded.

2

Justified Lies and Broken Trust

Morality is the culturally acquired art of selecting which harms to notice and worry about, where the worry takes the form of bad conscience or resentment.

Annette Baier, *Postures of the Mind*

TRUSTWORTHINESS AND DISCRETIONARY POWER IN HEALTH CARE

The next three chapters focus on relationships of trust within the context of institutional roles, this one and the next examining relations between health care workers and those they serve. In doing so, I reframe the discussion of rights and responsibilities vis-a-vis health care in terms of the harm involved in breaking the bonds of trust in a proper trusting relationship. Current literature in bioethics, while acknowledging the importance of trust to health care, neglects adequately to address the responsibilities that those with institutionally granted discretionary power have to try to sustain a relation of trust and to repair broken trust. I will argue that, when institutions fail to encourage us to do these things, they impede our ability to be fully trustworthy and therefore must themselves be critically evaluated. The discussion in the next two chapters will thus emphasize the role of institutions in our being or becoming as trustworthy as we can be. By examining trustworthiness in the context of an institutional setting, I raise questions about what it takes to be trustworthy within the constraints of an institution. In doing so, I draw out the idea that full virtue requires that our institutions and governing bodies be properly organized.

To reiterate the theoretical framework presented in the first chapter, we trust others when we allow them the opportunity to take care of something we value and when we have favorable expectations that they will not disappoint our confidence in them. Because we cannot, individually, take care of all the things we care about, we have to trust some things to the care of others (Baier 1986, 236). The prima facie good that we value and that we entrust another with, in the context of this chapter, is the care of our embodied health. It follows that, when we need health care, we should entrust the care of our health to those who can be counted on to provide that care well. Being trustworthy as health care workers will involve not exploiting patients' vulnerability and need as well as being competent in the relevant skills.

Trust plays a central role in health care in a variety of ways: for example, in organ and tissue donation, we trust that the distribution is fair, and we trust that donors are not coerced. When a doctor makes a pronouncement of death, we trust that she or he is determining death properly. And, as seekers of health care, we trust in the probity and knowledge of those persons who are in a position of power to promote our well-being in a variety of ways. When we trust someone, we become even more vulnerable than we already are, because we are placing in the hands of someone else something we care about. As Baier says, when we trust, part of what we are doing is having confidence that the person we are depending upon to take care of something we value will use discretion as to how to care and what the scope of that care is (Baier 1986 236). As I explained in chapter 1, much of our trusting is implicit, and we are not always fully aware that we are being vulnerable or holding certain expectations. A central phenomenological feature of most trust relationships—and one reason they can go wrong—is their relative "openness" with regard to the trusted person's expectations and responsibilities: the precise expectations, limits, and boundaries of caring for a particular good are often not articulated but, rather, are left to the trusted one to intuit, infer, or otherwise determine.[1] The combination of vulnerability, on the part of the trusting person, with some leeway to respond to the other's trust according to one's judgments, on the part of the one trusted, gives the (aware) trusted person discretionary power.[2] The point was that discretionary power, in the hands of the trusted, leaves the trusting one vulnerable to misuse or abuse of that power. Trust in the domain of health care, then, can be betrayed by the practitioner exceeding the limits and scope of her discretionary power or by the practitioner construing discretionary power so narrowly that she fails to care enough.

So, some power of discretion accompanies the trusting relation itself. But, in addition, in health care discretionary power is often awarded to practitioners via the institution. Rather than allowing the seeker of health care and her practitioner to establish jointly the scope and limit of the practitioner's discretionary power, its boundaries are decided by institutional policies and practices and are backed by our legal and economic systems.

(A word about terminology. I observe a distinction in health care between "patients" and "clients," where a patient is someone who seeks care of her "physical" self from medical doctors as legitimated by institutional practices, and a client is someone who seeks care of her "mental" self or whose health needs are addressed by a practitioner outside a legitimated medical field. For example, a person who goes to an internist or a psychiatrist forms a patient/physician relationship whereas a person who goes to a therapist or a chiropractor forms a client/practitioner relationship. Health care encompasses both kinds of relationships. When I refer to health care workers as an inclusive group, I use the term "practitioner." Note, as well, that by using the term "client," I am not suggesting that all client/expert relationships have similar vulnerabilities. There are differences in the kind and degree of vulnerability in any institutionally granted discretionary power. When we seek knowledge and advice or assistance from any expert, we are vulnerable in relation to their knowledge; consider the lawyer/client relation, or the businessperson/accountant relation. The kind of power difference in health care concerns health-related vulnerabilities. Even here, the difference in power in "physical" medicine may be one of being literally and physically more powerful, whereas in mental health fields, the difference may be centered on issues of self, subjectivity, and identity. There are problems with using this language and these distinctions, but there are also problems in collapsing the differences into one or another group.)

The values of the dominant culture are deeply embedded in western health care education, theory and practice. As I will show, these values often collude in the systematic oppression of those seeking health care, harming the one who is entrusting the care of her health to those working within the institution. Those who are inclined to place their trust in health care workers, then, would be wise to be skeptical not just with regard to knowledge-claims and expertise but with regard to the many ways that oppressive value systems intersect with health care and can adversely affect a practitioner's trustworthiness. If someone wants to be trustworthy in her role as a health care worker—and if health care is not to perpetuate harms to those it serves—then she will need to grapple with the insidious ways that misuses and abuses of power operate within this field institutionally and interpersonally.

As I discussed in chapter 1, we have a responsibility to be appropriately skeptical about whom we regard as sources of knowledge; naive trust in others' claims to knowledge is not a virtue. That idea pertains to the domain of health care, too. When we seek health care, we generally look for practitioners who are experts in their field. Then we believe that we can be relatively assured that our epistemic trust in them—trust in their knowledge about health and medicine—is well placed.

But questions about epistemic authority and expertise are not the only considerations involved in deciding whether or not to trust a health care practitioner. As patients, we are vulnerable to exploitation and harm even when narrowly epistemic questions are settled. Thinking about trust and skepticism only in terms of epistemic authority is, in fact, a misleading and impoverished way to characterize the relationship between health care workers and their patients or clients (or relationships between teachers and students, for that matter) (Brody 1992, 32). This is not only because there is more to legitimate power than epistemic authority (as I discuss below) but because, in health care as in everyday life, the greater burden of establishing and maintaining relations of trust stands with the person in the position of relatively more power. For these reasons, questions of trust are inseparable from those of power. In fact, Brody argues that "the central ethical problem in medicine is the responsible use of power" (36); he argues that the goal of practitioner/patient relations should be the ethical use of power, where it is recognized that the practitioner has the advantage and that neither of them wants to see that power advantage erased (47). I expand on Brody's point by homing in on a dispositional focus for the ethical use of power—that of practitioner trustworthiness.

When considering how discretionary power in health care can undermine practitioner trustworthiness, we need to think about power more broadly than in terms of practitioners' epistemic knowledge. Brody argues that epistemic authority (what he calls Aesculpian power) is only one of three kinds of power that health care practitioners hold. Aesculpian power refers to training and skill in health care, but health care workers also, to varying degrees, have charismatic power (power arising from personal qualities of character such as decisiveness or friendliness) and social power (power arising from social status and the authority to rule on sickness and health, rationality and irrationality.) These three kinds of power work together to form the institutional discretionary power of practitioners. Both practitioners and patients (or clients) realize that Aesculpian power is deficient and incomplete because medical sciences are unable to diagnose and treat every ailment, so many physicians see the power to heal as largely a matter of charismatic and social power. A skilled healer can facilitate numerous transformative changes in a person with an illness, but she can accomplish those changes best if she has a great deal of charismatic and social power in addition to Aesculpian power (Brody 1992, 34).

When people trust their practitioners, then, they may only be *trusting in* the practitioner's skill and knowledge, but they may be *trusting on the basis of* charisma and status as much as on Aesculpian power. And practitioners may exploit that ambiguity—with the ambivalent cooperation of their patients or clients. So, a broader scope of skepticism is required than that concerning epistemic matters narrowly construed. It may not be obvious to the person seeking health care what he is trusting in or the basis for his trust, and the practitioner's role in deciding what constitutes good caring in this context gives her a great deal of power that can be misused.

Both Brody and Schneider note that physicians and patients seem to disagree about the scope and limits of discretionary power that a practitioner should hold (Brody 1992, 35; Schneider 1998, chap. 2). Discretionary power could be limited by the autonomy principle which, Schneider argues, is unquestionably the dominant paradigm in the law and ethics of medicine today (3-9). But that route is complicated not only by differing views of the kind of autonomy practitioners should grant patients, but also by patients' preferences themselves. Schneider cites numerous studies that present convincing evidence that a significant number of people who seek health care do not, in fact, want to make their own medical decisions (chap. 2). Schneider cautions readers not to assume that *no* patients desire autonomy: "the attitude of even a single patient toward making medical decisions is likely to be ambiguous, ambivalent, and labile, and the preferences of patients as a whole stoutly resist facile generalization" (45). Some patients do have a deep-seated fear of the potential abuse of physicians' power. Brody's hypothesis is that patients try to assuage that fear by convincing themselves of the good will of their practitioners. Skepticism regarding health care workers is difficult for some patients, Brody suggests, because they are ambivalent about the freedom and responsibility that comes from having autonomy in this domain and, instead, want practitioners to heal with mystery and authority. They trust their doctors because trust, in this domain, is preferable to distrust and doubt about their doctors' knowledge and power.

There is another explanation: some patients are less concerned about their own participation in health care decisions because other issues raised by illness may, for the patient, be more salient than the consequences of one or another treatment plan. Schneider suggests that what most patients are concerned about is "what it means to be a person who is sick," with problems such as day-to-day coping and existential questions such whether they loved and were loved and whether they have lived a good life (84-85). These are questions about emotional and spiritual matters that, combined with practical concerns about how to adapt to illness, tend to take precedence over questions about rights and power. It's not that patients prefer being trusting to being distrusting, then, but that they have other things on their mind.

Either way, these bioethicists give weight to my claim that practitioner trustworthiness is crucial to bioethics. Preoccupied with one's illnesses and their effects in various ways and perhaps ambivalent about one's need for freedom in medical decision-making, one is vulnerable in ways that make one's trust ripe for misinterpretation or exploitation. Although Brody and Schneider focus on physician/patient relationships, much of what they say applies to other health care relationships as well. More bioethicists need to zero in on the intersection of trust and power in the patient/physician and client/practitioner relationship.

I take up this problem by reframing a typical bioethics discussion about moral issues on lying to patients. Moral questions tend to focus on which actions are the right ones to do, rather than to ask, as virtue ethics would have us, how we can be moral in this context. Rather than casting questions of morality in terms of justified right action where the value of patient autonomy comes into conflict with practitioners' commitment to healing, or where practitioners' commitment to patient or client autonomy comes into conflict with patients' or clients' preferences to cede decision-making in health care, I am framing the problem of justified lying as one that is insufficient to settle questions of trustworthiness. Clearly, how discretionary power gets used will partly depend on the relative values the practitioner places on autonomy and paternalism. A practitioner who views paternalistic actions as sometimes obligatory and, therefore, morally unproblematic, is likely to assume more leeway in the discretionary power granted him or her and may affect what sorts of acts he or she considers permissible. But my point is that current mainstream discussions in bioethics are framed in such a way that questions about trust and trustworthiness are not seriously considered.[3] To neglect such questions is to mischaracterize health care as an enterprise that is fundamentally about individual right action rather than one that is fundamentally about dispositions and relationships. When we fail to address adequately harms arising from misuses or abuses of discretionary power within such relationships, we leave open the possibility that, in worrying about some harms, we are failing to notice other important ones.

Training in ethics for those preparing for institutional roles, and professional codes of ethics, typically displace the issue of what it means to fail in someone's trust, from the perspective both of the one who is trusting and of the one who is trusted. Because the guidance in ethical practices draws at least implicitly on moral theory, I focus in this chapter on a problem in moral theory that I think leads to the neglect of matters of broken trust. Then, in the next chapter, I go more deeply into the ethics of policies themselves.

CRISIS COUNSELING AND BROKEN TRUST

There are a variety of settings and circumstances under which health care is practiced. Some contexts allow for and even require strong particular bonds of trust to be established (such as therapeutic relationships) while other contexts seem to call less for trusting relations and more for the importance of general practitioner trustworthiness (such as emergency room procedures). This discussion focuses on only one area of health care, that of crisis counseling, where the persons seeking health care are facing an immediate stressful or unmanageable situation. Some of the issues involved in a crisis may, therefore, be different from those involved in a routine visit with one's doctor, such as the relative urgency of the client's need. (Of course, it also sometimes happens that a patient visiting her doctor is in crisis. Crisis counseling and medical care are not mutually exclusive.) While this analysis is drawn from a particular area, it has implications for some aspects of general health care as well, in that many of the considerations for trust and trustworthiness generated in this discussion are relevant to the practice of health care as we currently understand it.

The agency for which I worked considers someone to be in crisis when that individual's anxiety and stress levels have exceeded his or her ability (or confidence in his or her ability) to cope with an immediate situation. The objective of a counselor is to help the client adequately to manage a crisis. (Objectives and policies of crisis counseling agencies, and effects on counselor trustworthiness, will be discussed in more detail in the next chapter.) A client can manage the crisis when his or her anxiety and stress levels are reduced sufficiently to get through the night.

People call crisis lines when they have been evicted; they call when they have been fired from a job; when a lover has just left. Women and men call with questions about sexual identity or with questions about the court system. Parents call whose children have been removed from the home, or whose child has just reported sexual abuse. Women call who have been threatened or beaten by a partner; raped; robbed; pathologized by a doctor, therapist, employer, or family member. Women (and sometimes men) with night terrors call. Depressed people call; lonely people call. And suicidal people call.

Although people can be in crisis for a variety of reasons, a widely shared feature of clients' lives is that they are socially isolated and lack adequate resources and/or information to deal with crises. Issues of gender, race, class, sexual orientation, and ability often heighten both the needs and the vulnerability of the caller, in part because the resources of people who face multiple oppressions are even more limited, and in part because they have often been previously betrayed by the dominant culture's health care and social services systems and their trust is particularly fragile. Where does responsibility lie in ensuring that client trust is not violated? Is a betrayal of trust a harm important enough to worry about?

There are, of course, individual counselors who are extremely conscientious about being trustworthy. However, an analysis of crisis counseling shows that *client trust* is treated far too lightly and that *trustworthiness* is not a primary area of accountability for those responding to people in crisis. I will argue that part of this complacency can be found in two features of much of mainstream moral theory: (1) inadequate attention to the moral residue when a morally questionable action has been justified (Williams 1988, esp. 49); and (2) a tendency to emphasize right action while not sufficiently worrying about character (Williams 1973, chap. 1).[4]

In the next section, I will contrast mainstream approaches to a problem in bioethics by setting the discussion in the context of a counselor lying to a client. In this way, I will tease apart some of the central concerns that discretionary power raises when crisis counseling is looked at from the perspective of a relation of trust. First, I will present what I take to be a very strong case for a justified lie—that of saving a life. I will argue that, even when it is clear that lying would meet the conditions under which it could be justified (to be discussed below), we may be left with unresolved moral concerns. What about other harms and worries that accompany the context of the lie?

This discussion will show that the intersection of moral theories on lying which prioritize right action with institutional discretionary power allows practitioners to dismiss, or at least not take seriously enough, the harm done when a patient or client's trust is betrayed. But as moral agents whose lives are grounded in complex social, political, and economic relationships with others, we sometimes notice that our lies, justified though they may be, raise questions about harms that are not resolved by satisfying ourselves and others that a particular lie was justified. That is, moral concerns may linger even after a lie has been justified, and we sometimes face persistent worries left by the aftermath of a lie. By attending to those residual concerns, we are in a position to explore the relationship between the bonds of trust in a relationship and the notion of a justified lie. I will argue that these residual concerns suggest that lying to one's patient or client needs to be looked at differently, and that when we do look at lying differently, the trustworthiness of the practitioner is called into question in ways that neither theories of right action nor contemporary discourse in health care attends to adequately. Finally, I will suggest that when we attend to the harm done to a client when she is lied to and feels betrayed, we also expose a flaw in crisis counseling—namely, that it prevents a vital aspect of trusting relationships from happening: the repair of broken trust. Then, in the next chapter, I will complicate this analysis by examining some of the underpinnings of health care that lead to abuses of discretionary power. The case studies and discussion will thus emphasize the idea that it is difficult to be fully trustworthy within the constraints of imperfect institutions.

Case Study

This case study involves a client of a health care agency who felt her trust had been betrayed. I was one of two outreach counselors that evening. (An outreach counselor does face-to-face counseling during the hours that regular clinics are closed.) We usually counseled people in their homes or in their neighborhoods, but before any visit we talked with the client on the telephone. So, some of an outreach counselor's work is done over the telephone.

A young female client called the crisis counseling agency after she had taken an overdose of pills about half an hour earlier. She stated that she felt sick and frightened but did not want to provide any identifying information. My outreach partner and I assessed that her life was in danger. While continuing to talk with her, I notified the agency's supervisor that I wanted the phone call traced so that an ambulance could be sent to her home. But, during the conversation with my client, she asked, "Are you tracing this call? Because, if you are, I'm going to hang up right now." I assured her that I was not; the phone call was traced, the ambulance was dispatched, and she was transported to a hospital where her life was saved. However, when the ambulance arrived and she learned that I had acted against her express wishes and in addition had lied to her, she indicated that she felt betrayed, and I wondered whether, in an important sense, I had in fact failed to be worthy of her trust.

This example raises important questions about relations of trust where the person trusted is in an institutional role. One of the responsibilities of a crisis counselor is to express care and concern for the client's situation. This care and concern might take the form of listening and providing appropriately sensitive responses, or it might involve working together to clarify and prioritize what the client's needs are, or it might require providing information as to the client's options, or assisting the client in understanding an experience or feeling by offering a context of similar experiences. (For example, a woman who is in a violent relationship is frequently assisted by learning that a pattern exists in most battering relationships and by having someone explain to her how the cycle of abuse operates.) Respectful and nurturing attitudes are essential in order to effectively counsel an individual through a crisis; when the client experiences the counselor's feelings of care and concern as genuine, a relationship of trust can be established and sustained. When a counselor violates the trust placed in him or her, that counselor is contributing harm to an already serious situation. A crisis counselor is expected to be a "person of refuge"[5]—someone who will listen attentively and respectfully to a hurting woman, who will believe her story, who will not judge her or blame her or pathologize her, and who will help her get through this moment better able to face the next.[6] In a society where sexism, racism, homophobia, poverty, and violence against women are so entrenched in our legal and social systems that most women cannot get redress or relief there, where the institutions which are supposedly in place to help the disenfranchised instead often fail them, where friends, family, and co-workers may have internalized harmful beliefs of the dominant culture, many women find it necessary to seek refuge in a stranger.[7] The client, vulnerable in her crisis, turns toward the counselor as someone whom she can count on to help her in taking care of something she cannot, at the moment, manage alone.

Inherent in the trusting relationship, I remind readers, is the fact that the person trusted is given some discretionary power about the limits and scope of caring, and inherent in the client/counselor relationship is the discretionary power that attends the institutional role of counselor. In the case study I presented, however, I/the counselor responded to the client's crisis by lying. That is, I used my discretionary power to make a decision about what I took to be my client's best interest. Did I use my discretionary power appropriately? To examine this question, we need to look at the lie, because how one responds to worries about a misuse of discretionary power in cases like this one will depend on whether one accepts mainstream moral theory on lying.

LIES AND JUSTIFICATION

As I argued in chapter 1, in order to be trustworthy one also needs to have other virtues. One of those virtues is truth-telling or, as many refer to it, honesty. Honesty is broader in scope than truth-telling because it encompasses both speech acts and other forms of communication such as body language (Baier 1990). Honesty, Baier suggests, is an intermediate between two extremes: liar/cheat/thief, on the one hand, and brutal frankness, on the other (Baier 1990).

Baier frames the virtue of honesty in terms of beliefs in the public domain. Honesty and trust are, as Baier puts it, "twin virtues," and a shared feature is what we believe others have a right to know and what we believe based on others. Baier argues that honesty is a difficult virtue to exhibit because speech, one of the main ways we communicate with others, greatly increases our ability to deceive, coerce, and manipulate others.[8] The special purposes of speech are to make story-telling possible and to give a superior way to hide what is naturally so readily available for all to perceive—namely, our emotions (Baier 1990, 273). Baier's claim is that we express emotions and desires through body language; we express beliefs through speech. This view is based on a Humean account of human nature that holds that we are naturally candid in expressing emotion, but naturally concealing in expressing beliefs, so that honesty in speech amounts to an artificial virtue.

I am not as convinced as Baier is that speech is the primary culprit in deception. As I argue in chapter 5, "intimate talk" is conveyed through gestures, body movements, sighs, and smirks as much as through speech acts, and honesty in institutional and in intimate relations requires that we monitor both spoken and unspoken communications for their ability to deceive or reveal. Still, Baier is right that honesty, understood as a kind of truth-telling, is difficult. It becomes even more difficult to be honest when one has discretionary power that permits one to deceive and when one's institutional role leads one to believe that one has a responsibility not to tell the truth in a particular situation. Trustworthiness and honesty, as twin virtues, do come together here, then, so an examination of the specific speech act of lying is called for.

To lie to someone is to assert to that person something that one knows or believes to be false with the intention that the listener will believe that statement to be true. We generally regard lying, and other forms of deception, as morally blameworthy; that is, lying seems to have some prima facie negative value. Lying is part of a broader category of deceit. It is distinct from other forms of deceit in that deceit includes the act of misleading others by communicating messages through more indirect means, whereas lying is the act of making a deceptive statement (Bok 1987, 14). When a questionable action has been performed, we require that some justification be given, and in the absence of that justification, we regard that action as culpable.

Literature on justification falls largely in the domain of principlist morality and underplays the importance of character but, nevertheless, it is instructive to consider it both for what it tells us about lying and for what it leaves out. Many moral philosophers have suggested that, in order for an action to be considered moral, it must be capable of standing up to public scrutiny (Bok 1987, 97). Rawls, for example, says that "certain principles of justice are justified because they would be agreed to in an initial situation of equality" (Rawls 1971, 21). Rawls proposes a two-part procedure by which rational beings can arrive at and confirm principles of justice that would govern a well-ordered society. In the first part of the procedure, one is asked to consider oneself in an original position in which certain stipulations hold; the idea is that, given these stipulations, one can arrive at principles of justice which do not presuppose any particular conception of the good, including an ideal of equality (137).[9] Rawls places five conditions upon the concept of right chosen by those in the original position: that the principles of justice selected by agreement should be general and universal, that they are chosen with the knowledge that they are to be made public, that the concept of right should impose an ordering when conflicting claims occur, and that the assessment of these principles would provide the "final court of appeals" in practical reasoning about moral questions. Thus Rawls writes:

> Taken together, then, these conditions on conceptions of right come to this: a conception of right is a set of principles, general in form and universal in application, that is to be publicly recognized as a final court of appeal for ordering the conflicting claims of moral persons. (135)

We can justify our actions to other reasonable and ordinary persons in the community, Rawls argues, by appeal to the principles of justice that would be agreed upon from the original position and within the constraints placed upon this conception of right.

Following Rawls' argument of the relationship between social contract theory and justification, then, if I want to justify a lie, I must be able to defend that action to the public; I must be able to offer good reasons as to why my lie was not wrong. An action is considered justified when it can be defended, when it can be shown that it was a right thing to do, and when the community's approbation for that action would be based on a Rawlsian original position.

But, in some cases, this guideline is not sufficient for justification. An action may be deemed morally permissible, but other actions may still be preferred because they are less controversial, less harmful, more beneficial in the long run, and so on. For example, I might have concealed the information the client requested, thus deceiving her without outright lying. This would be a better path to take, according to those who make a sharp distinction between lying and deception and view lying as more morally objectionable (see Jackson 2001). The question then would be why I didn't take the route of concealment rather than lying. When there is nothing prima facie wrong with what I did, I may not have to show that it was the best available alternative—but if what I did was prima facie wrong, the burden of justification shifts. In order to show that an action which was considered to be prima facie wrong was nevertheless the right one to do under the circumstances, we must also be able to show that that action was better than any other available alternative.

To show an action to be justified, it is not enough to show that there were good reasons for it; we must also show that it broke no authoritative rule, or that if it did, there was nothing better one might have done; nothing, that is, that had better reasons of a morally or legally acceptable kind (Baier 1985, 122).

I take this condition to mean that, given the questionable morality of an action, we have to show that other alternatives would have been even more questionable (or no better than the one chosen). For example, one would show that, even though lying is prima facie wrong, one had good reasons for doing so in this case (e.g., other, better avenues of prevention were exhausted) and one would argue that it is better to lie to someone than to let that person commit suicide. Part of what is required when we evaluate a morally questionable action according to societal norms, then, is that we determine whether there was no better action that could have been taken in the circumstances, all things considered. So, it seems that justification of a morally questionable action requires that two conditions be satisfied. One, the action must be able to withstand public scrutiny; and two, it can be shown that there was nothing morally or legally better that one might have done under the circumstances.

In the case discussed above, the client's age and the life-threatening nature of the situation suggest that I would be justified in having made a normative judgment to lie that reasonable and ordinary persons would agree upon. The client was a thirteen-year-old girl who was being victimized in her home and whose life experiences did not give her either knowledge or understanding of her own situation or confidence in other options for action. Furthermore, the agency for which I worked had been accredited by the American Association of Suicidology, which required it to comply with strict prevention and intervention guidelines in order to maintain the agency's accreditation. So, it seems that lying satisfies the "defensibility" condition.

However, I stated that a lie must be shown to have been better than any other moral or legal available options that a practitioner could take in those circumstances. An action may be deemed morally permissible, but other actions may still be preferred because they are less controversial, less harmful, more beneficial in the long run, and so on (Baier 1985, 122). Given the urgency and finality of the crisis in this case—she had already overdosed—it does seem that there was no other way to prevent her death than to lie. So, it seems that lying satisfies the "no better available option under the circumstances" condition as well as the former condition.

This discussion suggests a way that many moral systems intersect with institutionally granted discretionary power: together, they may serve to justify what are prima facie morally wrong actions. It looks as if, when one can justify a lie, then one has shown that one has not, in doing so, misused or abused one's discretionary power. But this conclusion depends, in part, on where one looks for justification and how the principles appealed to for justification have been established. If a member of an institution has both discretionary power and institutional responsibilities, those responsibilities carry some weight; institutional responsibilities, and those actions which properly fulfill them, are (or should be) capable of justification. On the other hand, those responsibilities that come with institutional roles are subject to criticism and sometimes ought not to be followed—justifying one's actions according to institutional responsibilities and practices isn't final. I take it that this is Rawls' point when he says that the finality condition places principles chosen from the original position, and not various institutional principles and practices *per se*, as the "highest court of appeals." One question, then, is whether or not the weight placed on various institutional responsibilities is warranted and whether or not the policies and practices of the institution would, themselves, stand up to public scrutiny (questions which are unfolded here and taken up again in the next chapter).

While it looks like one can justify having lied to one's client to save her life, there are reasons to examine this conclusion further. First, I want to take a closer look at the claim of justification in this sort of case and raise a question about what is appealed to in the justification process. My suggestion will be that it is not clear that justifying a lie to a patient or client by being able to defend that lie to the public actually meets the Rawlsian version of social contract theory where principles are arrived at from an original position.[10] Second, I want to raise some concerns about the "resting place" that much of mainstream moral theory seems to provide, and that bioethics literature replicates, when justification has been established. That is, I will argue that, even if justification for a lie to a patient or client can be established (including by Rawls' criteria), justification doesn't tell us enough about whether or not a practitioner was trustworthy with regard to his or her patient or client; yet many mainstream moral theories, which take right action to be primary, insufficiently attend to questions about moral residue.

It is important to note that I am not advocating that client autonomy ought to have prevailed in the particular case I set out. The point is that institutionally granted discretionary power, coupled with moral theory and professional training, leads to the view that it is sometimes justifiable to lie. While I concede that a lie can in some circumstances be justified, I think that that assessment only takes us partway in thinking about moral questions that arise when someone lies and trust is broken. For, on the prevailing view of justification for right action, a practitioner who lies to his or her patient or client when the patient or client's rationality is in question would be trustworthy. The practitioner is trustworthy, on this account, because he acts within the bounds of his discretionary power; he obtains his discretionary power, in part, because health care practices presuppose that certain norms of rationality are adequate standards by which we ought to evaluate judgments and actions. But this presupposition needs to be challenged.

One might see it as one's responsibility to intervene in any case where one considers someone to be incapable of making a rational decision. One evaluates the morality of intervention by considering whether or not it could be defended to the public; an action is justified when it could stand up to public scrutiny. A central part of justification for a paternalistic action, then, would require that the practitioner be able to show that the person intervened with was, in the practitioner's best judgment, irrational at the time.

But the notion of justification, as it is set out here, is a normative one; how does justification work in actual practice? My suggestion is that, although many practitioners may use some form of social contract theory in determining whether or not an action can stand up to public scrutiny, it most likely takes the form of determining whether those *within the institution* would justify a questionable action, or whether the public—defined and bounded in particular ways—would justify a questionable action.

As I suggested earlier, justifying actions by appealing internally to institutional norms and practices and without subjecting them to criticism from those not centrally involved in those institutions is not sufficient to establish justification, because it leaves open questions about the status of those norms and practices. Are the norms of rationality currently in practice in the institution of health care reliable standards by which to evaluate diverse people's rationality? I will argue in the next chapter that the current norms of rationality (as well as other ideological underpinnings of health care) reflect deeply embedded biases toward all women, men and women of color, sexual minorities, abuse survivors, and other socially marked groups, so at this point I will merely raise the question as a worry in the role of justification.

But even hypothetical appeals to those not directly involved in the institution may not provide a sufficient basis for justification. Supposing that one wants to justify intervention by lying on the grounds that one's patient or client was not rational, and that one wants the sort of checks and adjustments of practices that Rawls seems to have in mind, one might consider how others outside the institution would view a lie under these circumstances. Still, I claim, one is basing her or his assessment of someone's rationality on norms that are themselves highly political: what is considered rational depends upon who "the public" is. If restrictive notions of rationality are used, one can claim that anyone who wants to commit suicide isn't rational—but then norms for rationality may turn out to be prescriptions for socially acceptable desires.

The problem is that the norms of rationality have been established by a politically powerful public who have excluded certain groups of people from having a voice in either criticizing or expanding the norms. When marginalized groups attempt to offer arguments as to why the norms need to be expanded, the arguments are judged according to the very standards of rationality they are trying to challenge, and unless their criticisms stay within accepted boundaries, their arguments will likely be rejected as irrational. As a result,

these groups remain excluded from the discourse, while the norms remain secure. The result is that norms for rationality can seriously distort practitioner
discretionary power and thus threaten relations of trust in health care relations
(a point I return to in chapter 3). And the process of checking one's assessment
of a client's irrationality by appealing to the prevailing norms of rationality in
the public arena, given dominant patterns of discourse, doesn't guarantee that
the outcome is reliable for settling questions of justification.

Since I have raised the question of whether the norms for rationality currently in practice at the societal level aren't overly restrictive, one might conclude that what we need to do is to expand those norms and that the locus of
the problem is at the level of justification. One might argue, for example,
that although some forms of social contract theory might be inadequate for
justification for the practice of lying to save the life of the (irrational)
client—given current norms of rationality—Rawls' social contract theory
might provide justification for the practice of lying in order to intervene to
save the life of the client. Rawls argues that principles of paternalism would
be chosen in the original position to guide us to act for an irrational person
as we would act for ourselves from the original position. One constraint,
however, is that someone who has acted paternalistically must be able to argue that the person intervened with will (when his or her rational abilities develop or return) accept one's decision and agree that one did the best thing
for him or her. On such a view, one might argue, if we could resolve this
problem with how justification works in the case of lying (by expanding the
norms of rationality), then we would be able to settle questions of trustworthiness in such cases.

But Rawls also cautions readers: "Paternalistic principles are a protection
against our own irrationality, and must not be interpreted to license assaults
on one's convictions and character by any means so long as these offer the
prospect of securing consent later on" (Rawls 1971, 249-50).[11] While I do
think that a broader and more inclusive notion of rationality is called for, such
a change would not, by itself, resolve the tension between justification and
trustworthiness. First of all, as I will argue, no matter how justified one is in
having lied to a patient or client, by any norm for rationality, other moral concerns about the harms involved in broken trust may remain. For example,
even if the *patient* or *client* were to come to believe that that lie was justified,
she may not be able to trust that practitioner again. Second, even if the norms
for rationality were to be improved, there may be (nonpolitical) reasons that
some people would still fall outside those norms. But even in such cases, and
after justification in the case of a lie, residual moral questions about trust and
betrayal may linger. My point, then, is that questions of trustworthiness do not
reduce to questions of justification for what one has done.

This analysis leads me to suggest that *justification* for wrongdoing is not reliable as a measure of a practitioner's *trustworthiness*. This claim would seem to follow from the earlier account of what it takes to be a trustworthy person: a central feature of trustworthiness is that one gives assurances to *the trusting person*, and not just others (especially not just others whose interests, values, and beliefs are similar to one's own), that one is trustworthy. And one gives assurances of one's trustworthiness with regard to a patient or client by doing one's part to foster and sustain her or his trust or by attempting to repair broken trust. When one fails to do so, one fails to be fully trustworthy.

The discussion also might suggest a reason why much of mainstream moral theory seems to be inadequate to offer a full understanding of trust and trustworthiness—because being trustworthy isn't just a matter of doing the right thing but of being a particular sort of person, and to the extent that mainstream moral theory doesn't worry enough about questions of character, it is inadequate.

SALVAGED LIVES AND BROKEN TRUST

It is not clear what follows from a demonstration that lying is sometimes permissible in crisis counseling (or in other relationships both within health care and more generally). Such practices make it possible for practitioners to save the lives of potential suicide victims, it is true. Although Jennifer Jackson argues that the duty not to lie to patients is much more strictly binding than current practice would suggest (2001), she doesn't allow for justified lies even in life-threatening situations. I disagree with that position, but her explanation is that lying undermines trust, and that is precisely right. And thinking about justification *can* close off thinking about broken trust. Within moral systems where right action is taken to be primary, the counselor might be assured that her moral integrity has not been compromised by her having lied to her client. But nagging doubts and worries about broken bonds of trust call for a richer analysis of lying and institutional discretionary power than the process of justification seems to suggest or most theories of right action seem to provide.

As the defense of lying in matters of health care goes, a practitioner may lie when she feels that her responsibility to intervene overrides other responsibilities to her patient or client and when she can justify the lie according to the conditions discussed above. The implication is that the harm done by depriving a client of a right to information which would allow him or her to be self-determining is less than the harm which would have resulted had the counselor honored client autonomy and allowed the client, for example, to complete a suicide. But, while I firmly believe that suicide is, in most cases, both tragic and avoidable, I am skeptical about this way of framing issues of harm and justification. Has a counselor who justifiably lies to her client been trustworthy in this context?

Thinking about crisis counseling in terms of trustworthiness involves reconceptualizing the enterprise in terms of the vulnerability, power, and trusting that are central components of the client/counselor (and, indeed, the patient/practitioner) relationship. When the relation of trust is made a central consideration in determining whether counseling was done in an ethical and effective manner, we are compelled to pay attention to the broken trust of the client. Adrienne Rich eloquently describes the anguish and disorientation that can follow a betrayal:

> When we discover that someone we trusted can be trusted no longer, it forces us to reexamine the universe, to question the whole instinct and concept of trust. For awhile, we are thrust back onto some bleak, jutting ledge, in a dark pierced by sheets of fire, swept by sheets of rain, in a world before kinship, or naming, or tenderness exist; we are brought close to formlessness. (Rich 1979, 192)

But perhaps, one might suggest, I exaggerate the degree of betrayal a client might feel in a suicide crisis. One might argue that, when someone calls a crisis line and talks about suicide, he or she is placing trust in a counselor to help him or her to prevent that suicide; thus, an expectation that the suicide will be prevented is operative. That view might be supported by pointing out that the agency for which I worked broadcasts Public Service Announcements, one of which is about suicide intervention. A client who then responds to the offers for help could be viewed as having entered into an implicit contract where he or she understands that the counselor will help in any way possible (and that "help" includes preventing the suicide). Following this line of reasoning, a practitioner would betray her client's trust if she does not respond to such a call by doing whatever was necessary to prevent the client's death. Or, one could argue that, when someone calls a crisis line, she is ambivalent about taking her life and, in some sense, wants others to make the decision for her. That view could be supported by claims that patients are ambivalent about patient autonomy and may even sometimes want the health care worker to take charge.

I do not think that these are plausible lines to take, though. A client may be placing his or her trust in the counselor to help in any way possible, but that trust does not extend to the realm of permitting the counselor to transcend ordinary expectations of honesty. I contend that the client trusts the counselor to behave morally as well as to help, so that a call for help does not, in any way, grant a counselor implicit permission to do whatever she can to help the client. The client, at the very least, expects and trusts that the counselor will be honest with her—that is, the counselor will not lie or deceive her in the counselor's efforts to counsel—and, beyond that, the client hopes that the counselor can also help her.

The issue of trust and betrayal remains an important one. And one reason that a violation of trust is so serious in this particular example is that it has not occurred as an isolated experience but rather in the context of an ongoing experience of betrayal and violation. How far-reaching will the effects of broken trust be?

Contractarian versions of client/counselor relations (such as those I take to be currently in practice in crisis counseling) would deem that the formal obligation to a client was fulfilled when her life was saved. But a violation of a client's trust cannot be defended as an acceptable action by using the reasoning that deception, coercion, and trickery are regrettable but, in the big scheme of things, insignificant violations of trust. Although it is soothing to believe that a betrayed client will, with the help of others in the social services system, eventually be able to accept what happened and *perhaps even be grateful*, such a belief underestimates the importance of trust and the long-term pain of betrayal.[12]

A violation of trust is especially damaging to a woman who has already been a victim of abuse. Often, there seems to be no one to whom that person can turn for help and protection. As I suggested earlier, female abuse survivors are often diagnosed and treated by health care workers in unhelpful and demoralizing ways, for instance, by stigmatizing them as pathological, by not believing them, or by taking their signs of distress as symptomatic of their (putatively) manipulative or masochistic tendencies. Survivors' ability to trust, which has long been eroded as a result of repeated violations of trust, continues to be undermined because those in a position to care for them fail to do so. And, as I indicated earlier, most disenfranchised and marginalized women have survived daily exploitation and betrayal. By deceiving or tricking clients, crisis counselors victimize women one more time. Crisis counselors who coerce women to get them to do as the counselors and others want thus end up perpetuating the very social conditions to which these clients were reacting when they attempted suicide or otherwise expressed despair. In the case in point, others accepted the responsibility to decide for this client that she would live; but if her trust has been destroyed, she is left with even one less resource to turn to in her anguish. Who has responsibility for the ramifications of the broken trust?

It is not just mainstream moral theory that insufficiently attends to moral residue: this discussion points to an institutional failure to attend to the moral residue that accompanies crisis counseling. One of the shortcomings of current practice is that crisis counselors typically do not provide follow-up counseling. The formal obligation to a client is fulfilled when the crisis is over. And when we focus on justification of a lie in trying to determine whether a counselor's responses to a client's crisis were ethical, we approach the lie as an action that occurs at a given point in time. Some moral theorists lead us to believe that, once a questionable action is shown to be justified, we have cleared up the matter and can put it to rest. But it is a myth that justification is the end of the story: it isn't the end of the story for the client, and in some cases, it isn't the end of the story for the counselor or the agency either.

The bracketing of the time frame of the event enables moral theorists to overlook the constellation of factors in which the lie is embedded, including the power inequalities in the client/counselor relation, the ways that discretionary power can lead to exploitation of the client's vulnerability, and the broader sociopolitical context in which crisis counseling occurs. What social and institutional structures are in place—or not in place—so that people are brought to a point of crisis where the only alternative is to call strangers for help? What contributes to such isolation? What needs to be different in the legal system? What is lacking in the helping professions that workers end up prioritizing outcome-based solutions over ethically grounded relations? And how can we create a society in which community members care for one another when problems arise so that isolation, shame, demoralization, and despair don't set in?

Problems in living will arise. Natural disasters, as well as moral harms we do to one another, can create both material and existential difficulties and even crises. How we respond, when we are lucky enough to escape disasters, and when we are complicit in the harms done to others, reflects and shapes our moral character. Being trustworthy, like other moral virtues, requires that we are accountable—to those who would trust us, to communities of trust, and to ourselves—when particular relations of trust are disrupted. When we have harmed another's trust through our use of institutionally granted power and authority, we ought to do what we can to restore that trust. Part of being trustworthy, then, involves making reparations when we have harmed another. This restorative process, in the form of explanation, apology, critical self-reflection and transformation, allows each person to address the harm and heal the damage. But crisis counseling does not provide a means for clients and counselors to later discuss and, perhaps, anguish over harm, betrayal, and accountability, and so the counselor is unable to mend a broken relationship. This failure, then, is an institutional feature of crisis counseling that influences our ability to be fully trustworthy moral agents.

The point is this. If a client is lied to and feels betrayed by the lie, then even if the counselor can justify the lie to *others*, a harm is done when institutional practices do not facilitate the counselor offering a justification or explanation to the *client*. Given those conditions, the idea that the counselor's trustworthiness with respect to her client is not undermined, and that the client's trust in her counselor is not damaged, can only be sustained under a moral framework where doing what is morally right is enough for trustworthiness. This analysis also shows that, for it to be sensible for us to say of a counselor that she is a trustworthy person even though she is not trustworthy with regard to a client to whom she lied, that counselor would not only have to be *justified* in having lied to her client but would have to feel regret for having harmed her client's trust and would have to do what she can to restore that trust. That a counselor cannot, under the circumstances, do what is required to be fully trustworthy points to a deficiency in the institution and emphasizes the point that full virtue is difficult, if not impossible, to exhibit when the institutions are not themselves virtuous.

The lack of opportunity to restore client trust may have serious repercussions on the client. The lack of opportunity to restore client trust may also have implications for the counselor, who may struggle with an inexplicable bad conscience or an understandable sense of powerlessness to directly address harms she has inflicted. But in addition, current crisis counseling practices, where relationships are very time-limited, may foster in counselors an attitude of moral complacency about the harms done to clients. Entrenched ideas about discretionary power, as well as widely accepted beliefs about justified lies, make it possible for some counselors to be at least fairly satisfied that they are being good counselors, and the lack of opportunity (or responsibility) to face the client's broken trust give legitimacy to the idea that one should "let it go." Furthermore, the counselor has the power to walk away from the harm and not be concerned any more. These ways of responding to harms thus may erode the character of the counselor as well as the future trust of the client. In the last sections, I will elaborate on this point.

TAKING TRUSTWORTHINESS SERIOUSLY

By examining a justified lie in a case where the client's trust was betrayed, I am calling into question the assumption that justifiable acts where bonds of trust are broken do not undermine the trustworthiness of the practitioner. A practitioner who breaks the bonds of trust between her patient or client and herself by lying is at least prima facie untrustworthy. I also set out the argument, from mainstream moral theory, that a lie is prima facie wrong unless it can be justified by the two conditions. I have shown that a lie under certain conditions can be justified. But it doesn't follow from the justification of the lie that that prima facie assumption of untrustworthiness is reversed. I am proposing, therefore, to drive a wedge between the justification of lies and the virtue of trustworthiness. This discussion reorients issues in health care toward an examination of the intersection of trust and power, where the practitioner's character is placed center stage.

Trustworthiness is not an abstract and decontextualized virtue but rather is a state of character with respect to something or someone; hence, the problem of whether the practitioner in this case acted in a trustworthy manner depends upon how we answer the question "trustworthy to whom and with respect to what?" For example, one might be trustworthy as a representative of the agency's values, but then those values might themselves be questionable to patients or clients (if they become aware of them). In general, one might be "trustworthy" as a person who can be counted upon to have integrity concerning one's own values, but if those values to which one adheres do not include a value to avoid harm to others, or not to betray others' trust, then "trustworthiness" may not be a characteristic which applies to that person's relations to others. In other words, this sort of "personal integrity" doesn't necessarily lead to or include moral integrity (McFall 1987). And that would be an odd sort of trustworthiness. It seems inconsistent with common-sense morality to say "She is a trustworthy _____" (counselor, doctor, professor, etc.), but "She isn't trustworthy with respect to x," where x ranges over moral qualities such as truthfulness, integrity, kindness, and fairness.

The question is to what extent one can fail to be honest or kind or just and still be a trustworthy person. Can one be fully trustworthy and yet not be honest? Not, I suggest, if one acts from a disposition of dishonesty. But there is more to the question than this. As I stated, there is a tension in the compatibility between someone being a fully trustworthy person and yet not being trustworthy to another with respect to some specific value the other cares about.

One becomes a fully trustworthy person insofar as one, as a matter of character, is appropriately trustworthy to particular persons with regard to particular goods. But sometimes, through no flaw in one's character, one will prove not to have acted in a trustworthy manner toward others with respect to something they care about. Such situations, however, call for one to do what one can to restore the other's trust or repair broken trust. When this cannot be done, one's trustworthiness is, objectively, eroded. To the extent that one's trustworthiness isn't eroded, it will manifest itself in guilt or regret which one takes seriously—an attitude that, in the trustworthy person, provides the impetus to focus on the social structures which impeded one's ability to act in a trustworthy way toward another.

Just as social structures may impede our ability to act in a trustworthy manner, so they can provide an alternative focus for our cultivation of a trustworthy character. We may not be able, in some situations, to do what we should with regard to someone who has trusted us, but we can do what we can toward others, and we can work to change the problematic social structures. That is, tensions I identify (between being trustworthy and yet failing to be honest or between wanting to restore broken trust and being blocked by institutional practices) would be attended to and responsibly addressed by trustworthy persons. To the extent that a person does attend to broken trust in ways I suggest, that person is exhibiting central features of full trustworthiness. The person who is disposed to indifference about these tensions is calling into question the degree to which she has the full virtue.

One instance of lying does not call one's whole character into question. A lie might be "out of character," not the sort of thing one usually does. Yet there are a number of reasons why I think that one's trustworthiness is, nevertheless, shaken by such a lie. First, that the "one lie" *ought* to worry us is consistent with the framework for trustworthiness I propose. A virtue theoretic view holds that our individual actions and our character are in dynamic process. Our characters are shaped by the relationship between decision-making and action. Arguing that being virtuous is voluntary, Aristotle describes a circular dynamic between actions and character:

> we are ourselves in a way jointly responsible for our states of character, and by having the sort of character we have we lay down the sort of end we do. Certain actions produce virtues, and they cause us to do these same actions, expressing the virtues themselves. (Aristotle 1985, 1114b22)

Likewise, doing wrong actions shapes our character as well, influencing future decisions about what ends or goals to pursue. Although actions are different from states, both are voluntary and up to us, and we must take our actions seriously because we "do not know, any more than with sicknesses, what the cumulative effect of particular actions will be" (Aristotle 1985, 1115a). And, although one might not fully know the cumulative effects of lying to a client, crisis counselors are aware that they most likely will not be in a position to repair any damage done by broken trust. Trustworthiness is undermined, in particular, when one tells a lie without attempting to apologize, to make reparations, or to restore trusting relations, and it is especially undermined when one lies knowing that one will not be able to do those sorts of things.

This account of virtue and character requires that we take individual actions seriously. But in addition, the argument that a counselor's trustworthiness isn't called into question by one lie or one wrong action misses another point: that many of the virtues (and vices) are inherently social.[13] And, as I have argued, trustworthiness is a virtue that concerns *relations between people*; finding the mean for trustworthy relations, when one is a health care worker, cannot be done by appealing to abstract principles alone, independent of the trust relationship in which questions of trustworthiness arise in the first place. To pose the question of practitioner trustworthiness without examining the patient or client's betrayal is to misconstrue the nature of virtue.

Finally, to focus on the lie as an individual instance of a questionable action is to overlook the way in which institutionally granted discretionary power intersects with much of mainstream moral theory and, as such, creates certain dispositions toward the treatment of those they serve. Lying under these conditions is not a mere anomaly—it is a practice which is condoned (and sometimes justified) within health care. And practices, as MacIntyre argues, not only reflect particular standards for excellence and inform how we think about and evaluate things but they shape *who we are within those practices* (MacIntyre 1981, 175). Caroline Whitbeck puts the point this way:

> By practice I mean a coherent form of cooperative activity…that not only aims at certain ends but creates certain ways of living and develops certain characteristics (virtues) in those who participate and try to achieve the standards of excellence peculiar to that practice. (Whitbeck 1989, 52)

Responsible counselors and other health care workers who wish to become trustworthy with respect to those they serve, then, will not brush aside the effects that justified lying may cumulatively have on their character, as well as the devastating effects such actions may have on their patients' or clients' trust. Taking trustworthiness seriously, therefore, will involve reexamining the practice of crisis counseling in light of the various harms that may occur when discretionary power is abused. This critical examination will require that we do at least two things. First, we need to see if the policies that are used to justify such betrayals of trust are good ones. But this step will not be sufficient to address trustworthiness in this context; because trustworthiness also involves a certain sensitivity to and concern for harms done to trusting others, we also need to see how counselors and others respond to the likely harm done when a justified lie occurs within institutional constraints.

BETRAYAL AND FUTURE TRUST

It is an epistemic responsibility of each of us to be appropriately skeptical of whom we place our trust in and, in the field of health care, this applies to our position as patients or clients. I want to suggest a way that this responsibility intersects with the practitioner or counselor's responsibility to be trustworthy. The connection that I see is this: when a practitioner or counselor fails to be trustworthy with regard to the trusting one, she gives that patient or client reasons to be more skeptical about trusting in the future. As I have argued, the harm done to the client's already fragile trust may have significantly disrupted her ability and willingness to trust other social service workers. But if the client's needs for immediate care are overwhelming, she may be compelled to take risks that her "best judgment" tells her not to take. Thus she makes herself vulnerable unwisely, given that she is trusting in a context where she has been betrayed before and therefore has less reason to be confident that her vulnerability will not be taken advantage of. On the other hand, the client who has previously been betrayed might be just skeptical enough of counselors' trustworthiness in the future that she is not willing to be vulnerable and therefore does not seek help that she would otherwise seek. I believe this reasoning holds for patients whose trust is broken as well, although some of the factors in patient/physician relations are notably different (such as the likelihood of an ongoing relationship in which the physician has at least the opportunity, if not the incentive, to mend broken trust).

There are two points to note here. One, the degree of a present counselor's trustworthiness can constrain future client trust. Given the nature of crisis counseling, where it is unlikely that the client will contact the same counselor in the event of a future crisis, the client probably does not have to consider whether or not to trust that particular counselor. But she still has to decide whether or not to trust the crisis agency (or other health care provider) or other counselors. As I stated in chapter 1, trust is an inductive reasoning process: when we trust, part of what we are doing is generalizing into the future, projecting expectations about whom and what to count on, from what we have experienced in the past. And a client whose vulnerability has been exploited (intentionally or not) might generalize into a future where no one can be counted on.

The second point is that the degree of a present counselor's trustworthiness can constrain to what extent the client can balance his or her responsibility to be appropriately skeptical with his or her need to turn to others for help. A counselor's untrustworthiness might heighten the client's wariness and doubt—and the client may even expect herself to be prudently skeptical—but the client may still have to contend with another crisis, and sorting out whom to trust and whom to turn to may be complicated when she has already been betrayed and thus infers that it would be wise to be wary.

The ease with which one is able and willing to trust a health care worker depends upon the vulnerability we experience with regard to gender, race, ethnicity, class, age, sexual orientation, and able-bodiedness, as well as with regard to one's narrative history and one's former experiences with the institutions of health care and legal and social systems. For example, consider the following case:

Alice, a 30-year-old survivor of childhood sexual abuse who is now disabled due to a recent severe accident, required a counseling team to meet with her late one night. She lived in a residence hall for persons who require round-the-clock health care. One of the residents had sexually assaulted her and, although she was pressing charges, he was continuing to harass her. She was upset, anxious, and somewhat cynical; she felt unable to protect herself and yet both the police and the residence manager were failing to respond to her requests for further security. As she talked with us about her situation and possible coping strategies, however, she repeatedly interjected questions about our politics and our values. It's so difficult to get vegetarian meals—did we find that to be the case, too? Did we think that she should expect people to come to her apartment or that she should learn to get around into the city, considering her limitations on mobility? What did we think of the court system in terms of women? What did we think about the Gulf War?

This client was testing us to see whether she could trust us; she wasn't going to assent to a plan of action without being assured that we had her interests in mind. The other outreach counselor and I inferred that the sort of "interests" this client was looking for included shared sociopolitical values, since the problem she was facing was legal and political as well as practical and psychological. This example illustrates client distrust at work: she had been betrayed by people in the social and legal systems before and was not about to take unwarranted risks. Her wariness, together with her particular needs and vulnerabilities, led her to test the trustworthiness of individual counselors each time she needed assistance and to do so in a thorough manner. But other clients are not trusting enough even to test potential counselors' trustworthiness—once betrayed, they simply stop calling.

CONCLUSION

This discussion demonstrates the complex nature of trustworthiness where discretionary power is given—or assumed—and raises a number of questions about justification for prima facie moral wrongdoing. Although it might be tempting to try to resolve tensions in health care by focusing on the client's right to informed consent, that direction will not, by itself, address crisis counseling problems as I have laid them out. For the client/counselor relationship is not merely one where facts are exchanged, knowledge is disseminated, and choices are made: it is a relationship where the client, needing help in the care of something she values, allows herself to become vulnerable to a stranger in the hope that the stranger, the counselor, can do more help than harm. Although patient/physician relationships may be different (for example, some patients have a primary care physician whom they see regularly), the general point that it is a relationship of trust holds there as well. I have argued that we need to reconceptualize trust as a central component in relationships between health care workers and those they serve. In doing so, we recognize the role that patients and clients play in the development of discretionary power, and we reframe notions of harm and help in crisis counseling and other health care fields in terms of the trust relationship.

When we do not attend to the relation of trust, we may fail to notice harms brought about by misuses or abuses of discretionary power. But in attending to worry and bad conscience that linger even after conditions of justification have been satisfied, we see that dominant theoretical frameworks for bioethics fail to address adequately the complex questions raised in this chapter about how one can be trustworthy in the context of health care.

But we are not moral saints: we sometimes fall short of being morally good persons. Moreover, counselors and practitioners do sometimes have to lie to save lives. Given the reality of our moral lives, we need to be able to hold one another accountable when harm is done, and we need to be able to restore trust when it is damaged. Therefore, crisis counseling agencies and other health organizations need to be transformed to allow for such accountability and reparation. In the absence of these conceptual and structural changes, practitioners are at risk of continuing to use their discretionary power in ways that harm patient or client trust and undermine practitioner trustworthiness.

This chapter emphasizes two of the requirements of the account of trustworthiness given in chapter 1. First, a trustworthy person responds properly to broken trust. Even when it comes to matters with respect to which one *shouldn't* be trustworthy (for example, one shouldn't be trustworthy with regard to someone who "trusts you not to report her intent to murder so-and-so") one is still untrustworthy with regard to harm done to the trusting relation if one doesn't do something to attempt to redress the harm and restore trust. One expects a trustworthy person to care about having broken or disappointed his or her trust, and when the trusted person seems indifferent or callous to harm done to the trusting relation, it speaks ill of his or her character. But when one both feels and acts in ways that acknowledge the harm done and attempt to restore broken trust, one is trustworthy.

The second requirement that this chapter emphasizes is that one cannot be fully trustworthy without having the right sorts of institutions. Chapter 2 is an instance of the point that to be fully virtuous requires virtuous institutions. If part of being a trustworthy health care worker involves cultivating relations of trust and, when that trust is broken, doing what we can to restore that trust, then institutional structures must be such that this character virtue can be realized. In the next chapter, I will elaborate on the relationship between the individual person's virtue and institutional structures.

NOTES

1. Of course, sometimes the "openness" is only apparent, and the trusting person has quite clear expectations that are unspoken. The power of discretion, in these cases, is sometimes illusory, because the trusted person may be assessed as untrustworthy if she uses her discretion and it is out of synch with the trusting one's expectations. (At times, the apparent "openness" can function like a test of one's trustworthiness—or a setup.)

2. One doesn't have discretionary power if she doesn't realize she is being trusted.

3. Jennifer Jackson's *Truth, Trust, and Medicine* (2001) is a notable exception. Jackson writes that caring pragmatists need to follow a strict rule against lying, even in life-threatening situations, because it is the only way to sustain patients' trust, and because it sets a bad precedent (Jackson 2001, 88-93). As valuable a contribution as this book is to bioethics literature, it seems to assume rather than argue for the value of trust and trustworthiness in health care and, instead, analyzes the concepts of honesty, truth-telling, lying, and deception. Throughout the book, it's unclear what she means by trust and what moral motivations there are for placing the sustaining of trust as a high priority. Jackson's line of argument, therefore, is quite different from mine in that her primary focus is on distinguishing between truthfulness and openness as two separate virtues.

4. The conclusions Williams and I draw from this point, however, and the directions we go, are different.

5. The term "person of refuge" was introduced to me by Cassandra Thomas, director of Houston Area Women's Center and past president of the National Coalition Against Sexual Violence, but the description of it is my own interpretation of her meaning.

6. Of course, if the client is abusive or offensive, the counselor must set clear limits or terminate the call. A "person of refuge" (like anyone else) is not obligated to endure all forms of interaction.

7. I don't mean to suggest that women who are in crisis are always victims of others' crimes; some women call because they committed a grave mistake or a crime themselves. But women who break the law, or the moral code, are often met with the full force of multiple oppressions and they, too, often turn to a "person of refuge" to avoid victimization when trying to face their own culpability.

8. According to Baier, the reasons for this difference are that first, we have no natural urge to report what we believe like we have a spontaneous expression of emotion; second, there are built-in constraints on our power to deceive others about how we are feeling but no natural pre-linguistic constraints on our power to use words to deceive; third, our bodies and emotions are external and open to others, but our beliefs and thoughts are internal and stay there unless we choose to reveal them; and fourth, we can express all our emotions to an intimate, but we cannot express all our beliefs and thoughts to an intimate.

9. Rawls states that "The conception of justice eliminates the conditions that give rise to disruptive attitudes" (Rawls 1971, 144). To elaborate on this claim, he considers envy, and he argues that this conception of justice leads to social arrangements in which envy is not likely to be strong enough to call into question those principles. The avoidance of envy is just one psychological feeling which can serve as a desideratum

for a just society, however, and it would be interesting to see whether or not other psychological and phenomenal attitudes such as domination and submission, or trust and distrust, could serve as desiderata for a Rawlsian well-ordered society as well.

10. It is not clear that Rawls' social contract theory would adequately address the problems raised here, either, but I am not, at this juncture, taking on that larger question.

11. Whether or not Rawls' theory would allow the institutional practice of lying to save a life is not clear to me. (I am inclined to think not, because it doesn't seem likely that it would meet the publicity condition, but I will leave that argument for another time.)

12. As I pointed out earlier, the appeal to what someone would agree to after the fact is often found in practice and in some social contract theory, including Rawls', but as Rawls points out, it is not sufficient for justification (Rawls 1971, 249).

13. Such as truthfulness, friendliness, wit, justice, and friendship.

3

When Relations of Trust Pull Us
in Different Directions

In this chapter, I focus on questions of accountability for people in midlevel positions of power, where multiple loyalties and responsibilities create conflicts and where policies can push people into actions that reinstate hegemonic relations. As I argued in chapter 2, practices in crisis counseling are often dismissive of, and even antithetical to, concerns about clients' broken trust and questions about what it means to be a trustworthy counselor. That trust is not given a central place in the practice of crisis counseling has rather serious implications for the counselor who wants to be worthy of the trust of her client but finds herself counseling, not as an independent and autonomous moral agent, but as someone who stands in various relations of power with others in social services, legal services, and diverse populations. What complications do we face when we consider that a counselor or other person in an institutional role is also entrusted by the institution or agency to fulfill certain duties? This analysis, although focused on crisis counseling, has implications for other situations as well. As the discussion will illustrate, a counselor's loyalties may be pulled in various directions and her responsibilities may be conflictual. Many people in institutional roles face similar conflicts between institutional responsibilities, responsibilities to oneself, and responsibilities to those whom one serves in an institutional capacity. What counts as trustworthiness has to be considered in the context of tensions and conflicts within a network of relationships and norms in crisis counseling or other institutions, agencies, and organizations.

Policies play a critical role in directing counselors' responsibilities and settling conflicts about what is to be done in a crisis. That is, current practices, which employ an outcome-based model, can be seen to legitimize abuses of discretionary power through policies which prioritize "quick" solutions that are allegedly in the interests of the client but actually serve to reinstate hegemonic and oppressive relations. But, while it is tempting to conclude that the policies are faulty and therefore simply need to be adjusted, I think such a view would be misguided. An examination of these policies in the context of a particular case reveals deep ideological undercurrents that shape both policies and practices. These aspects of crisis counseling are operative in creating a web of abuses of discretionary power so that ethical counseling is undermined and counselors are impeded from focusing on being worthy of the trust of the client. I will argue, however, that a trustworthy counselor will do what she can to resist dominant ideological features in health care when her client's trust is at stake.

In the next sections, I will set out the policies of the particular agency for which I have been a crisis counselor, and then I will present a case study from my work that illustrates the policies as they were currently in practice. Although I will raise questions about policies and practices, the main focus of the paper is how those policies and practices affect the trustworthiness of the main crisis counselor in this case.

CRISIS COUNSELING AND AGENCY POLICIES

The policy of the particular agency for which I worked states that its objective is to provide "high quality crisis prevention and intervention counseling, which includes maintaining respect for the individual and empathy for their situation."[1] Its position statement reads, "In recognition of the need for immediate, anonymous and nonjudgmental assistance, we approach individuals with a spirit of respect, empathy and service."[2] The policy also states that the agency is committed to the "empowerment of the individual" and "ethical practices."[3] Thus, policy makes clear that one of the responsibilities of a crisis counselor is to be a "person of refuge"—someone whose ways of counseling are caring, constructive, and attentive to the needs of the client.

But this agency's policy also directs another responsibility of a crisis counselor, which is to provide *active intervention* when necessary. And the responsibility to intervene, in fact, bears greater weight than the responsibility to counsel a client in a respectful, empathetic, empowering manner. The agency for which I worked follows strict intervention guidelines for suicide prevention and considers it one's moral obligation to intervene in suicide attempts. These guidelines entail the belief that harm to oneself in the form of suicide ought to be prevented by whatever means are available. Hence, such a policy regarding intervention and prevention allows for abuses of discretionary power that are harmful to the client specifically in the area of trust.

For if, in the counselor's judgment, the client's situation calls for intervention, (institutionally granted) discretionary power gives the counselor the institutional *right* to intervene and the policy gives one the *responsibility* to do so. And, in the agency's policies and practices, this responsibility supersedes any other prima facie responsibilities for ethical interactions.

While I firmly believe that suicide is, in most cases, both tragic and avoidable, I am skeptical about this way of framing notions of help and harm. It is important to note that, as far as a relation of trust goes, discretionary power gives one, not the right, but the *opportunity* to intervene—at one's discretion, and *taking into consideration how doing so would affect the given relationship*. Being in a trusting relationship doesn't give one a right to use one's knowledge and power gained from another's trust in a way contrary to her wishes, and, under usual circumstances, if one does so, one will most likely be faced with the implications of the violation to the person violated and to the relationship.[4] But health care relations are not primarily conceptualized as relations of trust, and so health care workers tend not to think of the limit and scope of discretionary power as being bounded by anything other than institutionally driven criteria.

To illustrate the way these policies are implemented, I will again present a case study drawn from my work as a crisis counselor. This example, involving an adolescent girl who was actively suicidal, illustrates ways in which intervention policies and abuses of discretionary power intersect and, as a result, a young woman's trust is broken. But before I begin, I want to stress the relevance of this case to my more general argument. It will become clear, as I relate the story, that this narrative is dramatic and rather sensational; however, the underlying themes in this case are embedded in the policies and practices of many crisis calls. Secondly, this particular agency is by no means insignificant: it is a major counseling agency which served over 45,000 metro area residents in 1992, and over thirty mental health agencies and professionals count on this agency for back-up services;[5] it is a reputable, well-trained, and well-staffed organization. Neither is this agency an anomaly. The majority of major crisis counseling agencies have active intervention policies in effect similar to this one.[6]

Case Study

One night when I was on outreach call at the agency, one of the other workers (a white woman I'll call "Patty") counseled by telephone with a fifteen-year-old biracial girl (African American and European American) who reported that she had, in her hand, a loaded gun. The caller said she had been raped a few days earlier and refused to report the rape or seek any assistance other than this conversation. She stated that she could not live with the rape any longer, and that she could not and would not report it or talk with anyone else about it. She also reported that her mother had previously physically abused her and that her father (although no longer living with them) had formerly sexually assaulted her. The caller's mother was asleep in the house at the time, and the client stated that it was very important that her mother not get involved.

Because of the lethality of the situation, Patty put an immediate trace on the call and the supervisor contacted the police to advise them of the situation—standard procedure in cases like this. The police, in turn, dispatched a SWAT team to the client's home. The officers' reasoning, apparently, was that the client was considered to be "armed and dangerous." All of this was done without client knowledge or consent.

The supervisor at our agency remained in telephone contact with police outside the client's home and together they developed strategies for Patty to persuade the client to unload and put down her gun. In addition, the police wanted Patty to gather information; in particular, they wanted to know exactly where the client was in relation to the windows, doors, and stairway (I presume in case police perceived a need to fire a gun), so Patty had to repeatedly ask the client seemingly irrelevant questions such as "Where are you now?"

The only person actually talking with the client, however, was Patty; the client did not know that there were seven of us in the office working on this case or that her house was surrounded by a SWAT team. Meanwhile, the police said they were sending to our agency a *hostage negotiator* (their term) to "assist" Patty: the mother was viewed as a hostage and the client, a *terrorist*.

By the time these men arrived, two and a half hours had passed. Patty had been talking with the client the entire time, trying to persuade her to view the rape as something that she did not have to be ashamed of and for which there was recourse other than suicide. Although the client had not yet unloaded the gun or even discontinued her threat of suicide, the two of them had established a relationship where the client trusted Patty and felt cared for. For example, the client expressed dependency and vulnerability in her need to have Patty reassure her of her care and concern and of her commitment not to abandon the client. As soon as the police arrived at the agency offices, however, they demanded to take over the phone line, on the grounds that Patty was "inexperienced"—a judgment based on the amount of time Patty was taking to "resolve the crisis." Some counselors pointed out that such a strategy would not be advisable, as the client had explicitly stated that *she would not talk to police*. The hostage negotiator then told Patty to ask her client if she would talk with another female counselor while Patty "went to the bathroom." Patty agreed. After getting the client's (very reluctant) consent, Patty was off the phone to huddle with the police staff about the next step. The next step, she was told, was to inform the client that the law requires that a rape be reported, that the client has a choice of whether "to talk with the policeman *about the rape* or not, but she doesn't have the choice about whether or not to *talk* to the policeman" and then, the instructions went, Patty was to hand the phone to the hostage negotiator before the client had time to protest. Patty agreed.

When the hostage negotiator got on the phone, events proceeded rather quickly. The hostage negotiator told the client what she had to do: rape is bad, and someone has hurt you, and policemen think that is terrible. But we policemen are good men who want to help you. Now put down the gun and come out of the house.[7]

The client did not want to talk with the hostage negotiator. She kept asking where Patty was, couldn't she please talk to Patty, didn't Patty want to talk to her anymore? The hostage negotiator assured her that, "in a minute," she would be able to talk with Patty again. Eventually, the hostage negotiator told the client that, if she put down her gun and came out of the house, Patty would be there, and she could meet Patty.

The outcome was that the client did agree to come out of the house *under the condition that Patty would be there*. (Patty herself had not yet been consulted about this agreement.) It was then explained to the client that there would be one police officer there to greet her. She was not told that a SWAT team surrounded the house. From police phone connections to our agency, we were notified that she came out of the house, was told to hold her hands above her head, and was "searched and found unarmed." Of course, Patty was not there. From that point, the client was taken to the police station.

Meanwhile, back in the agency office, the negotiator then informed Patty that she did not really need to go with them to the police station, that he could "just get one of the female deputies to put on a white shirt and say her name is Patty."

ASSESSING COUNSELOR TRUSTWORTHINESS

The general feeling expressed among the volunteers by the early morning when we processed and debriefed the evening's work was that this case had been mishandled. All of us (especially Patty, since she was the central counselor for the client) were asking ourselves what we could have done differently. I do believe that things could have been otherwise and that Patty and others bear a responsibility for harms done. But, as readers will see, this analysis of harms and responsibilities draws in not only actions performed but conceptual frameworks and institutionalized attitudes and, although these things shape our character and conduct, they are harder to identify and hold accountable in others as well as ourselves. We assess the character of another by the way she lives her life; by the signs and assurances she gives of her commitments, her values, her projects and interests; by her loyalties; and so on. In other words, knowing another's quality of character takes time. I talked with Patty and worked with her, but did not know her well, and consequently have only a limited idea of her moral point of view or her political commitments. But I am not asking about Patty's overall character; the focus here is on a particular virtue, that of trustworthiness. Even so, what counts as a violation of trust is not a simple and straightforward matter. There are kinds and degrees of trust, and the expectations and actions of both truster and trustee must be considered in trying to determine when violations and betrayals have occurred. Trustworthiness is always with respect to something and someone and, as I indicated earlier, we are often placed in situations where expectations of trust pull us in different directions. Hence, in raising questions about Patty's accountability, I am not asking an abstract question about her trustworthiness. Instead, I am considering Patty's trustworthiness as a complex set of relations in light of what I know about her choices and attitudes, the client's expressed needs and reactions, and the larger institutional and political context in which this case occurs. Although it may not be possible finally to settle questions about Patty's role in this particular case, I believe a query about her accountability and trustworthiness is instructive.

Current ethical frameworks for health care, with their emphasis on justified right actions, imply that bonds of trust between client and practitioner can be broken and yet the moral responsibilities of a practitioner *qua* practitioner not be breached. But that view is inconsistent with the view that one of the responsibilities of moral agents in general is to be trustworthy, because if we consider trustworthiness to be a central responsibility of moral agents, then surely it is also a responsibility that falls within the domain of health care workers. So, when one is a counselor, part of being a responsible moral agent involves being worthy of the trust of the client who seeks that kind of care. Thus, when the client's trust is breached, morality requires further explanation in order to show that the practitioner did not fail in his or her responsibility to be trustworthy with respect to that client.

One way that is done in practice is by referring to agency policies. In Patty's case, the policies served to legitimize the hegemonic methods employed in "helping" the client; if Patty hadn't known the policies herself, the law enforcement officers, the supervisors, and her co-workers might have pointed out to her that they endorse active intervention and that is the stated objective of the agency. Patty did know these things, though, and this knowledge made it more difficult for her to disagree with the plans.

The fact that the policy seems to permit such actions, though, does not necessarily exempt Patty from accountability for having betrayed her client. Although agency policies toward "saving lives" can be offered as justification for what would otherwise be considered unethical conduct, they are trotted out far too quickly to satisfy this moral requirement. Since the betrayal of the client is not a harm that is taken seriously, others' judgments about what is necessary to "help" the client are not evaluated in the context of the trusting relationship but instead in the *context of the policy's norms of help and harm*, and pointing to them for justification presupposes that the policies have gotten it right. But it seems clear, in the case above, that the crisis team exceeded their discretionary power through the methods by which they responded to the crisis and prevented the suicide. And a policy that can be used to justify such excesses is not in the interests of the client. In fact, I suggest that policies may work more to inappropriately appease or negate counselors' discomfort about the ways in which they respond to crisis calls than to actually justify their actions.

Although the stated policy at the agency where this situation evolved is to provide empathetic, empowering, respectful services, it is an inadequate policy both in theory and in practice. In reality, as I have suggested, active intervention can trump respect and empathy, often at the cost both of the stated policy of treating clients with respect and of client trust. Policies which uphold intervention as a primary mission are bound sometimes to conflict with other stated values to counsel in an ethical manner, and, as such, typically relegate values such as respect and trust to a subordinate position.[8]

Furthermore, the policy of "active" rather than "passive" intervention gives weight to the counselor's responsibility to resolve crises quickly. While there are situations where time is of the utmost importance, the case above was not one of them. But crisis counseling practices reflect an interpretation of the policies that mirrors the model that health care, in general, is adopting—*outcome-based* care. This model rewards those practitioners who can quickly and efficiently address immediate problems, whether it is to diagnose skillfully and expeditiously and refer a patient or, in the case of crisis counseling, to stop a suicide attempt efficiently. There is reason to be concerned that, in the form of outcome-based care that the health industry is adopting, there is little room for the development of trusting relationships. The goal in health care is increasingly coming to be that of serving as many clients or patients as one can in a given period of time, and management teams and insurance companies reward such an approach. Practices and policies employed under this outcome-based model, especially those that prioritize active intervention, would seem to be antithetical to trust.

I am not arguing for a rejection of all outcome-based considerations of how one ought to be. Clearly, caring for another's health requires that a practitioner consider how to achieve good health. The worry about health care's approach to outcomes is the way in which it seems to allow—and even encourage—practitioners to separate the outcome of a given situation from the way in which that outcome is arrived at. The outcome, then, can be evaluated independently from the way that it has been brought about. But from the perspective of virtue ethics, both the ends we choose and the ways by which we promote them matter. To the extent that the independence of ends from means is built into the developing models of health care, this demarcation has the potential to undermine trustworthiness.[9]

The question "In trying to help the client, did I disproportionately harm her?"—a question in which we consider various harms and their consequences—is not the same as the question "Did I resolve the crisis?"—an outcome-based question that may very well ignore the possibility that resolving one crisis may be fueling another. And neither is the same as the question "Did I honor the client's trust?"—a question in which we hold ourselves accountable to the client for the use or abuse of our power in that relationship.[10]

But if the policies are themselves suspect, and we can see that power relations were operative within the crisis team, what can be said about Patty's role in deception and trickery? Was Patty a victim of power-tripping men with guns and holsters? Was she, in a way, being held hostage as those with more institutional power used her as "ransom" while they negotiated with the client? Who were the real "terrorists"?[11]

The nature of accountability, in this example, is extraordinarily complex. Patty needed to be worthy of the trust of the client, of her co-workers, and of the law enforcement officers. But being trustworthy with respect to the law, in this case, meant forming a deceptive alliance with them which undermined her trustworthiness with regard to her client; being trustworthy with respect to her client might have meant that she not only hindered her ability to get assistance from the law in this case, but potentially jeopardized long-term relations between our agency and law enforcement—relations in which cooperation is vital not only to funding but to effectively serving clients.[12] Furthermore, the law enforcement officers distrusted the counselors at the agency as well as the client's explanation of her situation. They seemed to view the counselors as rather incompetent do-gooders whose function was to pacify members of the dysfunctional subculture until the police could take charge and reestablish order—and they almost entirely discounted the client's story (for example, by commenting to the crisis team that her sense of victimization as well as her reports of assault were most likely spurious and motivated by a need for attention). This case is particularly apt, therefore, because it illustrates the ways in which crisis counseling intersects with the legal and economic domains.

How ought accountability for the deceitfulness and trickery be addressed? How many people bear responsibility, and to what degree, if harm was done to relations of trust between the caller and the others involved? Patty put the trace on the client's phone line and asked the supervisor to contact the police. But from that point on, the staff and volunteers at the agency were caught between a desire to assist the client in a fairly noncoercive manner and a need to acquiesce to the law enforcement officers who entered the case. In the judgment of Patty and some of the other counselors, such extreme paternalistic actions were not necessary in order to prevent the client's use of the weapon. But it is also clear that the actions undertaken expedited the resolution of the crisis. Furthermore, everyone complied with the evolving plan. Then again, although we at the agency knew that deception was involved, we also felt accountable to the law enforcement officers as well as to our own agency.

When a counselor uses deception, trickery, and coercion as part of her "helping" the client to manage a crisis, her trustworthiness is called into question. But the counselor's trustworthiness is connected both to other people's trustworthiness and to agency policies and practices. To understand more clearly what it means to be trustworthy to someone who has been harmed by violence, we need to look at the social and institutional contexts in which moral agency gets exercised.

Angela Davis, in thinking about the meaning of freedom in the context of the enslavement of Africans by European Americans, asked, is it possible for someone to be in chains and still be free? (Davis 1975) And, to extend the question, we can ask, is it possible for someone to be caught within systems of oppression and yet exercise agency in an ethical manner? "The first condition of freedom is the open act of resistance" (196). Resistance, Davis points out, includes not only a refusal to submit (to a flogging, in the case she discusses, or to law enforcement officers, supervisors, and policies, in the case I offered) but also a refusal to accept dominant ideologies' definitions. Resistance, then, is a rejection of oppressive institutions, their standards, and their morality.

As persons in varying positions of power, though, we are often unaware that we can be enslaved by our own systems (Davis 1975, 196). Patty is caught in a complex web of relationships that demand conflicting loyalties and responsibilities from her. She has power in relation to her client, but she has less power in relation to nearly everyone else on the crisis team. Patty might accurately be described as being in a double-bind: whatever she does, she will betray someone's trust.

Still, we must ask: why does she betray whom she does?

In pressing this question, I am suggesting that being in a double-bind is not the same as being in a moral dilemma. First of all, this case is not one of a classic moral dilemma between, say, preserving life and preserving trust; as I argued above, the sense of urgency was more contrived than real—the creation of a dilemma is a fiction resulting from an outcome-based model that emphasizes efficiency. In my view, given time—and a transformation of attitude and approach—Patty and the crisis team could have brought about the safety of the client and others while still honoring the client's trust (thus also honoring the agency's goals, minus efficiency). I will say more about this claim later. The point is that, with respect to the alleged choice between preserving life and preserving trust, this particular case does not appear to have the characteristics of a dilemma. Besides, I have grave reservations about framing crisis counseling in such a way, where the preservation of trusting relations is pitted against other, seemingly incompatible aims. This way of conceptualizing the problems of this case misses the point about the place of trust in crisis counseling. For a person to be in a moral dilemma, she must be faced with incompatible choices of action, each of which embodies values or principles which are taken to be equally right or good and the violation of which would each be taken to be equally bad. The dilemma, then, is that there is no way to decide what to do that will effect a morally better outcome, no clear moral ground for preferring one action over another. If there is a policy or some other systematic way of deciding which of two values or principles to choose when they come into conflict, and if there is also a practice of one value being consistently trumped when it comes into conflict with other values, then it seems to me that the conditions for a dilemma with respect to the subordinate value or principle do not arise. I have argued that, with respect to the value of trust, it is a subordinate value both in policy and in practice. Finally, to view this sort of case as a moral dilemma between preserving life and preserving trust is to mistake the richness and complexity of trusting relations. Let me emphasize that issues of trustworthiness in this case are not simply between Patty and her client, but between Patty and her supervisor, between the supervisor, the whole agency and the legal system, between that agency and its financial supporters, and so on. Like others in mid-level institutional roles, relations of trust are multifaceted and multidirectional.

So it is important to remind ourselves that many directions this case could have taken involved potential betrayals of trust between various individuals, groups, and institutions. Furthermore, it is important not to assume that the potential betrayals were on equal moral footing. It *matters* whom one betrays and whom one stands by: what we are trying to sort out here, in linking trustworthiness with nonexploitation and nondomination, is our ability to create a nonviolent world. This means that, if we are not to cast Patty as a victim—if we are to grant her some agency in this context—then we have to consider the ways in which she does make choices and what those choices mean.

Although I do not know exactly what Patty's thoughts and feelings were, I inferred from her actions, comments, and body language that she did feel caught in a predicament. And one way of understanding Patty's frame of mind is that this double-bind gives rise to ambivalence—about whose story to accept, whose interpretation of the situation to adopt, and whose picture of the world she herself should trust. It might be her experience, for example, that when the hostage negotiator and other police officers arrive, Patty and the whole scene get recast in a familiar script which nevertheless is discrepant with what Patty had, up to now, understood the scene to be. One might imagine that, with two disconsonant world-views, Patty's head spins: how is she to decide who has correctly interpreted the characters and roles in this scene? Is Patty right that her client has been victimized and needs the painstakingly slow building of trust in order to help her? Or are others right that the client is a dangerous terrorist who is holding her mother hostage? Conflicting moral claims collide with epistemic dissonance as Patty tries to attend to her client, co-workers, supervisors, and law enforcement officers all at once. In the midst of her client's crisis, Patty now experiences a kind of crisis of her own. Caught in double-binds, confused, and demoralized, a third interpretation occurs to her: maybe Patty is being "terrorized" herself. After all (one might guess) she feels bullied and scared.

That Patty might have experienced ambivalence, confusion, and powerlessness is not surprising. Neither is the way she momentarily resolved those feelings: policies, institutions, and people with power over her all colluded to pressure her into settling her ambivalence in the direction that resolved the crisis, quickly and finally. Although this case was a rather dramatic one with its themes of deception, coercion, and trickery—what I have called abuses in discretionary power—the tendency to devalue the importance of client trust is entrenched in much of current crisis counseling. Let me briefly mention two other kinds of situations. For example, a client who exhibits irritation at the counselor while seeming fairly unresponsive to the counselor's suggestions may be rather quickly categorized and referred to in reports as "a borderline," whereby the client's concerns are dismissed as a product of an intractable personality disorder. Rather than treating the borderline personality disorder as a diagnosis that requires training and careful consideration after considerable client contact, the diagnosis is used to label what seems to the counselor to be manipulative and frustrating behavior. Once a client is labeled a "borderline," the counselor's main goal may be to get off the telephone without getting hooked into the client's manipulations. While clients are sometimes difficult to talk with and assist, their concerns (even their irritation or misguided attempts to gain sympathy or control of the conversation) deserve respect and care, not dismissal or pathologizing.[13]

Another fairly common occurrence is when psychiatric patients call a crisis line. Agencies such as the one for which I worked often serve as backup services for outpatient psychiatric patients who live in residence homes. A list of clients in this category is provided to the agency for quick reference to the client's particular illness and the agency that oversees the client's treatment. When a client with a psychiatric illness calls our agency, that client identifies herself or himself and the counselor looks up the relevant information in the reference book. One of the most common responses of counselors, once they learn the status of the caller, is to inquire about the caller's medications. ("Have you been taking your meds regularly?" "Have you seen your doctor lately for a medication adjustment?") In other words, the caller's concerns are frequently treated as a medication problem, and the client is steered back to her or his main therapeutic route. There are reasons for this approach: crisis counselors are not qualified to treat psychiatric illnesses, for one thing, and it is important for counselors to recognize their limitations in competency to handle particular cases. But this approach is efficient, too, and I am not convinced that the value of efficiency is as consistently high as the place it seems to hold. Focusing on questions about the client's medications is a quick fix that frees up the counselor for other calls but may not address the needs of the client at all.

Clients who receive the kind of treatment I described in these situations may not feel betrayed, but I expect that many of them would feel dissatisfied with the quality of care they received and perhaps would feel rejected, judged, and, to varying degrees, distrustful of the help that was offered as well as of the agency in general. While it would take us too far afield to develop fully the ways that trust is impeded in these less dramatic cases, these examples are suggestive of the ways in which treating clients with disrespect, dismissal, or lack of sympathy can affect trusting relations between client and counselor. And this can happen even when the counselor is well-meaning and sees herself as upholding other values such as making efficient use of her counseling time or not overstepping her level of competency.

Moreover, in addition to the fact that most agency policies prioritize active intervention and outcome-based efficiency above other values and objectives, counseling practices both reflect and reinforce the values of the dominant culture—values which are deeply embedded in western health care. So when counselors do experience ambivalence or contradictions in the way they understand a problem, and they want to adopt one or another way to resolve their own moral and epistemic dissonances, the picture of the world that may "fit" best—or, if it is not necessarily a good "fit," the one that is least disruptive to the overall functioning of the crisis team—is the dominant view. This suggests that we must look beyond the policies themselves to the sorts of ideas and values that assent to and sustain those policies. Doing so will put us in a position to consider what else Patty could have done to develop and sustain various relations of trust while still responding to her client's situation as a potential threat to life.

IDEOLOGICAL UNDERCURRENTS

Abuses in discretionary power, such as those that occurred in the case study, don't just "happen." We might prefer to think that such cases are rare, or that only idiosyncratic power-mongers would exploit others' vulnerability, or that bad policies are to blame. In this way (we hope) we can isolate the problem.

But the underpinnings of abuses of discretionary power suggest that such explanations will not suffice. Endemic to crisis counseling (as well as western health care) and working their way insidiously into our everyday judgments and perceptions are dominant ideological themes that interlock and reinforce systems of oppression. Elsewhere I have discussed ways in which current health care is affected by a less-than-democratic epistemology, prejudicial and hegemonic standards of credibility, and an ontological commitment to women as essentially diseased in body and mind (Potter 1996). Crisis counseling, like other kinds of health care, is guided by norms of rationality that are, at least in part, political in nature. Who counts as rational and credible, who count as knowers, and whose complaints are taken seriously intersect with social and cultural markers of worth and difference. Those categorized as "Other" may be a priori pathologized, or intimidated into silence, or treated with suspicion. Here I want to discuss two additional points that also played a role in providing apparent justification for the counselor's course of action.

The notion of the "expert." One obvious way health care workers have power is in the role of "expert": the client turns to someone more knowledgeable or experienced than herself because she doesn't know what to do, or feels overwhelmed, with a particular concern or problem.[14] The caller trusts the counselor, then, to use her knowledge appropriately and not to exploit the client's vulnerability. But the practice of legally and morally sanctioned paternalism places discretionary power in the hands of these "experts" whose knowledge supposedly endows them with the ability to know what is in the client's best interest, and thus the power to deprive clients of their right to agency, even to the degree that it is sometimes permissible to lie or deceive.

The counselor is still trustworthy, on this account, because she acts within the bounds of her discretionary power. Note that, in the case study, the client didn't actually leave open the limits as to how the counselor could help her: she was quite clear on what she did not want. But her stated needs and expectations were overridden by "experts" who decided what the best course of action would be based on their "expert" knowledge.

Notions of "personhood." Dominant western culture is committed to a not always coherent set of notions of personhood, and this commitment carries enormous political, legal and moral significance. Historically, this commitment has entailed certain beliefs, varying from time to time and place to place, about what counts as being fully human—and, it need hardly be said, women and people of nondominant groups frequently haven't met the criteria. For example, in Patricia Williams's discussion of the intersection of racism with medicine and the law, she points to the ways in which whites hold partializing judgments of blacks:

> one of the things passed on from slavery, which continues in the oppression of people of color, is a belief structure rooted in a concept of black (or brown or red) antiwill, the antithetical embodiment of pure will. We live in a society where the closest equivalent of nobility is the display of unremittingly controlled willfulness. To be perceived as unremittingly without will is to be imbued with an almost lethal trait.
>
> I would characterize the treatment of blacks by whites in their law as defining blacks as those who had no will. That treatment is not total interdependency, but a relation in which partializing judgments, employing partializing standards of humanity, impose generalized inadequacy on a race: if "pure will" or total control equals the perfect white person, then impure will and total lack of control equal the perfect black person. (Williams 1991, 219)

This dehumanizing and partializing conception of people of color is operative, Williams suggests, when women of color are sterilized without their consent and without their knowledge. When counselors do not see certain groups of people as whole persons, it is likely that they fail to see them as deserving or needing respect, which can lead to abuses of discretionary power.

The underlying features of health care I have outlined above can be seen in the supposed lifesaving effort I described above, and they led to several forms of abuse of discretionary power: the "experts" that pull rank on epistemic authority (cops over counselors over client); norms of rationality that pathologize the client, followed by justification for use of coercion and deception; partializing judgments of the humanity of biracial people collapsing into "Blacks-are-armed-and-dangerous"; standards of credibility which led to a mocking dismissal of the client's reports of violent attacks against her; and an attendant criminalization of victims through an evocation of hostage scenarios—where girlchildren become "terrorists" when they attempt to express outrage at their exploitation. The pattern of violence, once examined, reveals an escalating problem in our responses: the person who has been harmed by violence grasps at violent means to end her pain and is subdued by more domination. And while this case may seem extreme, in fact the policies are typical and the underlying conceptual patterns I've identified are embedded in the practices of much of current crisis counseling. Consider, for example, the way the categories "borderline" or "psychiatric patient" can operate to dehumanize a client, assume irrationality, discredit, and so on. Policies often give lip service to the values of respect, empathy, and trust, while in reality allowing the values of efficiency and active intervention to trump—not to mention unstated values of upholding the status quo and hegemonic relations. Responses guided by current policies and practices, then, when a vulnerable client calls for help, may be disrespectful and disempowering to the client. They tend to devalue or altogether ignore the responsibility that attends the client's tenuous and fragile trust, and by treating her concerns lightly, or worse, by deceiving and betraying the client in her most vulnerable and desperate moment, may inflict a devastating harm.

TRUSTWORTHINESS AND RESISTANCE WITHIN MULTIPLE POSITIONS

As I indicated earlier, one might be inclined to argue that the locus of the problem in the above case is the all-male law enforcement team: they were the ones in power, they exploited their position of power, and they acted in an untrustworthy manner, one might reason. Cheryl Clarke writes that "men at all levels, of all classes and colors have the potential to act out legalistically, moralistically, and violently when they cannot colonize women" (Clarke 1981, 128). On that view, the law enforcement sphere would be the ones responsible for the harm done to the client and would be identified as the primary focus for change; if law enforcement officers could just purge their cognitive frameworks of a war mentality toward "Others," then this sort of situation wouldn't have to arise. Patty, though (one might suggest), wasn't untrustworthy, because she was just a pawn in an elaborate system: the culpable ones were the powerful ones.

Clearly, the law enforcement officers brought to the crisis undesirable attitudes and methods, and clearly, powerful systems of domination were at work. One could argue that the problem in this case was the agency's policy of drawing in the police. A solution, then, might be to revise the policy to one which allows for a diverse, heterodox set of responses to suicidal persons; this would involve creating a policy on police involvement that would require that the least-intrusive, trust-preserving means are exhausted short of completed suicide attempts before the police are brought in. Alternatively, though, one could argue that the very option of police referrals leads to trust-destructive or preemptive hegemonic responses by counselors and practitioners. The question of whether or not a crisis center is ever justified in turning over a case to a pure outcome-based police force is a serious one that must be carefully considered.[15]

But it is not the case that unethical practices seep into otherwise decent and honorable crisis intervention agencies via the legal sphere. This discussion suggests some of the ways in which the policies and practices of the institution of crisis counseling are infused with moral problems. An analysis of abuses of power and accountability, therefore, needs to take into account the ways in which discretionary power of the male law enforcement officers combines with institutional policies and practices and systems of oppression in general.

I question whether responsibility for abuses of discretionary power lies solely with those who hold the most power.[16] That way of thinking about power and responsibility is inadequate to clarify our understanding of the degree to which Patty's trustworthiness was compromised by her role in this case. Such a view misses a key point about Patty and others in mid-level institutional roles: that Patty occupies, not one position, but rather moves between and among multiple unstable positions, where her own trustworthiness is embedded within a complex pattern of relations and responsibilities. Patty, and others like her, is never simply one thing or another. Counselors and those workers who are employed in mid-level positions, then, will find that they are participating in practices and making choices which may reinforce hegemonic and oppressive structures and legitimize dominant ideologies even while they experience themselves as trapped.

By exposing the instability of positions within systems of oppression, I highlight a way of conceptualizing trustworthiness that allows for the possibility of resistance. As Biddy Martin and Chandra Mohanty point out in their discussion of Minny Bruce Pratt's article "Identity: Skin Blood Heart," power is most often conceptualized—wrongly—as totalizing. When we examine systems of oppression and the ways in which our positions in relation to power are unstable, we see how Patty is caught in double-binds about what it means to be trustworthy: "'the system' is revealed to be not one but multiple overlapping intersecting systems or relations that are historically constructed and recreated through every day practices and interactions, and that implicate the individual in contradictory ways" (Martin and Mohanty 1986, 209). This way of understanding Patty's role/s as fluid and ambiguous leaves open the possibility that Patty and other counselors can resist colluding in systems of oppression while moving within them. It suggests that there is a critical interplay between being trustworthy with respect to a client and resisting dominant ideology and practices, an interplay that requires attention in that most of the people who seek crisis counseling are disenfranchised, marginalized, and socially isolated persons who are vulnerable to being constructed as "Other" and responded to in ways that perpetuate harms to them through systems of domination and subordination.

Chinua Achebe, in an article honoring the contributions that James Baldwin has made to an understanding of what it means to be Black in America, discusses the claim Baldwin made that "Negroes want to be treated like men." Baldwin noted that this claim is "a perfectly straightforward statement containing only seven words" and then remarked: "People who have mastered Kant, Hegel, Shakespeare, Marx, Freud, and the Bible find this statement utterly impenetrable." Achebe, in commenting on Baldwin's statement, says that this failure to comprehend is a willful, obdurate refusal (Achebe 1991, 280). That refusal, Achebe says, is grounded in the recognition that such (thinly veiled) declarations of intent as Baldwin makes are profoundly subversive and that to acknowledge the meaning behind them would radically alter the ease and comfort with which those in power move in and through the world. It is not in the interests of the privileged, Achebe suggests, to listen to and comprehend the narratives of the disenfranchised.

Bernard Boxill makes a similar point in his analysis of self-respect and protest (Boxill 1976, 58-69). The statement by James Baldwin, straightforward though it is, might well be a kind of *protest*, as Boxill explains the concept. A protest, Boxill writes, is an expression of outrage at injustice; it is an unmistakable affirmation of a person's belief that she or he has rights and therefore claims self-respect. But a protest, a declaration of a person's belief in her or his own self-respecting self-worth, is a provocation to those in power relative to the protester: provocations arouse resentment because they challenge the moral claim to superior status that the more powerful enjoy and want to preserve.

Provocation of those in power relative to oneself may well bring on retaliation, and retaliation of those who protest injustice is one way in which the interests of members of dominant groups, and those who sustain systems of oppression, are protected. The threat of retaliation, persecution, or backlash suggests that it is not in one's interest to protest injury or to resist the coercive force of dominant structures and ideologies. Our interests are shaped, in part, by the ways in which we are rewarded or punished, praised or blamed, for our various choices, affiliations, and ways of being. Although many crisis counselors are deeply committed to doing ethical counseling, the complex structure of power relations within the crisis team as well as their own ideological frameworks may erode their efforts. Even a counselor who does not assent to dominant ideology's interpretation of a particular situation and who rejects racist and elitist explanations for a client's crisis may find herself acquiescing to tactics of domination and exploitation in order not to be "disruptive," for to cause a disruption, by questioning the accepted approaches to crisis intervention, would be to take the risk that she will be regarded as untrustworthy in the crisis team's eyes. Being regarded as untrustworthy by the crisis team and institutional supervisors may mean a bad review, less responsibility in the future, or even dismissal, which, to a paid employee, could be economically disastrous. The deliberation about whom to betray and whose trust to retain, therefore, may include considerations about how far the counselor or worker thinks her supervisors or employers might go in disciplining or demoting her for her resistance.[17] But, in avoiding disruption, she also makes a choice about whom she needs to regard her as trustworthy and whose assessment of her moral character is expendable. (This decision is also supported by the fact that a crisis counselor doesn't have to face a betrayed client, whereas she will most certainly be held explicitly accountable to the agency and to the crisis team if she disputes accepted practices and thereby causes a disruption.)

All of us who have grown up with western values have internalized, at least to some extent, the dominant culture's ideological undercurrents, and Patty and other crisis counselors are not immune from the force-fields of those ideologies. Fundamental concepts such as personhood, rationality, and credibility are embedded in largely unexamined biases and assumptions that, as raced, classed, gendered, and sexually oriented people, we carry into our relations. And ideologically grounded distortions about concepts of personhood, rationality, and so on, are often applied unevenly according to an individual counselor's privileges, her character, and the prevailing practices of the community. A counselor's ontological commitments, her adherence or resistance to the norms of rationality, as well as her underlying epistemological framework, will affect whether she conceives of the relationship as one where client and practitioner jointly engage in establishing a bond of trust and seeking a nonviolent course of action or treatment for the client. Whether she believes the client's story will depend on whether she accepts mainstream standards of credibility or whether she is able and willing to resist dominant ideological frameworks that seduce us into the value of "giving the benefit of the doubt" to members of dominant groups and the value of distrust and suspicion toward members of marginalized and disenfranchised groups.

If a counselor wishes to develop the virtue of trustworthiness, she must bring the moral values of that virtue into the particular relationships where she counsels. If she agrees that deliberately tricking, deceiving, or similarly betraying a client's trust is morally wrong, then even when there are reasons to do so—even when there are others who expect her to be trustworthy, who count on her to support their positions, and who might feel betrayed if she worries most about sustaining her client's trust—a trustworthy person will do what is within her power not to betray the client's trust. Because being worthy of another's trust requires that we take care not to exploit the power we have to do harm to the trusting person, and because the client population is particularly vulnerable to exploitation and betrayal, a trustworthy counselor will attend conscientiously and responsibly to the relation of trust that has formed between her client and herself, taking care to use her power of discretion both wisely and ethically.

This analysis seems to lead to the conclusion that Patty's commitment to take care of that which her client entrusted to her should be so central to questions about Patty's good character that even losing the trust of her co-workers and support team wouldn't deter her from keeping her commitment to the client. It suggests that, if faced with a choice between being trustworthy to her client and being out of a job, Patty has reasons to think carefully about what the virtuous path would be as well as what the pragmatic and economically sound path would be. But, while I hold that Patty and others in mid-level situations have reasons to resist (i.e., reasons to resist being coerced to betray the trust of a disenfranchised person who has placed her trust in them), there are other moral considerations that complicate this analysis.

Not all the considerations Patty or others might deliberate about, when faced with a conflict between being thought of as trustworthy by the more powerful and sustaining the trust of a disenfranchised client, are based on fear of retaliation. Suppose one is committed to working with those whose living conditions are oppressive; suppose crisis counseling is what Patty sees as her life's work. Maintaining cooperative relations with those in power is important to being able to continue to be trustworthy to the disenfranchised. Many people in mid-level positions have the responsibility to be a mediator between the more powerful and the less powerful. A legal advocate mediates between a woman who has been battered and the court system; a nurse (among other things) mediates between doctors and patients. Patty, too, might be viewed as a mediator between the client and the larger social services system. If one loses credibility with the more powerful, one may not be in a position to plead the case of a disenfranchised client, student, or patient in the future.

So another sort of question arises: how is it we are to be trusted and trustworthy in the world, not only at this moment, but in the future? I have argued that it is morally suspect to disregard the trust that a disenfranchised person has placed in us when the motivation is to avoid retaliation. I also argued that it is morally objectionable for us to appease those in power to the benefit of dominant structures and the detriment of the disenfranchised. But we also may need to consider the importance of maintaining trusting relations with people in positions of relative power when not to do so would jeopardize our ability to come through for those disenfranchised others who may, or may come to, count on us. It is important for people in mid-level positions to be seen as trustworthy by their peers, supervisors, employers, etc., in order to be able to be trustworthy to those whom they are responsible to serve and care for. Patients need to be able to count on nurses to communicate patients' needs to doctors; if a nurse isn't seen as trustworthy by the doctors with whom she works, then her ability to be trustworthy to her patients is likely to be impeded. Similar reasoning applies with regard to legal advocates, counselors, and others in mid-level positions: women who are battered need to be able to count on legal advocates to communicate with those in the court system; clients need to be able to count on counselors to communicate with those in social services—on behalf of the patient or client.[18]

So, although people in mid-level positions should take seriously the responsibility to sustain the trust of the disenfranchised who have trusted them—they should make their trust much more central to their deliberation—they may also need to consider how best to honor their position of trust, both now and in the future. Being trustworthy to their clients, patients, or students, then, may require that they do not completely alienate themselves from those whose cooperation they will need. And, although appeasing those in power is objectionable when doing so is to the detriment of the oppressed, one may be motivated to appease the more powerful for another reason—namely, that one also has the interests of the disenfranchised at heart.

This discussion needs a cautionary note, however. This last moral consideration leaves open the possibility that we may act in bad faith: it is possible to deceive oneself (about one's motivations or about who will be benefited or harmed by one's decision, for example). And it doesn't seem morally virtuous to deceive this person now on the grounds that relations with others in the future will be better protected against failures of trust. But the temporal question of how we can continue to be trusted so that we can be fully trustworthy does seem to be a consideration that needs to be included in our moral reasoning.

FINDING THE MEAN

When discretionary power is cast in terms of counselor trustworthiness, one is trustworthy when one's ways of caring are neither excessive nor deficient.

But being trustworthy must always be contextualized to the parties involved and their particular concerns and needs, and so the mean cannot be specified in advance. How excess and deficit are understood will be relative, in a central way, to the client's needs within a given situation. But counselor trustworthiness with respect to a client typically will involve wresting some discretionary power from its assumed domain of the institution of health care and returning it to the delicate and nuanced relationship between the client and counselor. Given the complex differences in power within systems of oppression and given the tendency for dominant groups, agencies, and institutions to exploit those differences on behalf of the powerful and to the detriment of the already disenfranchised, counselors who want to be trustworthy with regard to their clients will have to be especially attentive to the ideological biases and conceptual distortions and other impediments to being ethical counselors.

Patty did seem to have a fairly good understanding of what the client's world was like. But, as this discussion suggests, in order for Patty to have sustained the trust of her client, she would most likely have had to find a way to resist or subvert the dominant frameworks as they manifested themselves in the evolution of that night's crisis work. For example, Patty set in motion the chain of events that eventually led to her client's house being surrounded by a SWAT team without the client's knowledge or consent. When she requested that the call be traced, she could have stated to her supervisor what she advised as the limits of action. She could have strongly advised against the need for a SWAT team, on the grounds that she was making progress with her client and that that precaution appeared for the time to be unnecessary. Probably one of the most effective actions Patty could have taken, but did not, would have been to inform other counselors of her reservations about the police and hostage negotiator's methods, given her judgment of the client's frame of mind, and to request that other counselors step outside the room to discuss alternative measures for handling this case. Instead, Patty had to temporarily shift the counseling task in order to have a whispered and hasty conversation with the law enforcement officers, which left her in a weak position to disagree with their plans. In general, although her body language and facial expressions indicated some disagreement, Patty was not giving voice to her reservations or concerns in time for others to help her change the direction of events.

In other words, I am suggesting that Patty could have done more to try to protect her client. This is not to say that she would have been fully successful in her attempts. As I mentioned earlier, other counselors had spoken up on some points without much effect. But others were in a weaker position to argue in the interests of Patty's client when Patty herself was not explicitly and adamantly making her assessment or position known. Furthermore, even if Patty's efforts had not significantly altered the direction of events, her trustworthiness with respect to her client would have been less compromised if she had been less complicit. Knowing how the police respond to situations such as this, she went ahead and involved them without attempting to take charge of the parameters. She did not refute the insinuations and direct accusations that the client was malingering. She did not refuse to help the law enforcement officers set up a trap for her client. (She did, however, insist that she herself meet the client at the end of the night rather than sending a female officer in her name.)

It is my contention that the explanation for Patty's role in this case is that she, like others, had internalized attitudes, values, and perceptions that made it seem excusable or justifiable to sacrifice the trust of her client to other, supposedly greater values. Part of being a trustworthy counselor is knowing which aspects of a situation are salient to making good moral decisions. Patty could have (and may have) asked herself—even in the moment—how she was conceptualizing her client and what ideas about class, race, power, expertise, reason, and so on were operating that were leading her not to take a firm stand in defending her client's wishes. Whether or not she asked these sorts of questions, though, her decisions seem to indicate that she was informed and influenced by a value system structured and shaped by dominance and other repressive forces that function to maintain hierarchies of power.

But the time for resistance is usually not in the midst of another person's crisis, where one person's resistance may further jeopardize another person's safety. Although Patty could have disrupted the hostage negotiator's plans and challenged the norms upon which he and others where relying, she may have also worried about where such disruption would leave her desperate and despairing client. Counselors need to prepare for those times when their trustworthiness with respect to clients will be tested and strategies of resistance will be needed. And they need not to put off critiques of crisis counseling practices until the moment of crisis requires them to confront it.

Preparing for acts of resistance while attending to relations of trust with one's client, then, will require three sorts of things. One is that there needs to be a format for crisis intervention agencies and their support systems to critically examine practices, policies (especially those that empower counselors to engage nontherapeutic organizations like the police), ideologies, and methods of counseling. In this way, the structural and conceptual problems within the institution that I have discussed will begin to be explored. The second is that those working within the field need to engage in mutual critical reflection about the ideological biases and beliefs they bring to the workplace. Seeking knowledge about systems of oppression and locating oneself within them will enable counselors to be better prepared, when multiple positions destabilize them, to settle ambivalences with as much moral agency as possible. But from the perspective of virtue ethics, the objective is broader than to be able to exercise moral agency, for it matters what our character is, what our moral reasoning consists in, and what our moral psychology is like. Learning to be good, therefore, is a long-range task. What I urge is moral decision-making that aims to end the violence of institutionalized injustices and inequalities, and this requires the cultivation of good character and good institutions.

An Aristotelian notion of practical wisdom is useful here. Practical wisdom involves both knowledge about the specific goods of crisis counseling and understanding of what is most honorable; it involves both epistemic and moral knowledge (Aristotle 1985, 1141a20-1141b10). To be a good crisis counselor, it is not enough to develop good listening skills, to know available resources, and to be able to identify a caller's immediate needs; one must attend to the context of power and violence in which crisis counseling occurs and monitor oneself as someone situated within that context.[19] To do this requires a certain amount of self-awareness on a fairly deep level as well as awareness of sociopolitical, cultural, and ethnic dimensions of power relations as they play themselves out in our institutional and interpersonal lives. Critical self-reflection about one's conceptual framework in terms of the moral and political domain, and an openness to modification, are essential ingredients to being a good person. These two sorts of activities work best in a spirit of Aristotelian *philia*, where moral and epistemic inquiry that is undertaken between those who love justice, empathy, and other virtues will enable each of us to become better people ourselves through our joint activities and mutual correction (1172a14).

The third thing one can do to prepare for those times when one may need to resist is to form alliances with co-workers and like-minded members of the crisis team so that one does not end up in the position of resisting without any support from others. Knowing that there are at least one or two others whom one can count on not to undermine one's efforts at resistance may give one additional strength to resist even in the face of potential retaliation.

Qualities like cooperation, honesty, and loyalty are vital to the functioning of any organization or institution. After all, as I indicated earlier, if Patty is seen as consistently untrustworthy in relation to agency policies and practices, she will most likely lose her job. Still, as I have argued, the nature of trustworthiness as nonexploitative and nondominating presses the conclusion that counselors who wish to be trustworthy must worry most of all about the harms they might do to the already disenfranchised.

To reason well in these circumstances is not easy. Injustice and the threat of poverty, in an imperfect society, mean that many workers are, in fact, compelled by economic necessity to do what they would not otherwise do, and that fact is not to be taken lightly in conflicts at the workplace. The need to maintain cooperative relations with people in positions of relative power complicates, and sometimes compromises, our commitment to be trustworthy to the relatively powerless in a given situation. Considerations of what it takes to be trustworthy, therefore, point to the ways in which full virtue is constrained by our institutions and sociopolitical inequalities. Nevertheless, the question of how a trustworthy person would behave in particular situations is not only about discrete moments in time, because the person who deliberates about what to do and how to be for the moment is also one who, unless death intervenes, continues into the future. When we are deliberating about what trustworthiness calls for in a given situation, we should not only be concerned with our character, feelings, and actions in the moment but should project ourselves as future beings whose ability to be trustworthy over time is not compromised by current choices. Patty may not have been able to engage in long-term thinking about the implications of her actions when this situation arose, but it is crucial that she do so now if she wants to be more trustworthy in the future. Not only deliberation is involved: it is clear from this analysis that a central factor in Patty's future trustworthiness must include activity aimed at changing policies and practices so that the institutional constraints on trustworthiness are removed or at least lessened. For Patty to become more trustworthy in her capacity as a crisis counselor, she must work to ensure that those sorts of practices are no longer acceptable.

We cannot expect too much heroism of one another. This world requires compromise and negotiation. But it matters to our moral character—and to the future of more equitable, more compassionate communities and institutions—whom it is that we are negotiating with, where those compromises are being drawn, and who is getting sacrificed as a result.

CONCLUSION

This discussion challenges the notion that a person in crisis is best helped when counselors adhere to practices and policies which endorse counselor discretionary power to intervene on a client's behalf even when her trust is broken in the process. As I have suggested, the intersection of legal and economic domains with social services potentially, and sometimes actually, further violates and exploits the trust of already disenfranchised and socially isolated persons. Critical thinking about the underlying issues in crisis counseling indicates the need for counselors and clients to place issues of trust in a central position.

Clearly, current policies are, at best, inadequate, and perhaps the discussion points to the need for policies to be rewritten to reflect the value of creating and sustaining trustworthy client/practitioner relations. One might think that the policies are themselves at fault and that what we need to do is to tighten up the policy so that informed consent is given appropriate play. But I think that that wish is linked to an unconscious desire not to have to grapple with the deeper and larger social political and material ills that we are implicated in. We may desire to have the policy "tell us what to do." Like a desire for moral principles from which one theoretically can derive what one should do, a policy may reassure one that she is doing the right action and shouldn't have to worry that she is making mistakes or hurting people or that she might be blamed for something she should have known better than to do. But our moral and material lives are more complex than principles and policies can direct, and as I have argued, problems in crisis counseling do not start and stop at the level of policies.

As I have shown, training, practices, and formal policy are tipped in favor of intervention and thus make any policy statements concerning respectful, empowering, and trustworthy dealings difficult to carry out without conflict. So it seems clear that the tensions within agencies that value active intervention need to be examined critically in light of the other values held. When the value of trust is made more central to moral considerations, how will the principle of active intervention fare? How will the constellation of values shift when relations of trust are taken seriously? How can one be trustworthy under these complex and demanding conditions? In addition, this analysis also suggests that simply having a policy to be ethical is not sufficient when "being ethical" is defined by dominant groups whose ontological commitments and ideas about "experts," rationality, personhood, and credibility are deeply embedded in hegemonic and oppressive structures. As I have argued, *policies* are not the only determinant of people's decision-making, although they can be used as leverage and as justification.

But crisis counselors, while in a position to begin a revisioning of relations, will likely continue to be institutionally constrained unless they have the engagement of the bureaucratic levels of their agencies, the legal system, and the broader sociopolitical context within which individuals reach crises and seek responsible, trustworthy help. Thus, a transformation of such relations will entail that moral thinkers, counselors, social welfare workers and recipients, law enforcement officers, fund-raisers, and others work together to find effective ways to counsel people in crisis that take into account the value of honored trust.

NOTES

1. To preserve confidentiality, I have named the agency "Agency X." Agency X 1991 Annual Report.

2. Agency X 1991 Annual Report.

3. Agency X 1992 Annual Report.

4. Thanks to Anne Phibbs for prompting me to clarify the above claim.

5. Agency X 1992, 1991 Annual Reports

6. Conversation with outreach supervisor, Agency X, 1993.

7. This paraphrase is not intended as an indirect quote but rather is meant to convey the hostage negotiator's message the way I think it might have sounded to the client. Having been in on his conferences with other officers and counselors, I have the added perspective that he thought her claim of rape was spurious. Thus, the sincerity of his remarks is in question.

8. I am not arguing that active intervention is always wrong. The problem I am identifying is that of active intervention when a crisis team prematurely forfeits attempts to preserve values of trust and respect in the interest of some higher value that has yet to be shown to be at stake.

9. The worry I am pointing to is similar to a criticism of consequentialist theories. The criticism is that consequentialists take as their primary bearer of value "states of affairs," where the ranking and evaluation of various states of affairs are independent of how those states are brought about. (See Williams's critique of utilitarianism, for example, in Smart and Williams 1973). Note that act-consequentialists such as Samuel Scheffler reject such a criticism (Scheffler 1982, 1n).

10. Steve Miles, M.D., has pointed out that this discussion suggests an analogous abuse of trust that can arise in surgical harm. A radical mastectomy and a lumpectomy are both harmful in that they both involve incisions, exposure to germs and potentially harmful drugs, and so on, but a radical mastectomy is disproportionately harmful relative to the least harm necessary to benefit the person, which can be obtained from a lumpectomy.

11. I am not raising this question flippantly, although I do mean to convey a sense of irony. At the level of this case, as well as at the international level, the meaning of terrorism and the identification of terrorists are not based on objective and neutral facts. As Annamarie Oliverio argues in *The State of Terror* (1998), the construction of terrorists and its relation to ethnic and religious discrimination is a highly complex politically driven practice of the state. This case study is a microcosm of the larger activity of constructing terrorists and victims, good and evil, that is occurring in the United States as a result of the September 11, 2001 attacks.

12. For example, counselors rely on law officers to provide valuable police protection when the counselors are called to a scene of domestic violence to transport a battered woman to a shelter. Police officers agree to meet the counselors at the scene and escort the counselors and fleeing woman (and often children) out of the area safely. Without police protection, it is too dangerous for counselors to try to provide these services.

13. One way this problem arises is in a confusion between being effective and being efficient. With some clients, the counselor cannot be effective unless she gives up

the goal of being efficient. If a client is seeming manipulative and the counselor is experiencing frustration, it is going to take longer to get at the heart of the client's concerns. Counselors, in these situations, need not only the virtue of trustworthiness but patience and courage and intellectual virtue as well.

14. An "expert" is someone who has specialized knowledge, or is believed or assumed to have specialized knowledge, in an area. But "expert" here also means that those are persons who have the knowledge to implement certain policies and practices (that is, those who are trained and expected to implement institutional policies). I suggest that "experts" also, in large part, mold those policies and practices. As I say at the end of this article, while I think that health care workers (at every level) ought to play a role in setting policies and transforming practices, this task should not be solely the domain of "experts."

15. Comments by Steve Miles, M.D. Although I am not discussing in detail relations of trust between law enforcement officers and citizens, I believe those relations also cry out for critical analysis. Policemen and -women, although part of an outcome-based institution, are entrusted with certain responsibilities, and their conduct comes under scrutiny—increasingly, as examples of police brutality and racism are apparently ubiquitous. In this case, the officers would be blamed if someone were shot and they could have prevented it, so one might argue that they acted to sustain general "public" trust. A critique of that line of reasoning is beyond the scope of this paper. However, this discussion suggests that the social welfare system and the legal system need to identify and embody a more unified mission—one that gives nonexploitative and nondominating trusting relations a central place.

16. Clarke, as I noted earlier, suggests that male dominance is the axis of power, placing gender inequalities at the heart of systems of oppression. But there are reasons to reject such a view: a gendered analysis is inadequate to illuminate the complex relationships between trustworthiness and power.

17. There are positive reasons for her to worry about the effects of her being viewed as untrustworthy by the crisis team as well: a counselor needs to be able to count on the cooperation of her co-workers, supervisors, law enforcement officers, etc. If she is not trusted by them, she may be less able to adequately counsel and assist future clients, because her own resources and support may be limited. I will return to this point later in the essay.

18. I am not arguing that this reasoning applies to all cases where one is in a midlevel position and caught in a conflict between the more powerful and the relatively powerless. For example, should a mother whose child is being abused by the mother's partner continue to put efforts into maintaining relations with the offender, pleading the child's case to the offender, and trying to mediate between the two? Under what conditions would that be a virtuous thing to do? This sort of situation needs a separate analysis. (But it might also provide general suggestions for conditions as to when it would be reasonable to continue to try to cooperate with those in positions of relative power.)

19. In taking this position, I am suggesting that Aristotle is correct that practical wisdom involves an understanding of what is most honorable but is wrong about what, in fact, is most honorable. As I stated in the introduction, I am committed to the view that ending violence must be a primary goal and that our moral character is com-

promised when we are complicit in the maintenance of structures of power—values that Aristotle would clearly reject.

4

The Trustworthy Teacher

My 1957 college yearbook contains a photo of me in a graduate's black cap. From the way the picture is cropped, it looks as if I'm also wearing a black gown. That is an illusion because only my head went to college. My severed head.

Sylvia Fraser, *My Father's House: A Memoir of Incest and of Healing*

It's a sad story as I am an old-fashioned human being who had a few dreams; I liked books and I would have enjoyed a cup of coffee with Camus in my younger days, at a cafe in Paris, outside, we'd watch the people walk by, and I would have explained that his ideas about suicide were in some sense naive, ahistorical, that no philosopher could afford to ignore incest, or, as I would have it, the story of man, and remain credible.

Andrea Dworkin, *Mercy*

As a survivor, my experiences in the classroom have been largely negative.

A women's studies student and a survivor of incest.
Used with permission.

Increasing awareness of the prevalence of sexual harassment in the academy and an appreciation of students' diverse backgrounds and needs have highlighted the importance of attending to the relationship between knowledge, power, and trust in the college classroom. Members of oppressed groups may find that their sense of themselves as knowers and participants in an educational community is undermined; neglecting the existential reality of such students fosters a hegemonic classroom and perpetuates systems of oppression.

Despite an increased awareness of these issues, especially in feminist circles, racism and other systematic oppressions remain fairly entrenched in pedagogical methods. This chapter focus on one specific group—survivors of long-term or chronic incest—and on the responsibilities that teachers have to create a learning environment where incest survivors are not subjected to further harm.[1]

Very little attention has been given to incest survivors as students, even in feminist pedagogy. But although this chapter is concerned specifically with survivors, it raises epistemological, existential, and pedagogical questions that are relevant to members of other oppressed groups as well. In fact, incest cuts across every socioeconomic, racial, and religious category and, for many people, is experienced in the context of multiple oppressions. As Debi Brock writes: "Everyday conditions like poverty, racism, or neglect, or traumatic events like the early death of a parent also shape who we are. These cannot be simply dismissed as separate issues. Any of these factors may do more to shape our identity (and our pain) than the experience of sexual abuse. We need to be more aware of how all of our experiences intersect and merge" (Brock 1993, 112). In focusing on incest survivors, then, I am calling attention to a neglected area in pedagogy, but one that is situated in the context of students' narrative histories as they intersect with various and multiple systems of oppression.

Research indicates that approximately 30 percent of females and 10 percent of males have been sexually abused by family members before they reach college age (Herman 1992, 30). A significant percentage of any class, therefore, consists of students whose histories are imbued with disrespect, violation, and degradation, and whose experiences with persons in positions of authority and trust were detrimental to self-development. How do current pedagogies employed in philosophy, women's studies, and other classrooms affect students with experiences of socially sanctioned interpersonal abuse? When does the classroom further entrench survivors' existential dissonance, epistemological conflicts, distrust, stigmatization, silence, and marginality, and how might such an environment interfere with learning? Finally, what can educators do to be trustworthy with regard to survivors in the classroom? What sorts of things should teachers attend to, and what sort of person should students be able to count on teachers to be?

Drawing upon conversations I have had with student survivors in classes I have taught, as well as narratives written by survivors, I identify some of the central problems of trust and knowledge in this context and provide an initial theoretical framework within which to begin to address these pedagogical issues. I argue that part of being a good teacher involves creating an environment conducive to nonalienated learning and a space in which survivors' experiences in the classroom can be enhanced. This claim entails that the teacher cultivate trustworthiness in relation to her students while she attends to the dynamics of knowledge, power, and trust in the classroom. This chapter thus frames current pedagogical questions in terms of being a trustworthy teacher so that survivors' knowledge claims and experiences can be taken up in a morally and epistemically responsible manner.

It is important to note that I am not arguing for the more general claim that survivors' experiences should be able to be taken up in any and all epistemic communities; the centrality of a survivor's experience may vary from epistemic community to epistemic community. But the point is that there are some epistemic communities—namely, the classroom—where survivors' existential reality is likely to be relevant and, furthermore, there are some classrooms—for example, those in the humanities—where survivors' worlds are likely to be central. How we, as teachers, enhance or undermine the intersection of knowledge and trust, then, may have significant effects on survivors. But although the specific pedagogy that needs to be developed may vary from classroom to classroom, I suggest that considerations for trustworthiness as a teacher with respect to survivors are relevant to the teacher of any subject. This claim suggests that teachers who do not teach in subjects directly related to humanities are not exempt from the moral demand to become the sort of persons who would be trustworthy to survivors. Subjects such as mathematics, logic, and the so-called hard sciences can be taught in ways that are epistemically and existentially alienating as well. Being fully trustworthy as a teacher requires, among other things, that one takes certain epistemic responsibilities seriously regardless of whether or not one's course subjects fall under the domain of the humanities. This claim holds for teachers whether we are considering student survivors of incest or other student populations. In this chapter, I am raising questions about what it means to be a trustworthy teacher using incest as an example. This chapter, then, develops two aspects of trustworthiness in particular: first, it highlights the requirement that we take epistemic responsibilities seriously by focusing on the epistemic responsibilities that one has as a teacher; and second, it illustrates how the mean can be employed as a conceptual device in moral reasoning while not relying on it to stand in for the messier and more complicated work of determining how to become trustworthy teachers with respect to *this* particular person in *this* situation.

THE CLASSROOM AS EPISTEMIC COMMUNITY

Lorraine Code argues that knowledge is *commonable*, which means that human beings are cognitively interdependent and that the creation of knowledge is dependent upon the attitudes and cognitive practices of knowers (Code 1987, 171). According to this view, endeavors to construct knowledge are always located within communities; in order for something to count as knowledge, it must be possible for at least some members of a community to locate, refer to, or symbolize an item in some shared or shareable way, making connections between it and a currently recognized body of knowledge. Communication systems, then, develop through the cognitive interaction of knowers in their various communities.

Code, making an explicit connection between epistemology and trust, draws upon the work of Ludwig Wittgenstein. Wittgenstein argues that the act of doubting requires a background of propositions that we take to be true in order that a judgment can be made. Although he allows that skepticism is sometimes an important epistemological attitude, he rejects as spurious such questions as how I can know my left hand from my right or whether this color is blue:

> If I don't trust myself here, why should I trust anyone else's judgment? Is there a why? Must not I begin to trust somewhere? That is to say: somewhere I must begin with not-doubting; and that is not, so to speak, hasty but excusable: it is part of judging. (Wittgenstein 1969, 22e)

Trusting in at least some things, then, is logically necessary in order to make judgments at all. Being a member of a community of knowledge, Code argues, allows us to draw upon a body of unarticulated assumptions through which we, for the most part, take for granted the reliability of others' words.[2] As she emphasizes, epistemic communities are bound together by an assumption that the trust placed in others' testimony is, in general, properly given, and thus it is of central epistemic and moral importance that members of an epistemic community sustain that trust. Indeed, Code says, "it is a condition of viable membership in an epistemic community. In fact, the very possibility of epistemic life is dependent upon intricate networks of shared trust" (Code 1987, 173).

Expanding on Code's discussion of trust as an integral feature of an epistemic community, I apply these notions to the classroom. To what extent can the classroom be a kind of "epistemic community"? Given the shared and shareable nature of knowledge, it becomes clear how important it is to have some degree of trust in (at least some) members of a community of knowers in order to transform oneself from a would-be knower to an active member of an epistemic community. But what happens when one's potential to participate in an epistemic community is undermined by distrust? To what extent should teachers and students strive to create an environment of trust—and trust with respect to what? And, specifically, how will those questions be answered regarding incest survivors?

TRUSTWORTHINESS AND TEACHING

As I discussed in chapter 1, being worthy of another's trust involves, among other things, that one take care not to exploit the trusting person's vulnerability. This is particularly true when the person who is trusted is also in a position of power or privilege relative to the trusting ones, as in the case of teacher to students.[3] Here, the vulnerability that accompanies the inequality of the teacher/student relationship increases the risks that inherently attend trust, so that students' risk in trusting may be significantly heightened. The power granted by her institutional role confers upon a teacher, then, heightened responsibility to be nonexploitative and nondominating with regard to her students' (potential) trust. This responsibility is especially critical when, for instance, the student is a woman of color and the teacher is European American, or the student is lesbian and the teacher is heterosexual, or the student's class background stands in contrast to the teacher's mastery of academic discourse. Where multiple oppressions of students interface with the teacher's institutional power and sociopolitical privileges, students' distrust may be (at least initially) warranted. With an understanding of the nature of trusting relations in mind, I stress the responsibility of teachers to develop a trustworthy character in relation to their students.

As a starting point, I propose that a trustworthy professor is someone who can be counted on to fulfill certain pedagogical responsibilities as well as epistemic and moral ones that comprise her institutional role. This proposal entails that educators attend to questions of their own character as well as to particular responsibilities and expectations of teacher-student relations. Such questions of character might include clarifying with whom and what one is in alliance, where one's loyalties lie, what one believes in and is willing to defend, and so on. A central feature of being a trustworthy educator will also involve understanding how authority works in the classroom and what effects institutionally granted authority, as well as sociopolitical power, have on students. It must also be recognized that some students also hold more "authority" in the classroom than others. How the professor and other students respond to—and even establish—these varying degrees of authority, voice, and visibility affect trusting relations in the classroom as well. By attending to the particular needs and issues of survivors in college classrooms in the context of power relations, one can begin to identify the intersection of pedagogical, epistemic, and moral responsibilities which a trustworthy teacher will strive to fulfill.

This definition of a trustworthy teacher once again employs the mean as a starting point for thinking about virtue in this domain. Applying the mean to teaching, I suggest that one can exceed one's responsibilities as a teacher (for example, by trying to be a quasi-therapist; by doing students' research for them; by teaching basic writing skills to individual students instead of sending them to specially designed writing labs) and one can fall short of being a responsible instructor in a myriad of ways (in more obvious ways, by failing to know what one claims to know or by consistently returning students' work later than one has committed; and in more subtle ways, by perpetuating silences and marginality in already oppressed and harmed student populations). But a trustworthy teacher will work hard to find the mean; she will see herself as the sort of person who can be counted on to be an authority and a teacher in the classroom in ways which are neither too much nor too little but are "at the right times, about the right things, toward the right people, for the right end, and in the right way..." Just what this claim entails with regard to survivors of child sexual abuse must be explored, first of all, in the remainder of this essay, and more particularly, in dialogue among the members of philosophy, women's studies, and other departments. It is important to note that the relational nature of trust in the context of liberating pedagogy suggests that teachers have responsibilities to trust their students as well. Finally, I reiterate that trustworthiness, whether we are talking about co-workers, friends, or teachers, is not something for which there is a universal principle to follow. There are characteristics which a trustworthy person will have with respect to particular others and specific goods, but how those characteristics get embodied will depend on the particulars of the situation and the parties involved. So what it means to be a trustworthy teacher cannot be decided only by sketching the extremes and suggesting one find a mean between them: we need to use practical reasoning that involves sensitivity to particular others and the context of each situation. This kind of attentiveness involves thinking both locally and more broadly, and is oriented both toward the historicity of a situation and future implications.

THE SEVERED HEAD

In this section, I draw on an autobiographical account of a survivor whose experiences as a student in philosophy exacerbated her already fragmented self. Sylvia Fraser is an incest survivor whose childhood experiences of sexual abuse resulted in a splitting of the self at an early age. This process, called dissociation, is a complex psychological mechanism that is common for people to engage in to some extent; it includes such operations as dreaming and fantasizing, projecting positive and negative aspects of the self onto others, and so on. Clinicians consider dissociation to be found on a continuum ranging from healthy to unhealthy, from positive to negative, and from less to more severe. But when a child's experiences and environment are those of prolonged terror, captivity, and violation of the self, she may develop a dissociative reaction, where "certain faculties, functions, feelings, and memories are split off from immediate awareness" and compartmentalized as separate entities (Courtois 1988, 154).

Courtois's characterization of dissociation fits Fraser's self-description in her memoirs of a split-off or fragmented self: reacting to a severely abusive environment, the self becomes segmented and, as Courtois says, "the information flow from one to the other is impaired sufficiently to disturb the person's sense of selfhood" (Courtois 1988, 154). Thus, when Fraser entered college, she had no conscious memory or knowledge of the incest or of an "other" self—the "Child Who Knows" (Fraser 1987, 223). Fraser's description of her academic experience as a philosophy student raises important questions about the relationship between epistemology and pedagogy as it pertains to survivors, and thus an analysis of her narrative serves as a starting point by which to explore the notion of the classroom as an epistemic community and the ways in which its members (and the teacher in particular) are accountable to one another.

Fraser describes her college days as a philosophy student:

> I burrow into the library stacks for my second term. While my roommates giggle over threatened panty raids, I swing on syllogisms as if they are monkey bars, weave intricate spider webs of logic from my own substance to see what they will catch, rub premises together to strike fire, chase down intuitive possibilities as if they are rare butterflies, crack open the bottle of dialectics to let the genie loose.
>
> It comes as a revelation that abstract ideas can dynamically alter my universe.
>
> When rationality fails, and I find myself plummeting into familiar snake pits, I rescue myself by an old rope, newly woven: the myth of my own specialness. Thus, through the ego needs of my severed head, Descartes' confirmation of existence, "I think, therefore I am" becomes, "I think, therefore I have worth." Verbal cartwheels: the cheerleader as philosopher. (Fraser 1987, 125, 127)

Fragmented in a way that allows her to engage intensely in academic scholarship while splitting off the experiential knowledge of the embodied girl-child who was abused, Fraser searches in philosophical discourse for explanation, confirmation and understanding of her existential dissonance:

> Later, Immanuel Kant provides the definitive loophole through which I shoot from the strictures of the rational into the stars: if time and space are not real in themselves but are merely projections of the human mind then anything is possible—immortality, *simultaneous existence of past-present-future, parallel worlds*. (Fraser 1987, 131, emphasis mine)

Hungering for a rational world where she could make sense of her experience intellectually while unconsciously denying it at another level, Fraser found that abstract philosophical theories both *permitted* and *required* her to be disembodied—a "severed head."[4] Although her academic experience enabled her to experience the power of abstract ideas, it was ultimately unable to transform her being from one of existential and epistemological dissonance toward synthesis of her disparate worlds. In fact, her education only served to entrench her further in her fragmented state. Fraser's understanding of Kant's theory of metaphysics allowed her a *degree* of existential comfort in its suggestion of "parallel worlds," but nothing in her academic experience brought her knowledge of philosophical theories together with her existential reality. As Judith Herman notes, Sylvia Fraser is a woman with remarkable gifts which enabled her to develop multiple personalities as a creative response to severe trauma (Herman 1992, 97). But, although Fraser's engagement with philosophical discourse suggests her passionate quest for some resolution of the conflicts in her internal world, the world she *inhabited*—the one in which she attended classes, voraciously read and analyzed and critically examined and debated with professors and other students—seemed to have no place for the split-off self with whom she was unconsciously sharing her body. Cognitive and existential dissonance could only be warded off by stronger efforts to maintain her disembodied state.

> Sometimes my head aches. Sometimes I can't sleep, but when I do I seldom dream. *My other self is bored with my new life. For a time, at least, it's as if the tapes of her adventures have been wiped clean.* These days, when I get angry, it's intellectual rage, so much safer than the real thing. (Fraser 1987, 127, emphasis in original)

But the fragmentation she experienced living her life as a severed head/philosopher finally created an existential crisis. Confronting her reflection in a mirror, she didn't recognize the disembodied image looking back: "In an instant I realize: I'm tired of living in the past and future. I want to live in the present tense. I'm tired of abstract reasoning with its pursuit of false accuracy...My severed head swivels looking for its discarded body" (Fraser 1987, 135).

Fraser left the academy, locating the explanation for her existential crisis not with the academy, not with traditional philosophical discourse, and certainly not with her father, but *within herself*: "I am haunted. I don't see things as they are" (Fraser 1987, 137). And even when, many years later, she learned to "see things as they are" and she recovered the memories of incest and the other self (the "Child Who Knows"), Fraser acknowledges the devastating effects of her psychological world on her ability to have confidence in her role as a member of epistemic communities: "My pride of intellect has been shattered. If I didn't know about half my own life, what other knowledge can I trust?" (137).

EXISTENTIAL DREAD: EPISTEMIC COMMUNITIES AND PEDAGOGY

Fraser doesn't seem to hold the academy or philosophical discourse accountable for failing to provide the necessary link between her internal world and the world in which she moved. (But a critique of the academy wasn't the focus of her writing, either.) Her strategy for coping with her history represents a common one for survivors: unconscious selective amnesia about the past enables them, for a time, to develop other important survival skills (such as skills acquired through work, education, and social relations). Still, nagging questions emerge from the telling of Fraser's story: What was happening, pedagogically speaking, such that in all the philosophy courses she took, she was able to keep her own experience at a distance? How did her sense of fragmentation ultimately affect her sense of herself as a viable member of an epistemic community?

Fraser's memoir raises the question of whether her confidence in herself as a knowing subject (threatened, in part, by her failure to know about her other self) was also undermined through education. Even though she was able to experience herself as intellectually facile and philosophically knowledgeable, she was unable to draw upon her own existential reality as a resource for knowledge—or to confirm it—and thus eventually called her own capabilities as a knower into question. One wonders whether her education could have been experienced differently—in a way that helped bring to consciousness, rather than to exacerbate, the split within her. Would that have been a good thing? Is that a proper goal of education?

To address the questions I have raised, I return to Code's notion of knowledge as commonable. As I stated earlier, Code says that, in order for something to count as knowledge, it must be possible for at least some members of a community to refer to or bring into social consciousness an item or idea in some shared or shareable way. That is, the process by which knowledge claims are offered and assented to requires that would-be knowers be able to *make reference to* potential knowledge claims in a way that connects them with some currently *recognized* body of knowledge.

Student survivors, like Fraser, are often unable to do that in the classroom with respect to their experiences and knowledge-claims as survivors. Although in Fraser's case, it would seem that part of the explanation could be found in the inaccessibility of her own self-knowledge, such an explanation fails to account for the fact that, in all likelihood, there was not a reference point in academic discourse for the kind of existential pain and anguish she was in. Furthermore, as I have argued, Code's theory of knowledge as commonable suggests that the adult Fraser's inaccessibility of the Child Who Knows can *itself* be explained by the absence of a point of reference that could be recognized by others: even self-knowledge is not an individual enterprise but is integrally connected to one's knowledge as a member of some epistemic *community*. These claims are clearly also relevant to students who are experiencing racism or other forms of oppression in the classroom. The absence of a reference point for existential anguish excludes such students from making explicit connections between some central aspects of their experiences and classroom knowledge-production and may even prevent the conscious awareness of oppressive dynamics within the classroom.

This point is related to Andrea Dworkin's criticism that those who engage in philosophical discourse about such existential issues as suicide and mercy (or, I might add, desire, bad faith, or even trust) but fail to take incest into account are not credible (Dworkin 1990, 292). Expanding on this point, I suggest that conceptual analyses of human experiences and meaning-making where the analysis neglects incest as a reality of women's lives also loses credibility. In courses where the subject matter is the humanities, then, where aspects of survivors' existential reality are especially relevant, it is particularly important to consider these questions about epistemic communities and trust in the classroom. Survivors cannot locate themselves within such discourse or theorizing when the topic of incest is neglected, for there is no such reference point, and the theory becomes an epistemological system that provides no knowledge of the survivor's reality—except inasmuch as it reflects the *absence* of any acknowledgment of the social sanctioning and horrors of incest. This absence is the source of a critical problem of trust in the classroom, because some things that are essential from the survivor's point of view cannot be assumed to be shared by others. She cannot assume trust regarding a central truth of her existence. Thus (applying Code's theory) the survivor finds herself outside of the epistemic community with regard to her existential reality—an intolerable position, especially when the classroom subject concerns aspects of human experience. Often, the only way to resolve the epistemic alienation is to repudiate the existential survivor-self and assert oneself as a member of the epistemic community—or drop out of school. Similar conflicts may arise for students who are experiencing other forms of oppression in the classroom.

The process of constructing certain bodies of knowledge, then, requires that survivors be able to make reference to their existential experiences. Women's studies classrooms are, perhaps, less likely to entirely ignore the subject of incest and, therefore, it is more likely that a survivor would find a common reference point through which she could feel included as a survivor in classroom knowledge-production. But there is more to this epistemological and pedagogical problem than providing reference points for inclusive discourse. The other side of the process involves the ways in which others in an epistemic community fit what survivors say into their world-view. Non-survivors, in trying to "make sense" of what is outside their own experience, often translate survivors' reports in ways that are in keeping with their current body of knowledge, thus distorting or "falsifying" knowledge-claims that do not comfortably join the existent body of knowledge.[5] The result is that, when survivors' reports are taken up at all, they are most often taken up in ways that fail to actually expand the body of knowledge in an epistemic community in the direction of survivors' worlds.

The problem of the absence of a reference point for survivors is not remedied simply by introducing "survivor discourse" into the classroom. Survivor discourse, I suggest, as it has been promoted by the media and popular culture, creates an illusion that incest is being taken seriously. What Sue Crowley calls the "disguise of openness," where there is *talk about* survivors but that talk actually inauthenticates survivors' existential reality, transforms the survivor into the "Other" and often prompts an inappropriate response of pity for her rather than outrage at the numerous practices which permit sexual abuse to continue.[6] The "disguise of openness," in fact, can be profoundly disorienting, since the student at once feels that, for all the talk about survivor's issues, her existential reality has not been genuinely taken up, yet because there is *a* discourse about survivors being engaged in, she cannot quite point to its inadequacy. A similar phenomenon occurs in much of the current discourse on racism in women's studies.

My point, then, is that epistemic and psychological harm is done to survivors by the persistent distorting, ignoring, minimizing, or disclaiming of the reality and pervasiveness of institutionally sanctioned incest. Even feminist pedagogy, which is committed to the demystification of various oppressions in womens' lives, often fails to acknowledge the serious and endemic features of course materials and methods and classroom dynamics which may distort, deny, or conceal facts about incest and its legacy (a claim I elaborate on later in the chapter). Student survivors in classrooms, then, feeling themselves outside the epistemic community with regard to their survivorship, may experience a kind of *existential crisis.* How can a survivor hope to resolve such a genuine existentialist conflict with its attendant feelings of dread, hopelessness, and despair as long as the politics of incest are ignored?

A responsible teacher is one who creates a space in which potential knowledge claims of survivors can be located, referred to, or symbolized in some

shareable way. This responsibility entails that the teacher employ communication systems in the classroom that are inclusive of survivors in their diversity. Paulo Freire's work is suggestive here. As he points out in *Pedagogy
of the Oppressed*, the process of unlearning oppressions

> must always be with men [sic] in the "here and now," which constitutes the sit-
> uation within which they are submerged, from which they emerge, and in which
> they intervene. Only by starting from this situation—which determines their
> perception of it—can they begin to move. (Freire 1992, 71)

But student survivors may discover that classroom experiences can be a
way of "domesticating" reality (Freire 1992, 68). Reality becomes what the
texts and the dominant members of the classroom, including the professor,
acknowledge as reality (an experience that women of color may also have,
whether incest survivors or not). The reality of the legacy of incest—where
children have been betrayed by those in authority, where they learn to simultaneously hold disparate views of the world in order to survive, where they
distrust their own ability to know and understand what is going on around
them, and where they learn to doubt or assent to ideas and knowledge claims
on the basis of how they can best *survive*—is all too frequently glossed over.
Freire argues that educators who are truly committed to *freeing* students
rather than further entrenching them in oppressive structures will directly address the existential issues central to their ways of being in the world. Such
pedagogy—where one strives to create an epistemic community of sorts in
the classroom—"involves a constant unveiling of reality...the *emergence* of
consciousness and *critical intervention* in reality" (Freire 1992, 68) which allows students to "develop their power to perceive critically *the way they exist* in the world *with which* and *in which* they find themselves" (70; emphasis
in original). When this vision of the student's existential world as epistemically relevant is appropriately taken up, the demystification of incest and its
exposure as a central practice for engendering and perpetuating relations of
domination and subordination contribute to the student's ability to participate
in epistemic communities and to experience themselves as knowers whose
histories and lived conditions under oppression are vital items in the process
of communal knowledge-seeking.
The creation of a space within which students—including survivors—can
openly embrace their existential reality has to be undertaken in a nuanced
manner sensitive to context, however, and cannot be done by simply formu-
lating a universal principle applicable to all classrooms. One shouldn't, for instance, just bring up the subject of incest out of context, or introduce it into a
discussion where virtually no one can make sense of its relevancy (even survivors), or otherwise force the topic. This sort of unexpected singling-out of

the subject may result in further stigmatization of survivors. This caution should not be taken as a simple one, though, for many, if not most, teachers are socialized to think that the subject of incest is nearly always "out of context" and are less able to see when they have been neglecting it. One has to find what it means to be trustworthy relative to the particular epistemic community or classroom.

The creation of this kind of epistemic community calls for a revisioning of several elements of pedagogy that a trustworthy teacher should consider with regard to survivors. One shift toward trustworthiness involves the restructuring of the teacher-student relationship. Freire says that

> the humanist, revolutionary educator's...efforts must coincide with those of the students to engage in critical thinking and the quest for mutual humanization. His efforts must be imbued with a profound sense of trust in [the students] and their creative power. To achieve this, he must be a partner of the students in his relations with them. (Freire 1992, 62)

On this view, then, the professor and her students are jointly responsible for the process of seeking, criticizing, acknowledging, and making knowledge claims (Freire 1992, 67). The importance of having some autonomy over knowledge-seeking, as Herman notes, is especially critical for many survivors, who often become objects of inquisition rather than the subjects of their own quest for truth (Herman 1992, 97).

Another step in becoming a trustworthy educator involves transforming the way in which teachers, as well as students, conceptualize survivors. Extending Freire's ideas, I suggest that a pedagogy which is truly liberating for all students will structure the course or the classroom environment, taking into consideration the particulars of the setting as well as the local and historical contexts, in such a way as to make explicit that the practice of sexually abusing children, like racism and heterosexism, is institutionalized in our society and that, far from being marked, deformed, or wounded creatures who need to be nurtured back into "normal" society, incest survivors are already in the social systems whereby we stand in relation to, and are shaped by, various structures of power and oppression.

> The truth is...that the oppressed are not "marginals," are not men [sic] living "outside" society. They have always been "inside"—inside the structure which made them "beings for others." The solution is not to "integrate" them into the structure of oppression, but to transform the structure so that they can become "beings for themselves." (Freire 1992, 61)

Particularizing Freire's theory to survivors, I suggest that incest—and the child upon whom it is practiced—is structurally part of the systems of oppression in our society, and that, as Freire argues, it is these systems that need to be transformed to accommodate their experiences (and, ultimately, to eradicate further abuses). Furthermore, taking Fraser as an example once again, I also suggest that many survivors are part of epistemic systems/communities via the repudiation of a part of themselves, although, as I argued earlier, they, paradoxically, may not experience themselves as such and, unless an epistemic system creates a space for the acknowledgment of the existence and experience of incest, survivors may not only experience themselves as "outsiders within" but simply as "outsiders."[7] But, extrapolating from Freire, this view is mistaken, and it is the responsibility of teachers to correct this misconception.

A trustworthy teacher can be counted on to resist the notion that student survivors are somehow marginal, that the incidence of incest is low, or that child sexual abuse isn't really a part of oppressive structures of our society. The practice of incest is widespread and cannot be separated from other forms of oppression, victimization, and exploitation upon which current societal structures depend.[8] Counter-hegemonic pedagogy which takes into account survivors' experiences will have, as an underlying objective, the transformation of structures of oppression so that survivors are no longer "beings for others" as they were as children.

Integrally connected to the last point is the responsibility of teachers to acquire the knowledge and understanding necessary to be appropriately inclusive of, and responsive to, student survivors: one begins to reconceptualize members of a group as one gains knowledge about the misinformation and distortions one has learned and replaces those views with an understanding grounded in the diverse experiences, coping methods, and perspectives of survivors themselves.

One of the central pedagogical responsibilities of trustworthy educators, I have argued, requires that we teach material in ways that allow students to make those significant connections in their own lives. In many ways, feminist pedagogy has already been practicing this method. But in feminist pedagogy, as well as in other pedagogies, this theory has been largely neglected with regard to student survivors. For those students whose existential reality includes a history of childhood sexual abuse, this pedagogical responsibility entails that, as educators, we must create a space in which it is possible for student survivors to consciously, if privately, acknowledge and have confirmed the truths of institutionalized sexual abuse and its legacy.

This last point requires elaboration. In order to develop the teaching and learning methods necessary for creating such a space, educators need to gain knowledge and comfort about these issues themselves. Others' arrogance, ignorance, and fear are sources of much harm done to survivors. This, plus (for some teachers and students) the felt need to be defended against the knowledge of bodily violations, not only leads many to be silent about the subject altogether but, when it is addressed, often leads to responses by others which leave survivors feeling misrepresented, stigmatized, pathologized, or otherwise further alienated.

> I have tried to ask professors about sexual violence. One instructor was very disrespectful. She gave a reply and then ended the conversation. She didn't even ask where the question was coming from or why I may be thinking that way. (Student comment)[9]

This problem is particularly salient in any classroom where student survivors' histories and experiences seem to be radically different from theirs (and from other students'). But it may also occur when a survivor's experiences are all too familiar, and class members (including teachers) wish to distance themselves from memories and truths about incest.

This discussion illuminates the relationship between pedagogical and epistemic responsibilities: a trustworthy teacher with regard to survivors is one who has acquired sufficient information to be able to open up the subject in the classroom when appropriate; who continues to gain understanding through a search for knowledge that is both cognitive and self-reflective of her own fears, prejudices, and experiences; who develops a comfortable, confident, and grounded understanding of the interplay of psychological and political structures that perpetuate abuse; who explores the intersection of the legacy of incest with students' diversity; and who is committed to doing her part to undo the effects of abuse on adult learners. Educators who are trustworthy will familiarize themselves with the growing body of literature on child sexual abuse and will make their own connections between this information and learning as it pertains to students of great cultural diversity as well. Just as it is European American people's responsibility to educate ourselves about (for example) African-American and First Nations cultures, literatures, histories, political conflicts, and so on, and to teach in nonethnocentric and antiracist ways, it is every teacher's responsibility to educate ourselves about survivors and to teach in ways that acknowledge this form of oppression. It is important to stress that "every teacher" includes both nonsurvivors and survivors. A significant number of teachers are survivors, too, and need to seek actively knowledge and understanding about this legacy and to learn to appreciate the specificity of their experiences so as not to assume similarity of experiences or responses.

THE LEGACY OF CHILD SEXUAL ABUSE: WHAT STUDENT SURVIVORS BRING TO THE CLASSROOM

Clinical research shows that a victim of chronic or long-term incest has profoundly disrupted relationships and thus faces formidable developmental tasks. Herman describes the double-bind survivors contend with: for example, the child has to try to develop trust and safety with caregivers who are untrustworthy and unsafe, to develop the capacity for initiative in a context where the abuser demands that her will conform to the abuser's will, and to forge "an identity out of an environment which defines her as a whore and a slave" (Herman 1992, 101). Herman states that the conditions of chronic childhood abuse lead to fragmentation as the central principle of personality organization. This is important because, as Herman points out, fragmentation in consciousness not only prevents the development of a secure sense of autonomy within connection and inhibits or prevents the integration of identity, but also "prevents the ordinary integration of knowledge, memory, emotional states, and bodily experience" (107).

Most survivors of incest, then, come into college classrooms with difficulties in basic trust, autonomy, and initiative, as well as, for some survivors, difficulty in cognition and memory (Herman 1992, 110).

> The pathological environment of childhood abuse forces the development of extraordinary capacities, both creative and destructive. It fosters the development of abnormal states of consciousness in which the ordinary relations of body and mind, reality and imagination, knowledge and memory, no longer hold. (Herman 1992, 196)

Active learning, as envisioned by Freire and others, may become difficult and sometimes contradictory. As one student wrote:

> To be an active learner of knowledge, a survivor must challenge all that was told to her/him by the perpetrator. Often, survivors are told that they are not worth anything, they're too sexual, not sexual enough, dirty, stupid...etc. A survivor must challenge all of these messages to learn new messages. At times the old messages may be more powerful than the new ones, and active learning is not possible, just passive learning. (Student comment)

For some survivors, complicated alterations of consciousness such as dissociation and memory barriers (amnesia) interfere with the cognitive skills necessary for successful coursework; the deeply internalized belief that one is worthless, bad, or stupid exacerbates these problems. Other survivors compensate for feelings of worthlessness by developing a highly competent intellectual self. Fraser, readers will recall, expressed an almost jubilant relation to abstract philosophical discourse and logical reasoning. For Fraser as well as many other survivors, however, the competent intellectual self can become equated with one's self-worth so that criticism of one's coursework is tantamount to an assault upon the self. One survivor wrote:

> I am constantly trying to prove that I'm perfect to rid any doubt of my own about my responsibility in the abuse. If I'm perfect in all areas then I couldn't be responsible for something so bad. If I'm perfect then I can't be those things my brother said I was. Every time a teacher gives out overly harsh feedback, a survivor will have to try and "survive" not only the abuse but the new messages of being less than OK too. (Student comment)

The central place some survivors give to their intellectual capacities imbues their coursework with a high degree of significance and leaves them particularly vulnerable to criticism; teachers are seen as having the power to affirm or deny the self-worth of the student. The fact that survivors attribute such power to teachers suggests that criticism of a student survivor's work or ideas must be carefully presented. One incest survivor expresses a sentiment shared by many students, survivors and nonsurvivors alike:

> Instructors should make sure that their suggestions are thoughtful and encouraging. It's not OK to just say "you could have done more." (Student comment)

Many survivors were consistently undermined and humiliated as children, and as a consequence are starving for praise. Others have experienced praise and other forms of compliments as a method of manipulating and controlling the victim; these survivors are eager for genuine praise where there are no conditions attached. As with any student, praise and positive comments help build confidence in one's ability to participate as a member of an epistemic community, and professors need to be respectful and supportive both in classroom discussions and in responding to written work so that student survivors receive enough encouragement to be in a position to counter abuse-related beliefs.

Many adult survivors are particularly vulnerable to people who are (or who are perceived to be) in positions of authority. As one survivor wrote:

> The professors hold an almost excruciating amount of power over me. They have the power to reinforce all the old messages if they choose to. I realize that I have the control not to hear some, but if I choose not to hear some messages, how can I trust that the ones I do take in—are valid? For me, I need to trust fully for the new messages to be valid. (Student comment)

Herman explains the adult survivor's vulnerability to those in positions of power as a consequence of their traumatic experiences, where chronic abuse prevents the child victim from forming, and then being able to call upon, inner representations of trustworthy authorities in times of distress—a developmental task necessary to gain a secure sense of autonomy (Herman 1992, 107). The result is that, even as adults, survivors rely more upon external sources of comfort and solace and many continue to seek desperately and indiscriminately for someone to depend upon. And, Herman argues, an underdeveloped sense of independence leaves survivors at risk of repeated victimization. Survivors may

> seek out powerful authority figures who seem to offer the promise of a special caretaking relationship. By idealizing the person to whom she becomes attached, she attempts to keep at bay the constant fear of being either dominated or betrayed. Her empathic attunement to the wishes of others and her automatic, often unconscious habits of obedience also make her vulnerable to anyone in a position of power or authority. (111)

This aspect of the legacy of incest highlights the need for educators to be aware of the potential of students to idealize them and to attach to and become dependent upon them.

For example, while I was teaching a course on sexuality, one female student confided in me that, when I came within a certain distance of her, she started to feel "small." She offered, by way of explanation, her hypothesis that those negative feelings had something to do with her experiences as an incest survivor. Upon further discussion, she told me that the perpetrator had been her mother. Because her respect for me as a teacher and authority figure had merged with her past experience of an abuse of power in a primary relationship with an authority (her mother), the student-teacher relationship became, in her psyche, charged with the potential for the utmost betrayal. She found herself vacillating between idealization of me and intense fear and repudiation. Consequently, her coursework became increasingly infused with a desire to please/placate me (teacher/mother) alternating with feelings of resentment and confusion.

This example illustrates the difficult dynamics a teacher can sometimes encounter with survivors, where a relationship of transference develops which interferes with the student's ability to learn and work in the classroom. Although there is no guarantee that a student survivor will learn to trust a teacher even if the teacher is cautious about her position as an authority, a trustworthy teacher is one who is alert to potentially disruptive teacher-student dynamics and can deal with these issues respectfully and responsibly. Teachers must try to maintain a delicate balance between assuming responsibility for the student's past (an excess) and courting indifference to their potential to trigger former abusive relationships (a deficiency). This may mean that teachers will need to work through issues of their own concerning abuses of power, victim-blaming, guilt, caretaking of others, and other unhelpful or harmful ways of relating to others.

Teachers who are themselves survivors will most likely benefit from addressing those issues as well. An unworked-through abuse history on the part of the teacher can exponentially complicate already complex issues of power, authority, and trust in the classrooms. Teachers who are incest survivors need to engage in an ongoing reflective relationship between their teacher role and their legacy as an abuse survivor and the ways in which the intersection of these positions affects classroom dynamics. This process is important because survivor teachers may bring to the classroom issues similar to the ones student survivors do or, alternatively, they may assume that other survivors' legacies are similar when they are not.

Student survivors seem to flourish in educational settings where the instructor maintains clear and consistent boundaries that express a friendly professional relationship. A teacher who appears detached from a survivor's expressed pain and rage, perhaps by minimizing it or by subtly disapproving of an outburst of emotion, or who distances herself from survivors, may be experienced as hostile, and most students cannot learn well in a hostile environment. On the other hand, over-involvement and concern for students' private lives is also problematic. As I indicated earlier, many survivors are dependent upon external sources of comfort and mirroring of self-worth. As a result, they may invite and welcome more personal relationships in an attempt to be "rescued" by the teacher. Although personal or "special" attention is sometimes desired by survivors, it also, paradoxically, may be experienced as intrusive (and it may be harmful even if the student continues to perceive it as desirable). Teachers, then, need to find a delicate balance between detachment and over-involvement in student survivor/teacher relations. This particular issue, which in therapeutic relationships is closely attended to and carefully moderated through team consultations, supervision, and other professional strategies, is underexplored in many women's studies departments as well as in the overall academy.[10] One important way to extend the work of this chapter would be for teachers to develop similar consultations where they can critically examine and explore individual classroom dynamics and, with others, cooperatively and creatively engage in becoming trustworthy teachers.

One way in which the legacy of incest may intersect with teacher/student dynamics involves the negotiation of coursework. A student survivor who finds her teacher open to discussing survivor issues may confide her inner turmoil and ask to be evaluated independently of other students or given special

considerations because of her difficulties as a survivor. Once again, responsible teachers must find the mean between being rigid and dogmatic, on the one
hand, and so flexible as to be unfair to other students and sometimes unhelpful to the student survivor as well. A system of rigid and inflexible rules often
mirrors the original abuse dynamics in the mind of the survivor, who may
then experience the classroom as a kind of captivity. But a survivor may also
*dis*trust a teacher more who treats her in a "special" way—after all, the violation of rules on the grounds of "specialness" or "exemption" is often one of
the founding principles of incest. I suggest that being responsive to students'
needs may mean that an instructor can tailor an assignment to fit the needs of
a particular student but that no student, and especially a survivor, benefits
from being held to standards discrepant with that of other students' required
coursework. Teachers have the responsibility to be worthy of all students'
trust in teachers *qua* teachers, survivors and nonsurvivors alike; although this
is a rather obvious point, it is worth emphasizing that, as teachers, we must
avoid cultivating trust with one student if in doing so we jeopardize the ability of other students to count on us to fulfill our teaching responsibilities in a
professional and just manner.

I have been discussing the legacy of child sexual abuse and what survivors
bring to the classroom. My last point concerns the relationship between
power and sexuality. The early sexualization of relationships of authority
leads many survivors to equate power and authority with sexual relationships,
and they may unconsciously sexualize the teacher-student relationship.
Teachers, of course, may sexualize such relationships as well, and most uni-
versities have policies against sexual harassment. But conceiving of this issue
in terms of standard forms of sexual harassment will almost certainly leave
the relationship unguarded against more subtle forms of sexualization that
can harm the trusting relation and, hence, the student's learning in the classroom. It should be clear that the classroom (as well as the academy) is no
place for sexualized teacher-student relationships, in whatever way they are
formed. However, I want to stress the importance of this point in cases where
the student is a survivor, has already been subjected to sexual exploitation and
abuse by someone in power, and is particularly vulnerable to further abuses
of power. Since teachers may not know who is and is not a survivor, I suggest
that teachers be particularly aware of and work to defuse both sexualizing and
the sexualization of any student-teacher relations.[11]

On all of these points, it is important to consider the question of what students are entrusting to teachers, what their expectations are, how reasonable
those expectations are, and so on. Although the prima facie good that students
value and that they are entrusting to teachers is their education, survivors may
be entrusting much more, or much less, than that. How educators respond to

the combined vulnerability and expectations of survivors will, in part, depend upon clarifying what counts as reasonable expectations. But, in my view, this project cannot yet be done. Most teachers primarily work in isolation from one another, and many teachers aren't clear on what students are entrusting to them (or even that trust is involved). This means that educators aren't, individually, in a position to evaluate student expectations and teacher responsibilities. Once again, I remind readers of the therapeutic model, where professional guidelines have been established to characterize the therapist/client relationship and where therapists spend considerable time establishing relationships which are healing and trusting but nevertheless clearly delineated and bounded.[12]

A final word on the relationship between authority, boundaries, and responsibilities. I do not mean to suggest that student survivors have no responsibility to set or observe boundaries; nor do I mean to suggest that survivors are not autonomous and therefore need to be paternalistically cared for by teachers and others. As Freire says, liberating pedagogy requires the reconceptualization of the teacher-student relation, a central component of which is to trust students enough to return some authority to them. My reason for emphasizing teacher responsibilities is that, given the intersection of trust with power relations and the vulnerability involved in trusting another, the person who stands in a position of power bears more of the burden for establishing trustworthiness and cultivating trusting relations. The responsibility of teachers is to be in the classroom in ways that allow for the possibility of student survivors to experience authority figures as people who can be counted upon not to exploit their power and who can be depended upon to do their part to maintain clear professional boundaries.

EPISTEMIC COMMUNITIES, TRUST, AND DISCLOSURE

This last section concerns the relationship between the classroom as epistemic community, trust, and personal disclosure. The central question is whether and to what extent the classroom *can* be an epistemic community for all its members, and for survivors in particular. Although this discussion will focus on women's studies classes, where personal disclosure often plays a vital role in pedagogy, the central question is relevant to other disciplines in the humanities as well.

Responsible teaching involves employing a counter-hegemonic pedagogy which makes room in the classroom for the conscious analysis of the material conditions of diverse women's lives,[14] including the realities of incest. In many ways, feminist pedagogy has gone furthest to address problems such as inclusiveness and power in the classroom, but it, too, may be fraught with problems. Geiger and Zita, in discussing general strategies that a "good feminist teacher" employs in the classroom—such as relinquishing exclusive epistemic authority on course subjects and divesting herself of the role of judging the quality and authenticity of students' lives—argue that such practices often "work against the validation of Black women's experiences and lead to the marginalization and silencing of Black women in our classes" (Geiger and Zita 1985, 111). When the teacher attempts to respond to each student's subjective reality with nonjudgmental acceptance or to receive each student's statements as "true for her" and therefore exempt from comment, she leaves herself little or no room to question or challenge racist remarks and attitudes. The denial of power as teachers, then, can lead to the repetition of oppressive and abusive dynamics and represents a *failure* of responsibility (117).

Particularly relevant to this section of my chapter is Geiger and Zita's criticism of the way in which the divestiture of power intersects with the strategy of using personal experience as a resource for knowledge. According to their analysis of current feminist pedagogical theory, a "good feminist teacher" aims to "create a classroom context in which every woman is comfortable expressing thoughts and feelings based on her own experience and using perceptions gleaned from that experience to understand or critique the material being studied" (Geiger and Zita 1985, 112). Such a goal seems consistent not only with Freire's reconceptualizion of power relations in the classroom, but also with Code's analysis of epistemic search and inquiry as a community endeavor grounded in shared and shareable ideas. Even the earlier discussion of the academic life of Fraser as a philosophy student suggests that, were this strategy to have been employed in her classrooms, Fraser's fragmentation might have been lessened rather than heightened. The creation of a "safe" and "trusting" classroom environment where each student can self-disclose those experiences, feelings, thoughts, and beliefs she deems relevant to the process of knowledge-production, then, seems like not only a laudable, but an epistemologically necessary, goal.

But, as Geiger and Zita argue, experientially based responses are socially constructed and, as such, are infused with institutionalized racism, sexism, heterosexism, ageism, and class-bias. Furthermore, they note that "personal disclosure requires—especially if the disclosure is threatening or self-revealing in significant ways, a trusting alliance among students in the class. But why would a Black woman feel any trust toward a group of new white acquaintances?" (Geiger and Zita 1985, 112).

Why, indeed? And why would a survivor feel any trust toward nonsurvivors, whose revulsion and horror at the idea of incest are often transformed into revulsion and horror toward the incest survivor, and who may react with silence, pity, blame, or distancing? As one student survivor wrote:

> I often find myself on the edge of rage in classroom discussions. When I hear another woman share how she fended off her near attacker by persuading him not to rape her by having him picture her as his mother or sister. I'm all for fending off possible assaults. I don't understand what the implications of her statement are. Is she evoking even more shame for me by saying how disgusting incest is—somehow worse than rape? Is she saying that a flip comment can fend off assaults?
>
> I question whether or not it would be alright for me to respond in class. Just to ask what about victims whose perps were in the family. Then what? As an incest survivor I don't want to be forgotten. It's important to remember that there are different issues for different crimes. So at times I don't feel that my reality is reflected/included. (Student comment)

As this student points out, although survivors' experiences are often not taken into account, personal disclosure, which may call needed attention to others' obliviousness and misinformation, is also fraught with difficulties and conflicts. Classroom disclosures of incest are often met with painful silences or declarations of disgust that carry a tone of blame. Frequently, nonsurvivors construct survivors as "Other" by remarks about their own good childhoods and great families, patronizingly stating that they "cannot imagine" what it would be like for a father/brother/mother to do *those things* to them. Such reactions can close down communication and reinstate general distrust, often interfering with later learning in that classroom due to the student survivor's hypervigilance and concomitantly depleted resources available for incorporating coursework into her world-view. And some survivors, in anticipation of further stigmatizing responses founded upon previous attempts to disclose, simply are not willing to risk disclosure.

> The environment must be right for me to disclose. Only when the situation is highly controlled and respectful will I disclose what sexual practices were used in my abuse...Elements of trust and respect are crucial. A discussion also needs to follow the disclosure to help rid any fears the survivor has about being "out." Does that person think I'm dirty? Are they saying it was my fault? (Student comment)

Not only do many survivors not trust the other students enough to risk disclosure, but they do not trust the instructor to address stigmatizing and victim-blaming remarks appropriately. Teachers who abrogate power in the classroom in these situations by denying responsibility for students' reactions, by claiming neutrality, or by pleading ignorance on survivor issues, contribute to an environment of distrust. Survivor students must be able to count on the intervention, assistance, and validation of teachers when they disclose; this is a responsibility of teachers and one of the features which, if consistently present, would make a teacher an ally worthy of a survivor's trust. But the *bond of an alliance* needs to be carefully examined in the context of survivors in the classroom.

As I discussed in earlier chapters, one way in which we indicate who can trust us is by giving signs and assurances of our commitments and loyalties. In alternative pedagogies, such signs and indications may be employed as a strategy whereby the teacher forms an alliance with some oppressed or marginalized subset of the class. Such alliances are felt both through explicit articulation as when a teacher says "we" in a way which marks group identity and excludes some students from the group, or through less overt expressions of alliances as when a teacher responds more affirmatively, energetically, or thoroughly to students from a particular group.[14]

But, as I discussed above, such alliances between teachers and students are sometimes formed, not between the teacher and marginalized students, but with those from privileged groups (i.e., middle-class teacher with middle-class students, white teacher with white students, even along disciplines or "party lines,") to the exclusion of other students. The formation of alliances is clearly not part of liberating pedagogy when it reinstates hegemonic relations in the classroom; teachers need to be on guard against oppressive alliances and resistant toward those who attempt to draw one in.

But there is another reason to be wary of alliances in the classroom as well. One might think that, given the discussion so far, alliances between the teacher and self-disclosed survivors would be beneficial to survivors in the classroom. Such a strategy might backfire, however; a common dynamic in abusive families is the formation of liaisons and alliances which play members of the family off one another and serve to isolate and insulate the victim(s) from making trusting connections with others. These alliances, in a family where children are incestuously assaulted, are a key factor in protecting and perpetuating betrayals and reinstating fear and dependency in the victim. When an adult student survivor feels herself becoming part of a "special" alliance, she may, in fact, distrust the teacher *more*. Teachers need to be careful, therefore, that they do not inadvertently draw students into quasi-personal, "special" relationships, while at the same time they need to demonstrate to student survivors that they can be counted on to intervene on behalf of survivors, when circumstances call for intervention, and to ensure that personal disclosures are dealt with respectfully and appropriately.

Professors must also recognize that disclosure of abuse histories ought not to be expected or implicitly required. Nor should it be assumed that, if disclosure of incest does not arise in the classroom, it is not an issue for at least some students. This possibility is unlikely. But as Geiger and Zita show regarding differences in trust and disclosure between white and African-American women in women's studies courses, the degree of comfort and confidence in personal disclosure is related to students' varying sociopolitical as well as psychological backgrounds. Also relevant to a student's decision to disclose survivor-related information may be the composition of the class—that is, how many students in the classroom are similar to or different to herself, and her knowledge or sense of other survivors in the room—and the length of time she has been consciously aware of being a survivor.

Furthermore, when incest is disclosed, it may constitute an act of disloyalty to one's home community (Geiger and Zita 1985, 113). In the eyes of the perpetrator(s) and even within the larger kinship system, naming incest almost always constitutes an act of disloyalty. However, Geiger and Zita's point is especially salient with regard to women of color, who are daily inundated with racist stereotypes, distortions, and myths about their communities and cultures. These students may feel caught between a fear that exposing someone from their home community will play into white racist beliefs and a concern that others from their racial background will distrust them if they address sexual offenses within their own community. Teachers need to be aware of the particular conflicts that racial minorities face as student survivors and to be prepared to address both racist stereotypes and the student's unique conflicts, should she decide to discuss her own abuse history in the classroom.

I have argued that it is the responsibility of teachers to teach in ways that begin to undo the harms done by an oppressive culture rather than to inflict more harm. But the counter-hegemonic pedagogical strategy of validating each student's personal experience by creating a classroom environment where every woman is comfortable disclosing personal thoughts and feelings seems to overlook not only the ways in which positionality and authority in many classrooms work to the benefit of white women and to the detriment of women of color, but it also seems to overlook survivors' wariness about trust and disclosure. For many survivors, the classroom simply is not an environment in which they believe it is reasonable to be vulnerable with regard to their histories and their existential realities; the risk of entrusting others to *take care with their survivor-selves* is too great. But with regard to personal disclosure in classroom, the dynamic quality of trust is once again highlighted. A trustworthy teacher will *trust the student survivor* to know when she feels comfortable and trusting enough to disclose a history of sexual abuse and when she prefers not to reveal it.

So we return to the question of whether the classroom can, indeed, be an environment of trust. As Geiger and Zita state, "the relationship between professed or apparent openness and vulnerability and actual power and control within the context of classroom dynamics should be recognized by all who participate in the group" (Geiger and Zita 1985, 117). Although epistemological pursuits have, as background conditions, the assumption that much of what its members claim can be relied upon, it does not follow that such assumptions are made with equal ease, comfort, and confidence by all members of an epistemic community. The rich diversity of students means that establishing a classroom environment which creates a sort of epistemic community grounded in trust is a far more delicate task than might have appeared. Given the diversity in students' sociopolitical, economic, cultural, and ethnic positions as well as their histories and psychologies, teachers committed to becoming trustworthy with regard to their students will not gloss over the role that various power imbalances play in hindering trusting relations and will, instead, address both the assumption of trust and its absence.

CONCLUSION

In this chapter, I have illustrated how the Doctrine of the Mean can be employed in a specific area of moral and intellectual life—the classroom. Students have diverse histories, with different ways of knowing and learning, and different senses of themselves. The educational environment ought to be sensitive to those differences, and a trustworthy teacher will find the mean with respect to diverse students. I have argued that it is the responsibility of teachers to conduct teaching and learning in a way that begins to undo the harms done by an oppressive culture rather than to inflict more harm. In arguing for this claim, I have emphasized epistemic responsibilities that a teacher has—responsibilities that are a central part of being fully trustworthy as a teacher. Although the diversity of students precludes an easy assumption of trust in the classroom, a trustworthy teacher can nonetheless work to create the space in which distrust might be eased sufficiently for student survivors, as well as students in other oppressed groups, so that they can begin to experience themselves both existentially and intellectually as valuable members of an epistemic community.

NOTES

1. I characterize incest as sexual contact between familial relations where the age difference between the parties is at least five years. Familial relations need not be legally formalized; many familial relations are social ones where members consider

one another as kin. The five-year gap is generally thought to create sufficient power differentials to suggest nonconsensual sexual relations. Sibling sexual relations where the siblings are close in age may or may not be incestuous, depending on other factors that influence power relations between the siblings, such as gender or physical vulnerability, that affect children's ability to work out for themselves what kinds of body activities they want to engage in.

Incestuous assault may occur once, for a period of time in one's childhood, or over one's entire childhood, and single-even trauma is, in some respects, different from long-term trauma (see Terr 1990). Recognizing that distinctions regarding different experiences of incest need to be drawn, I am primarily addressing the incest survivor who has undergone chronic captivity and long-term trauma. But some of the issues raised in this chapter may also be relevant to survivors of one-time incestuous assault, and some may be relevant to survivors of long-term childhood sexual abuse and ritual abuse, where experiences of captivity, secrecy, and terror may be similar to that of some incest survivors.

2. Code cites labels on bottles, maps in atlases, and medical reports as examples of assumed good faith (Code 1987, 172).

3. I am not suggesting that all students innocently trust their teachers, but that some trust is always involved in taking a class from someone (e.g. one trusts that the teacher knows something one doesn't know or that the teacher is in a position for others—and perhaps even the teacher--to learn something that they don't know).

4. It is interesting to note that philosopher Iris Murdoch wrote a novel titled *A Severed Head* in which Honor, the heroine, has an incestuous relationship with her brother. It is, perhaps, no coincidence that Fraser's self-description has clear resonances with Honor's (although Murdoch's treatment of brother-sister incest tends more toward a critique of the cultural taboo against incest than of the practice of incest itself). In the following passage, Honor dissuades an interested lover who earlier interrupted a scene between Honor and her brother: "Your love for me does not inhabit the real world. Yes, it is love, I do not deny it. But not every love has a course to run, smooth or otherwise, and this love has no course at all. Because of what I am and because of what you saw I am a terrible object of fascination for you. I am a severed head such as primitive tribes and old alchemists used to use, anointing it with oil and putting a morsel of gold upon its tongue to make it utter prophecies. And who knows but that long acquaintance with a severed head might not lead to strange knowledge. For such knowledge one would have paid enough. But that is remote from love and remote from ordinary life. As real people we do not exist for each other" (Murdoch 1961, 182).

5. See chapter 3 for examples, both in the case study and ensuing analysis.

6. Sue Crowley was the commentator for a shorter version of this essay that I read at the April 1994 conference of the Society for Women in Philosophy.

7. The term "outsider within" comes from Linda Carty (Carty 1991, 15).

8. See Louise Armstrong's "Making an Issue of Incest" for a scathing critique of the legal and social systems' endorsement of incest and a discussion of its history as a patriarchal prerogative (Armstrong 1990).

9. All student comments quoted in this essay are from women's studies classes

and are used with permission.

10. Thanks to Karen Heegaard for bringing home to me the importance of consultations and supervision in therapeutic relationships and the absence of such activity in the academy.

11. This discussion raises important and difficult questions about the place of eroticism in our work such as those Audre Lorde discusses (Lorde 1984). This is an area that calls for exploration by teachers in the light of the various and complex issues discussed in this chapter which may arise between incest survivors and teachers.

12. I should add that it is not obvious to me that women's studies instructors should pattern teacher-student relationships after therapeutic relationships, and that is not my point. What I think women's studies instructors can learn from the therapeutic model is the practice of consultation and careful thought about what constitutes a health, constructive, epistemically and morally responsible teacher-student relationship.

13. Wording extrapolated from Weiler (Weiler 1988, 52).

14. Weiler gives a positive example of a feminist teacher at a public high school demonstrating her position as an ally in a mixed-gender class in which the teacher "overtly identifies her own gender with the girls in the class through using 'we'" as a way of signaling her non-neutrality to the girls. In this example, the minority group (girls) were assured that the teacher stood in loyalty with them and, if need be, in opposition to the dominant group (boys) in the class (Weiler 1988, 136).

5

Trustworthy Relations among Intimates

I hesitated at the offer of a ride. Simon was world famous, at least famous on the Spokane Indian Reservation, for driving backward. He always obeyed posted speed limits, traffic signals and signs, even minute suggestions. But he drove in reverse, using the rearview mirror as his guide. But what could I do? I trusted the man, and when you trust a man you also have to trust his horse.

Sherman Alexie, *The Approximate Size of My Favorite Tumor*

So far, I have focused primarily on the idea of what it means to be trustworthy in the context of institutional settings. Here I turn my attention to relations of trust in intimacy. My view is that we are deeply influenced by social practices and institutions such as family or kinship systems, the workplace, and education to become the sorts of persons we are and that relations of power virtually always infuse even our most intimate relations. For this reason, intimate relations are not exempt from difficulties in fostering just, equitable, and mutually flourishing relations.

Being in a genuinely intimate relationship is not a matter of geographical and long-standing togetherness, or of legal contracts, or of public recognition that parties are committed to one another. I will argue that intimacy requires a quality of relation captured by the concept of *connection* and that being connected in intimate relations requires that we be trustworthy. Being in an intimate relationship, therefore, involves an ongoing effort to be trustworthy and to sustain trust with one another. Because a trustworthy person is nondominating and nonexploitative and exhibits further features of the virtue, a person who consistently falls short of trustworthiness hampers the likelihood of mutual flourishing and is not a good partner in intimacy.

This view of intimacy contrasts with the idea that, in intimate relations, one can just relax and be appreciated for who one is (Govier 1998, 25). A normative notion of intimacy is not a retreat from moral struggle. The longed-for "home" that Bernice Johnson Reagon talks about, where one is barricaded from political and psychological struggles, and where one goes to be revived and readied to return to the struggle elsewhere, should not be sought in intimate relations (Reagon 1992, 506). If we want to find "home" in intimacy, we are likely to impede the very closeness we seek. Genuine intimacy requires that we engage in moral struggle with our loved ones and with ourselves and, to be able to do that well, we need the virtue of trustworthiness. Linking intimacy with trustworthiness puts into stark relief the mistake in thinking that intimacy, or even "being in relationship," is necessarily good. Whether or not a particular intimate relationship is a good one depends on the degree to which mutual flourishing develops—and that depends in large part on the dynamics of trust and trustworthiness of the parties involved.

There are many characteristics that need to be considered in intimate relations. We have needs, expectations, and hopes that center on the intimate, yet we may feel ambivalent. We long for companionship, affirmation of our centrality to the intimate, yet we also require boundaries and space. We want to be empathetic and empathized with, yet we may also find ourselves judging the intimate one and being criticized by him or her. We ache for harmony and a sense of unity, yet we also must deal with difference and conflict. And like Simon who only drives in reverse, we can be quirky.

At the heart of intimate relations is the delicately shaped relation of trust. Being trustworthy in intimate relations involves many of the features of trustworthiness I've already discussed. We need to indicate to our friend or lover the ways in which we are trustworthy and be willing to reassure; we need to take seriously the responsibility to know things relevant to the life of the other and to know that person in his or her particularity; we need to handle social and psychological power, as well as discretionary power, responsibly; we need to respond properly to broken trust; and we need to have other virtues such as forgiveness in order for our close relationships to thrive. In addition, in intimate relationships, being trustworthy is an ongoing process of making and recognizing reciprocal efforts to sustain connection and repair disconnections. A normative notion of intimacy concerns the quality of connection we experience. Mutual flourishing is constituted in part by sustained connected close relations. Staying connected in relations requires being able to keep trusting each other. And it requires that the participants be trustworthy in ways particular to the relationship. In other words, if we want to experience sustained connection with particular others, we have to be trustworthy in those relationships. Of course, being trustworthy doesn't guarantee that connection will be sustained. But trustworthiness is a central part of what makes connection possible. I identify and discuss four features of trustworthiness that facilitate connection among intimates: commitment to the relationship, commitment to mutuality, being honest, and responding properly to hurt. Each of these features, like other aspects of trustworthiness, must be contextualized and particularized to the individuals concerned. In particular, it is crucial to understand that a commitment to any relationship that does not also express both parties' commitment to mutuality is not a demand of trustworthiness and may even call one's trustworthiness into question. That is to say, an absolute commitment to a relationship in which one cannot flourish is no virtue. I'll say more about this point below. But first I begin by saying more about what I mean by "intimacy."

THE SCOPE OF INTIMACY

The scope of intimacy is both narrower and broader than one might think. I indicated that intimacy without connection is not really intimate after all, and the majority of this chapter fills out that idea. By bringing together the psychological and moral components of intimacy, I narrow the scope. At the same time, I think that the sustained connection of intimacy is possible for a wide array of relationships, and I want to resist a reductionist and hierarchical account of close relationships such as Aristotle's account of complete friendship. The etymology of the term "intimacy" suggests that it characterizes relationships that are meaningful, deep, and close.[1] Following that general lead, I include in intimacy a range of friendships, lover relationships, and coupling. Although there are differences between those kinds of relationships (coupling is more socially valued than the others, norms for exclusivity apply less to friendships), many of the qualities of a trustworthy intimate are relevant whether one is a friend, a lover, or a partner.

For now, there are two main ideas about intimacy that I want to counter. One is the idea that disclosure is a central criterion for intimacy, and the second is that intimacy is nearly impossible among unequals. While disclosure does sometimes play an important role in strengthening bonds of closeness and in facilitating deeper understanding, I argue that it should not be overemphasized to the detriment of other forms that intimacy can take. And, although it is true that inequalities make genuine intimacy difficult, I argue that that awareness suggests that we make greater efforts to be trustworthy as I have defined it, rather than that we eschew attempts at closeness among unequals. This section, then, moves toward broadening the scope of intimacy by suggesting its rich potential in our lives.

The first idea about intimacy that I think needs clarification, then, concerns the role of disclosure as an identifying feature of intimate relations. Part of countering that view will involve correcting what I think is a mistaken assumption about disclosure—that it is largely a linguistic act. It is true that different human relationships are, in part, constituted by different degrees of sharing (Reiman 1976). But some thinkers argue that what makes intimacy different from other human relationships is that quantitatively and qualitatively more *information* is shared (Rachels 1975; Fried 1970). Reiman argues that that view casts intimacy as a market good. In contrast, Reiman says, intimacy involves "a reciprocal desire to share present and future intense and important experiences together, not merely to swap information" (33). Although sharing of personal information is part of intimacy, it is the context of caring that makes the sharing of information significant. What is important is who cares about that information and to whom we want to reveal it (34).

Strikwerda and May would seem to agree with Reiman's claim, but still place a high value on disclosure. They distinguish "fellow feeling" from intimacy by the experience of mutual self-disclosure (Strikwerda and May 1992, 101). In a similar vein, Govier says that a special feature of friendship is "intimate talk" (Govier 1998, 25). Such claims imply that intimate knowledge is largely linguistic. This seems wrong to me. The term "disclosure" seems to mean the deliberate revelation of previously hidden aspects of ourselves. If this understanding is right, the definition of "disclosure" doesn't say anything about the *means* of disclosure. Yet usage typically assumes that the means of disclosing is through talk.

But we can reveal things to others—even deliberately—without talking. I can allow my anxiety, or my sadness, or my excitement, to be felt and discerned by another without using words. Lovers may reveal feelings and attitudes through tactile communication. Friends use conventional signs such as gift-giving to convey feelings of affection, appreciation, or knowledge of a loved one's needs and delights.

I am making two points about disclosure, then. First, I am pointing to a broader understanding of what disclosure is: disclosure is sometimes unspoken and can sometimes be quite subtle, requiring the other carefully to attend to expressions of feeling and to interpret them with the intimate other. For example, my friend Judy knows that, when we are scouting a rapids, I am likely to look worried. My facial expression and body movements say to her that I am feeling anxious. She knows this about me because I don't attempt to disguise my anxiety with bravado and because, upon seeing the unspoken changes in me when we are scouting a rapids, she has asked me if her understanding of my feelings is correct. I am more comfortable revealing to Judy my fears about wild rivers than to some other canoeing partners, because I trust her not to ridicule me or minimize my anxiety. "Intimate talk" plays an important role in intimacy, and at critical points of difference and misunderstanding, talking is usually necessary. But "intimate talk," understood as speech acts, shouldn't be the sole criterion for determining whether or not a relationship is intimate, because it unnecessarily restricts the domain of disclosure.

In fact, disclosure—however it is understood—shouldn't be the sole or central criterion for intimacy. This is the second point I am making about disclosure. I think Reiman is right to point out that the context in which sharing occurs is important to intimacy, but I also think too much emphasis can be put on disclosure as a sign of intimacy. Knowledge of other people—and the closeness that comes along with it—involves more than the mutual disclosing of thoughts and feelings (Code 1991). I emphasize the importance of sharing time and experiences, as well as of sharing thoughts and feelings. Intimacy includes cognitive, emotional, and behavioral closeness and is structured by a complex web of expectations, hopes, memories, caring, and trust (Martin 1993, 501). The insight about "intimate talk" that is crucial is that revealing ourselves to another (however we do that, and whether it is deliberate or not) makes us feel vulnerable, and so, in order to be willing to take the risks involved in being more vulnerable or vulnerable in ways we haven't been before, we need to have signs of the other's trustworthiness (Strikwerda and May 1992, 101, 103). Expanding on Reidel's point, I suggest that what marks off the intimate from the less intimate is the quality of connection that exists. Connection, then, turns out to be central to intimacy. I develop this claim below.

The other idea about intimacy that I think needs clarification is the question of how inequalities affect the degree or likelihood of intimacy. Trustworthiness, readers will recall, requires that we attend to inequalities and take care not to exploit vulnerabilities that arise from social and other inequalities. Trustworthiness does not require that we *be* equals but that we work to minimize inequalities and their effects. Intimacy does not require that we be equals, either, although from the time of Aristotle, many thinkers have recognized the ways in which inequalities can impede intimacy. Govier, for example, excludes parent/adult-child relationships from potential friendships on the grounds that they can never be psychological equals (Govier 1998, 27). Govier is right to point to psychological inequalities as another source of inequalities in relationships. Not only must differences in gender, race, or class be navigated in order to sustain intimate relations, but differences in personal histories. Just as student survivors bring to the classroom a legacy of abuse that complicates their learning and engagement styles, so do all of us, with our various experiences of hurt and injury in earlier life, bring to relationships histories that complicate our styles of interacting, loving, and giving to one another. Idiosyncrasies and quirks also vary; some people just are reserved, or laid back, or jumpy.[2] Socially shaped positions of inequality, combined with our historical and idiosyncratic selves, make for difficult times within intimate relationships. But they do not make intimacy impossible. How to navigate those difficulties in a trustworthy manner such that intimacy is sustained is the subject of this chapter.

THE CONCEPT OF CONNECTION AND BARRIERS TO IT

Human flourishing is not possible unless we take an interest in others for their own sakes, and intimacy is the primary way by which we can attend to the particularity of others in a fuller sense (Govier 1998, 21). But what kinds of relationships lead to the positive psychological development of the people in them, and what kinds of relationships diminish and destroy people and can even lead to pathology (Miller 1986, 2)? In this section, I situate connection culturally and show how the sustained connection of intimacy is dependent on the trustworthiness of the participants. This view rests on the idea that flourishing is dependent on healthy psychological states as well as on just, joyous, and compassionate social and political environments. Intimacy is good to the extent that sustained connection between parties takes the form of mutual flourishing, but given social stratification and interlocking systems of oppression, in tandem with individual idiosyncrasies, disconnection is rampant. While sometimes disconnection is the wiser path because flourishing is consistently impeded, as a social phenomenon it is a loss. Some people remain in unsatisfying friendships or coupling relationships while experiencing disconnection; others feel lonely, alienated, and depleted of energy. By examining connection—that somewhat amorphous psychological concept with normative weight—we can better understand what genuine intimacy looks like and why transforming disconnection and staying connected requires that we be trustworthy.

A genuinely intimate relationship is built from many, many growth-fostering interchanges (Miller 1986). According to Miller, five "good things" occur in a growth-fostering interchange: each person feels more zest, vitality, and energy; each feels more able to act and does act; each has a clearer understanding of herself and the other person; each experiences herself as having a greater sense of worth; and each feels more connected to the other person and feels greater motivation to seek connections with others beyond the specific relationship (3). Although Miller doesn't explicitly say so, I think that for interchanges to count as growth-fostering, we need to experience more than just zest, vitality, and energy. One form of zest comes from erotic power (Lorde 1984) and, in some contexts with certain people, is marvelous. But domination and subordination are also eroticized and can give us a rush of zest and vitality that, because they rest on nonmutuality, undermine the possibility of fostering growth. I take it this is one reason why Miller includes the other "good things" in her characterization of growth-fostering interchanges. When zest, vitality, and energy intertwine with the erotic, it is crucial that the parties are also committed to mutuality, an aspect of trustworthiness I discuss shortly. The point I draw from Miller is that, taken together, the good things that come out of growth-fostering exchanges are vital for us to experience on an ongoing basis with at least some others in order for us to flourish.

Connection has a dynamic phenomenology that isn't captured by serial representations of the participants' attitudes and actions. To be "in connection" is to *be with* another person in whatever feelings and thoughts that person is having, seeing that person in the moment and sensing that she is feeling seen— and sensing her being with you and you feeling seen by her in the moment as well. It is not mere "mirroring" of another's thoughts and feelings, however, because a growth-fostering interchange adds something positive to the interaction. People are connected through the interplay of their feelings and their thoughts, thereby creating something new together that is built by both of them. This bridging experience is the "connection between" (Miller 1986, 9).[3]

Crucial as it is to human flourishing, staying connected is sometimes quite difficult. Disconnection (from the intimate other, but also from oneself, from one's own responses, needs, and yearnings) is a primary source of human suffering (Jordan 1995, 1).[4] I identify three barriers to connection—stratification, other fears about difference, and the expectation that the connectedness of intimacy should be unambivalent—and show how thinking about what it means to be trustworthy in the face of those barriers can help us transform disconnection and stay connected through difficulties.

Jordan identifies disconnection as a cultural problem that is reinforced by our fears of being hurt. She notes several forces that push us toward withdrawal and isolation:

1. normative emphasis on defensive disconnection as a means to feeling strong and self-sufficient (e.g., "becoming your own man," "standing on your own two feet");
2. contextually produced disconnections including societal forces that suggest certain "different" or "minority" groups are "lesser than" (e.g., women, people of color, lesbians and gays, older people);

3. individual pathological disconnections which result from repetitive and ongoing violations in close relationships, particularly those that involve dependency and inability to self-protect, such as between small children and parents. (Miller 1995, 2)

Disconnection is often a feature of cultural meanings of difference. Stratification of people based on racialization, norms for sexual expression, and class markers present barriers to mutual trust and, hence, to connection. Women's love for other women, for example, can be distorted and even thwarted by heteropatriarchy. Women who want to sustain female friendships must not only be trustworthy friends but must contend with social forces and barriers that make such trustworthiness difficult and sometimes suspect.

As women form friendships across sexual difference, they come face to face with the effects of homophobia and heterosexism. Friends whose mutual trust is fairly well developed begin to reveal at a deeper level some of the ways their different positionalities and experiences threaten disconnection. A nonlesbian might learn what it feels like for her lesbian friend to be treated as invisible, for example, or what it is like to be blamed for others' homophobic discomfort, or what it is like to be continually disappointed in nonlesbian friends' ability and willingness to come through for her on issues of justice and friendship. A trustworthy friend in this case is one who is willing to work through with an intimate other the very personal ways in which institutional injustices and inequalities invade our lives.

Homophobia and heterosexism are social practices which operate together to support patriarchal institutions and dominant ideologies (Hoagland 1990, 29; see also Pellegrini 1992, 51; Pharr 1988; Rich 1980). The construction of the categories of homo/heterosexuality serves not only to reward those whose participation in heterosociality places them in the category of value, but also to signify women's loyalties to patriarchy, to exacerbate homophobia, and to further entrench divisions between women. The pervasiveness of these sociopolitical problems makes women doubt and distrust themselves and each other and fuels disconnection. But subtle changes in one's ways of being in the world can provide, to loved ones who are attentive to those realignments, important assurances that one is committed not only in her overtly political life but in her everyday personal attachments to eradicating oppressions.

Intimate relations between women across racial divides also are strained by the larger social context. Racialized stratification creates dynamics of exclusion, marginality, and internecine oppression that work against many women's desire to strive for good connection (Walker 1999, 1). Subtle forms of racism make women resistant to making themselves more available to growth and change within cross-racial friendships (2). For example, Walker explains that differences in matters of taste get turned into normative judgments that parallel background assumptions of racial superiority and inferiority. These normative judgments not only invoke aesthetics but also psychological health. As an example, Walker discusses Amy, a white woman, who gives an interpretation of African-American women's hair grooming as a sign of African American women's "low self-esteem" (3). Amy is engaging in stratified thinking about matters of taste that follow racial lines; she is also engaging in stereotyping. These activities impede connection across difference. Each of us brings to an encounter our own conception of what we want to do, could do, and should do. But racialism and other forms of oppression deny the oppressed access to full participation in meaning-making in those systems (4).

The effects of a stratified social system make it very difficult for women to grow together through conflict and across racial divides (Walker 1999, 4). Walker discusses the fracture of a friendship between two undergraduate women who suddenly started avoiding each other and making caustic comments about one another.

> Sue, who describes herself as a Korean American woman, had darkened her skin and chosen to wear something that she called an "Afro fright wig" for Halloween. Stacy, an African American, felt insulted and betrayed by her friend, whom she perceived to be making fun of African racial features. She retaliated by suggesting that she would go and find a yellow mask with slanted eyes. Sue accused Stacy of being too sensitive, and worse, needing everyone to be politically correct. Stacy accused Sue of being racist, and worse, really wanting to be white. Both women, fearing that their connection had been irreparably ruptured, remained distant from each other for the next several months. (Walker 1999, 5)

Walker notes that the templates that Sue and Stacy bring to their relationship make it difficult for them to be together through the conflict but also that the larger "culture of disconnection," where connection is devalued and explicitly discouraged across difference, makes it difficult for them even to understand their difficulties. I return to this example later to consider how the disruption of their friendship called into question each woman's trustworthiness with respect to the other and how distrust and disconnection can feed on one another.

Yet female friendships across difference and in the midst of larger oppressive structures are vital sources of energy, hope, and renewal.

> Female friendship gives women the context in which to be 'life-glad.' It creates a private and public sphere where happiness can become a reality. It provides encouragement and environment for the full use of one's powers. And since the

profession of friendship means that the one who befriends has a greater interest in her friend's happiness than in that of others in general, female friendship strives for the full use of the friend's powers. (Raymond 1986, 239)

Friendship is an intrinsic good, and connection that identifies and sustains it is good as well. Yet we have seen that sustained connection across stratified social differences is difficult. Skepticism about the good will of others in the face of power and privilege gives rise to distrust and fear. Distrust and fear feed disconnection.

There are other ways that connection is difficult, too. Connection is an integral component of intimacy, an experience many people long for. A longing for connection may keep someone in an unhealthy relationship, a problem I discuss in the next section when I talk about the value of being committed to a relationship. Here I want to focus on ways that a longing for connection can turn on us, in particular when we lose sight of the importance of being trustworthy in our attempts to be connected to others. My point will be that, although connection is generally a good thing, it must be sought in conjunction with features of trustworthiness.

The second barrier to connection, then, is a fear of difference—its meanings and implications for intimacy. Consider this exchange between Loots and the narrator after the party where they first met.

"Tell you one thing," [Loots] said as he walked me to the car, "I'm not drinking any more of that plum brandy. I was sick as a dog."

"Me too," I said. Not because it was true, but because I liked him and I wanted us to have things in common. (Thomson 1996, 93)

The narrator rationalizes his misleading statement by his need for connection. Yet he thwarts his own purpose. The narrator could not experience connection—at least not with respect to the "common ground" he pretended—because he had to hide from Loots the past self who, in fact, did not get sick from the plum brandy. Furthermore, if Loots were to find out that the narrator says things to please him rather than to be honest with him and see how the friendship develops, Loots is unlikely to trust the narrator. Not only would the narrator's trustworthiness be called into question, but so would the experience of connection Loots thought they had had.

A longing for connection may motivate us to act in ways that hamper the very thing we want. And we may want connection so badly that we lose sight of what it means for us to be trustworthy to this person in this moment. This sort of thing can happen when we are confronted with differences that we believe will threaten a connection. Intolerance of or fears about difference do not only arise in the context of structural or societal hierarchies. Many people have difficulty in intimate relations when values and ideas clash. Trusting another involves allowing another to take care of something we care about, but even in intimate relations, we are sometimes uncertain that what we most care about will be cared for well by the intimate other. When this uncertainty arises, we might feel threatened enough to press the other to think the way we do, or value what we value, or interpret things the way we have done. Differences between Alice's view and her friend Jay's view of how to interpret and respond to the Bush Administration's "Operation Enduring Freedom," for example, might be experienced by Alice as disconnection, so that she pushes Jay to accept her views. Persuasive argumentation about political and other differences is part of many intimate relations, but sometimes a line of respect for the intimate other's perspective is crossed and disconnection then occurs.

Low tolerance for differences doesn't only show up in politics. Many differences are matters of taste and we can be quite petty, or quite nasty, about our own opinions. Which movies we want to see, or what kind of music we want to listen to, can be a source of friction between intimate others because tastes differ and sometimes those differences are irritating or threatening. Because part of being close involves spending time together and sharing experiences, too many or too significant differences in taste may not allow enough moments of connection to sustain intimacy. But often the problem is more a matter of mistaking difference for disconnection and similarity for connection. As Walker's example of a white woman's interpretation of a so-called African-American hair aesthetic suggests, we often turn matters of taste into hierarchical moral judgments and then treat those moral judgments as objective. Statements or nonverbal messages like "anyone who could enjoy that film must be sick!" close off conversation and at least temporarily sever connection between intimates.

A third difficulty with connection in intimate relationships that I want to mention is that some people feel ambivalent about intimacy. Fear of being hurt sets up a paradox for people; the yearning for connection and the terror of connection can be paralyzing (Jordan 1995, 3). We communicate indirectly, for example, in order to maintain a self-defensive reserve, to promote the pleasant experience of rapport without having to spell out everything, and to protect relationships from the potential hurt of bluntness (Martin 1993, 498). Sometimes our efforts to protect ourselves and foster closeness are rewarded, and sometimes they backfire. And when we think we perceive ambivalence in a loved one, we may be confrontational about its meaning in an attempt to clarify the status of the relationship, or we may require excessive reassurance that, paradoxically, pushes the loved one away. I suspect that, often, the problem with connection isn't so much the ambivalence itself, but rather the assumption that feelings of ambivalence are an indication of trouble in the relationship. Feelings of ambivalence even in the best of relationships are fairly common at least occasionally, and an interpretation of ambivalence as trouble may, in some cases, be more likely to cause disconnection than the ambivalence itself. If you or I want intimacy, we must make and sustain connection with others in ways that allow for ambivalence and fear. Being trustworthy in ways that sustain connection involves an acceptance of a certain amount of ambivalence both in ourselves and in our loved ones. It is a way we indicate to a loved one that we will allow a degree of mixed, vacillating, or confused attitudes and feelings (even when they concern us) without demanding that the loved one "settle" things one way or another. Like other features of trustworthiness, though, how much ambivalence should be accepted must be contextualized to the particular people involved.

ELEMENTS OF TRUSTWORTHINESS THAT SUSTAIN CONNECTION

The kind of connection involved in intimacy is not an easy quality of relation to sustain. In analyzing the concept of connection and discussing some common barriers to staying connected, I have also begun to identify what *trustworthy* connectedness looks like. The next section identifies features of trustworthiness that sustain connection: a commitment to the relationship; a commitment to mutuality; being honest; and responding properly to hurt.

Two commitments are basic to connection: a commitment to the relationship itself and a commitment to mutuality. Although people may hold other commitments within intimacy as well, those others can emerge from the particular relationship and can vary widely.[5] I take the two commitments I discuss to be central to a normatively intimate relationship. Although I discuss them separately, I argue that these two commitments work together and that a commitment to mutuality is vital in order to set parameters on relational commitments.

Commitment to the Relationship

One important way to be trustworthy in a relationship is to be committed to the relationship. Although ambivalent feelings about being in intimate relationships can be fairly common, they can call into doubt the degree to which one is committed to the relationship. Ambivalence is more easily tolerated when it exists in conjunction with affirmation that the relationship is valued. Similarly, conflicts, misunderstandings, and disappointments are much more easily healed when the parties are confident of each other's continued commitment to the relationship. The trustworthy friend or lover indicates through her commitment to the relationship that she recognizes its value. An intimate relationship is not merely the joining of two individuals; over time, it becomes something with intrinsic value that both parties work to foster. In a relational metaphysics, it is the *relating* that is the primary relation, and the *relata* are co-derivatives (Oliver 1992, 44). While this makes my point rather too strongly, I think there is merit in conceptualizing the relation itself as requiring commitment and care. We more readily trust those whom we believe to value their relationships with us. We see those people as trustworthy with respect to the relationship. The trustworthy intimate other, then, is someone who can be counted on to do what he or she can to help the relationship, and the participants in it, thrive.

Women's development occurs within a culture that both valorizes and denigrates the relatedness of sustained connection. Even though some women are not particularly good at sustaining intimate friendships, most women come to believe that their development requires intimacy and connection and that meaningfulness will (or should) arise out of relationships. Many women, then, do not merely "have" relationships—they *invest relationships with their spirit* (Josselson 2000, 88). While surely this should not be a gendered practice (if it is), it is a vital one. A sign of one's trustworthiness in an intimate relationship is that one imbues the relationship not only with value but with zest and vitality.

There are limits to this claim, however. Being in relation isn't unequivocally good, and to think so is to romanticize relation (Card 1990, 202). This is because being in relation doesn't necessarily entail being in connection. Socialization into ideals of love, loyalty, and forgiveness—liabilities for women—as well as a longing for connection that can lead us to want to downplay differences or suppress ambivalence can keep us stuck in debilitating relationships.

A single-minded commitment to a bad relationship doesn't reflect one's trustworthiness but one's bad luck and bad judgment. "Not every passionate attachment to persons is valuable, any more than every passionate espousal of principles is. The nature and basis of the attachment matters" (Card 1990, 215). Sometimes nonmutual, chronically disconnected relationships need to be ended, because they derail our development (Jordan 1995, 5). Being trustworthy in one's commitment to a relationship, then, doesn't mean that one remain committed regardless of the quality of the relationship or its effects on one's own development. Card points out that moral philosophers need to develop an "ethic of attachment" that indicates how to discern the difference between good and bad attachments. A beginning for such an ethic might be found in Miller's early work. Miller states criteria for interactions to count as growth-fostering: "Does this interaction lead to a greater sense of connection with the person(s) directly involved rather than less? And does this interaction lead to a motivation for more connection in general rather than the reverse—that is, a decline in motivation for connection or a turn toward isolation" (Miller 1986, 7). Good quality of connection not only imbues the relationship with zest and vitality a significant amount of the time, but also sparks the participants to expand their connections with others. Sustained connection is not privatizing but instead is a primary source for broadening the scope of love, compassion, and care toward other particular others.

Commitment to Mutuality

A second important commitment is to mutuality. Such a commitment makes possible the flowering of intimate relations between unequals and is at the heart of flourishing both at the interpersonal and civic level. Within intimacy, a commitment to the relationship *must* be accompanied by a commitment to mutuality in order for mutual trust to grow and thus connection be sustained. Carter Heyward characterizes deepest, most profound friendship as "right relation." By this she means relations in which "all parties are empowered to be more fully who they are as persons (or creatures) in relation" (Heyward 1989, 193). Wrong relation, in contrast, perverts and distorts all participants, turning them around from what they have the potential to become, and disempowering (trivializing, diminishing, abusing) one or more participants in the relation. Given barriers to connection such as those I discussed, a commitment to a relationship without an attendant commitment to mutuality is likely to turn into wrong relation. Wrong relation, Heyward argues, is the root of evil in our lives together, and a primary cause of wrong relations is "fear of the scope and depth and passion of our relational possibilities" (193). "We yearn to be true to ourselves in relation, touched by and touching one another in the soul of who we are together and in each of our deepest places" (93), but, she says, many of us don't even partially relate to one another in this manner, because we are stuck in "the fear of mutuality and its consequences, sadomasochistic relations, which characterize not only the might makes right credo of our national government but also, not infrequently, our own most intimate friendships" (92).

Mutuality is vital to connection. Mutuality, and thus connection, can be threatened in a number of ways; for example, when one's boundaries are so rigid as to impede openness, when one uses others to bolster one's self-esteem, when one withdraws into the self to repair damage, when one exhibits frequent helplessness and wishes for ministrations from others, or when one person in the relationship begins to do most of the accommodating and giving. Finally, an investment in domination over another clearly interferes with mutuality (Jordan 1991, 92-93). When mutuality is absent, trust diminishes and connection falters.

Mutuality is not only the experience of being in right relation. It is also (and perhaps primarily) a process by which persons in relation move toward right relation. Mutuality involves making efforts to share power "in such a way that each participant in the relationship is called forth more fully into becoming who she is—a whole person, with integrity" (Heyward 1989, 191). Mutuality requires a mutual attunement to, and responsiveness to, the subjective cognitive and affective experience of the other. When we are committed to mutuality in an intimate relationship, we are motivated to understand the other's meaning system and inner experience from the other's perspective. It is, as Jordan says, a "holding" of the other's subjectivity (Jordan 1991, 83).

But this attunement and responsiveness are never entirely independent of systems of meaning and experience. As Heyward explains, mutuality and right relation are not only interpersonal commitments and practices. They are intrinsic to our efforts to seek justice. The scope of justice ranges from friendships, families, local and larger communities, and the global world. Right relation is reflected in human justice to the extent that we are willing participants in creating a broader domain for justice on the earth (Heyward 1989, 191).

The kind of knowing that comes from being in relation "fundamentally alters one's experience of 'Otherness' and hence one's experience of self in the world" (Josselson 2000, 92). "The capacity to embrace difference in relationship enlarges the self, expanding the repertoire of representations that we carry of people who inhabit the world we share, both sharpening the boundaries of the self and connecting the self in deeper ways to others" (96). But mutuality isn't easy, and often isn't continuous even when it is present. We can at one moment recognize the full subjectivity of a loved one and, at the next moment, experience that person as an extension of oneself or a gratifier of one's needs (94). As Miller says, "mutually growth-fostering interactions cannot occur if one person has an overwhelming amount of power to determine what happens in the interactions and uses the power in that way" (Miller 1986, 10). This is why we need to be committed to mutuality. As imperfect beings, we will flounder and fail one another, breaking trust and breaking connection by misuses of social and psychological power, by ignoring power differentials within the relationship, and by neglecting to tend to harms the other has experienced through social inequalities and injustices. A person who is committed to mutuality in relation indicates that she can be counted on to try to regain "right relation" with her intimate other.

An indication that one can be counted on to take seriously the relationship is that one reflects on it, worries about it, and attends to its strengths and weaknesses. Martin mentions what he calls "meta-truthfulness," which is a commitment to communicate to one's friend or beloved about one's attitudes toward the other and about the relationship (Martin 1993, 498). In order to do this, we need to develop what Jordan calls "relational awareness." Relational awareness allows one to move toward greater clarity about the quality and shape of the relationship. To be relationally aware is to notice patterns in the relationship, such as patterned ways of connecting and disconnecting, and to work toward transforming the flow from disconnection to connection (Jordan 1995). Relational awareness is not a matter of analyzing relationships but rather of an openness to learning about relational patterns. And this openness involves a willingness to be vulnerable to the other person. "Essential to the transformation of disconnection," Jordan says, "is an openness to being moved by the other person. Also essential is an openness to being seen by the other person" (6).

Relational awareness isn't only a matter of being concerned about problems in the relationships. It requires that participants in an intimate relationship pay attention to the resiliency of the relationship as well as to its rough edges (Jordan 1995, 7). The deep vulnerability we experience in close relationships is mitigated by the recognition of the strengths and creativity manifested. It is good—joyous even—to celebrate together the delicate but sturdy fabric of a relationship woven over time. Honoring relational resilience is a way of being trustworthy. Such honoring says that you or I can be trusted to see not only problems but strengths and to balance frustration with hope. This hopeful and valuing attitude allows even difficult and sometimes disconnected relationships to have a current of zest and vitality that is so vital to their continuance.

Being Honest

Honesty is the third element of trustworthiness in intimacy that I will discuss. Being trustworthy in one's commitment to the relationship and to mutuality, and developing relational awareness, requires a fairly deep level of honesty. We have to be able and willing to be honest with ourselves, for example, in assessing how we are feeling about the relationship, and we have to be able to be honest with ourselves and others at particular moments within that relationship. But being honest in this deep way—about how one is feeling, about what one needs and wants from the other, about what is satisfying in a relationship and what isn't—is very difficult when we don't trust the other person. In order to be honest in ways that foster connection and transform disconnection, the participants have to be trustworthy. The link between honesty and trustworthiness, in other words, is dynamic rather than causal and linear.

When philosophers have discussed intimacy, most of what they have focused on is the importance of disclosure and honesty. Like disclosure, honesty has different dimensions and different significance within intimate relationships than in more formal or institutional ones. If we want our relationships to thrive and to shift from less connection to more, we have to be willing to be honest with our loved one about our perceptions, feelings, thoughts, and experiences past and present. This claim doesn't amount to an absolute, as I will discuss shortly. But if we take seriously the link between trustworthiness and the honoring of commitment to the relationship and to mutuality, it is vital to be honest in the relationship as well.

Jennifer Jackson takes the Kantian duty to keep a promise to permit and even sometimes require us to conceal things from others. In other words, in Jackson's view, part of being trustworthy may require that we sometimes conceal things. She makes the point that trustworthy people do not betray secrets; they conceal them (Jackson 2001, 47). Even friends hide their thoughts from one another at times, and this is no more than prudence, she suggests. While we might think that reserve or concealment indicates lack of trust in the other, "there are plenty of reasons for hiding your thoughts, etc. from friends that do not imply the least doubt of their trustworthiness" (35). That suggestion seems to miss the point of her own argument. What we want to know is whether or not *my* reserve or habits of concealment affect *my* trustworthiness. In intimate relationships, can the participants conceal things from one another and still be trustworthy?

One answer can be found in Martin's article "Honesty in Love." Honesty, he says, is a far richer notion than simple truth-telling (Martin 1993, 498). "When we call people honest in their speech we praise them for uttering appropriate truths or their views on pertinent issues…We do not praise people for honesty when they chatter about irrelevant matters; indeed, chatter can function as a dishonest evasion of truth. Nor do we praise individuals as honest when they are utterly insensitive, callous, or cruel" (498). David Nyberg argues that, even in truth-telling, we must make choices about what to reveal and what to edit out.

> There is choice in truth-telling; we do have a range of truths to tell. Many questions do have more than one truthful answer. It may sound strange to say so, but I think the virtue of truth-telling is determined by just this kind of selectivity. We ought to try for the right truth in the right amount in order to produce the best effect for the people involved. In other words, it is probably better to tell the right truth rather than the whole truth or no truth at all. (Nyberg 1993, 158)[6]

Martin's view, though, is that honesty does not require us always to say the right thing at the right time, but that "as a character trait and as a feature of truthful communication, honesty is a prima facie moral good" (Martin 1993, 498). Truthfulness and trustworthiness usually go together because they both involve avoiding deception, and deception undermines trust (500). Martin would agree with Jackson, though, that concealment isn't always a threat to trustworthiness (504). This is because he defines trustworthiness as a general concern for maintaining trust, and he thinks that general trust can be sustained while withholding some information. In fact, he suggests, some contexts may require concealment in order to sustain general trust and intimacy. How much candor is too much, and how much concealment or reserve threatens connection?

Figuring out what it means to be honest in ways that reflect trustworthiness and sustain connection is probably one of the most difficult aspects of intimacy. When the participants in a relationship know one another well, there is much to take care of—much that each has entrusted to the other—that inclines them to protect one another. Concern and empathy for the other, coupled with fear of disapproval, anger, blame, or rejection, make honesty in speech and behavior difficult. Martin, Jackson, and Nyberg are certainly right that being honest is a much more nuanced value than an absolute principle would allow. Still, a great deal of honesty is needed in order for relationships to shift from stale and static patterns of disconnection and frustration to more mutually flourishing ones. When participants adopt a reflective stance toward the relationship, honesty with oneself and with the other is vital. Moving through hurt, disappointment, and misunderstanding, not to mention betrayals both large and small, requires that we be honest in the moment about our feelings, attitudes, and thoughts. Note that honesty, in my view, is not restricted to what is said or how it is said but also includes what is revealed to the other in nonverbal communication.

Of course, the analogue of being trustworthy with respect to honesty is that one needs to be able to trust the other with one's honesty. If we show our anger, or our doubts, or our defensiveness, we must be able to count on the intimate other not to take advantage of our moves toward openness. Honesty is an easier virtue to embody when the receiver of our honesty has another virtue—the virtue I call "giving uptake." This virtue is so central to trustworthiness that I devote the final chapter to it. The virtues of trustworthiness, honesty, and giving uptake work together to assist us in maintaining reciprocal and rewarding intimate relationships. The moral demands of honesty might also appear less opaque when the relationship is centered. Being trustworthy in an intimate relationship requires attending to the flourishing of the relation, so that the participants are not solely focused on what is good for themselves, or the other, or some vacillation between the two.

This discussion about honesty is especially important to remember in light of structural inequalities and power imbalances that affect even our most personal attachments. Differences between people which center on race, class, gender, sexual orientation, age, ability, and ethnicity often put a strain on trusting relations. These kinds of diversity between and among us are framed by institutionally sanctioned imbalances in benefits and burdens and give rise to interpersonal relationships infused with dynamics of privilege and injustice, opportunity and exploitation, recognition and marginality. Differences that are less institutionalized but nevertheless threaten disconnection (such as matters of taste that are transformed into moral or psychological judgments) also interface with power because we can use them against one another. If we understand trustworthiness to be an enduring characteristic of being nonexploitative and nondominating in the ways that we take care of what is entrusted to us, we cast honesty in a different light. Trustworthiness with respect to honesty includes, for example, that we pay particular attention to the ways concealment can be used to regulate power in the relationship, as when one person conceals information about an action that, if known, would be detrimental to the relationship. Concealing feelings of vulnerability in order to appear strong, or even concealing feelings of strength as an attempt to keep the other in a caretaking position, are also ways to regulate power. Both the giving and the receiving of honest communications undermine trustworthiness when they threaten or destroy mutuality.

Being honest does require that we be open and vulnerable, yet those aren't always good ways to be, and not only because openness and vulnerability sometimes aren't wise in the face of another's potential to hurt us. Both too much vulnerability and too little vulnerability within a relationship can impede connection over time; both extremes involve controlling the other (Hoagland 1990, 111). Hoagland argues that vulnerability can be turned into a tool for manipulating another, for example by consistently revealing feelings of anxiety, fear, need, or desperation. One's vulnerability, then, takes the form of revealing just one theme of one's emotional life and serves to defend against connection even while seeming to engage in it (111). Disconnection occurs when expressions of vulnerability function as a means to manipulate or exploit the other. One cannot be both connected in a relationship and exploitative of the other. It is sometimes difficult to tell when we are making ourselves vulnerable for the wrong reasons, and this is another reason why self-reflection coupled with honest dialogue with the intimate other are vital to sustained connection.

Responding Properly to Hurt

The fourth element of trustworthiness among intimates concerns how we respond when we hurt others and are hurt by them. Baier implies that friendship facilitates flourishing when she says that the proper use of intimate knowledge is to enable better reciprocal aid and comfort, and more satisfying shared enjoyments (Baier 1989, 273). But our ideas of how to aid, comfort, and enjoy one another come into conflict, even when we know one another very well. When we trust someone, we give her some leeway to use her discretion about how to care for what is entrusted to her and, in intimate relationships, both the scope of what is entrusted and the range of leeway are much broader than in most other kinds of relations. I argued in chapter 2 that trusting gives the trusted one discretionary power that can be abused. The vulnerability that comes with giving another implicit discretionary power is even more pronounced in intimate relations. The mutual trust that is integral to intimacy gives intimates, with their shared experiences and knowledge, greater potential to hurt us. An irony of intimacy, though, is that although we become more vulnerable with increasing intimacy, the more we experience connection—with its (assumed) solid trustworthiness—the less we tend to notice the vulnerability. That is, our experience of deep mutual trust that is so central to connection tends to obscure the vulnerability (274).

Not only are our positionalities, histories, psychological compositions, and idiosyncratic needs different, but our ways of interpreting the same event can sometimes be radically divergent. We need relationships and so must form them, but those others in relationships with us retain a reality independent of our mutual representations and misrepresentations (Josselson 2000, 93). Or, as Lawrence Cahoone puts it, the self is incompletely social in its identifications (Cahoone 1992, 65). Broad discretionary power, plus social and personal differences, leave us open to being hurt in varying ways and degrees.

Some hurts and injuries are inevitable, and we accept them as part of intimate relations. But responding in a trustworthy manner to the hurt we experience as well as the hurt we do to others involves more than merely accepting that we will sometimes hurt and be hurt by our loved ones.

Hurt and issues of trust are closely related. When we are hurt, we make attributions (of intent or of the other's character, for instance) in order to reconcile our assessment that someone hurt us with our subsequent attitudes toward the person who hurt us (Vangelisti 2001, 50). Being hurt by another, especially someone close to us, raises the question of future harm. We want to assess whether or not there is a threat of more hurt to come. The question is whether the hurt done to us suggests that our trust in the other is misplaced, at least with respect to the domain of that hurt. Putting our trust in another involves making inferences to the future about the other's capacity and good will to take care of things we value, and when we are hurt, the warrant for that inference is called into question. We feel the vulnerability that comes from having trusted the other deeply (something we tend not to notice in intimate relationships until we are hurt) and then we experience that vulnerability heightened by getting hurt. For example, we may no longer be confident that the other has the good will toward us that grounds our trust and, without that good will, we fear we may be facing more hurt in that relationship.

One way to respond to a perceived threat is to reconstrue the relationship in a way that decreases the hurt one's vulnerability. Distancing oneself is one obvious way to accomplish that (Vangelisti 2001). Distancing is a kind of disconnection, and it occurs within the context of intimacy (42). Distancing is the mode that Sue and Stacy settled into in response to the hurt and disruption in their friendship when Sue had darkened her skin and worn an "Afro fright wig" for Halloween. As we saw from that example, being hurt, or feeling hurt, affects a relationship through how we respond to it emotionally, how we construct the hurt within the relationship, how we talk about it, and how our overall responses are received.

Dialogue can facilitate understanding; it can also prevent it, exacerbating the hurt and assessment of threat. (The latter seems to be what occurred with Sue and Stacy, and I'll return to this point shortly.) The reason is that explanations we generate for the source of our emotions about hurtful interactions themselves become part of the social environment. The way people think about and explain their hurtful experiences affects the way in which they interact with the people who hurt them (Vangelisti 2001, 42). For example, if the hurt is perceived to have been done intentionally, it is judged more harshly than if it is perceived to have been done inadvertently. Even where nonintentional hurt is assessed, one is more likely to distance oneself if the other is perceived to be self-absorbed or if hurting others (due to insensitivity, for example) looks like a character trait. Finally, judgments of intent and other appraisals are made against a backdrop of relational quality. Interpretations of an intimate other's behavior are linked to the hurt one's feelings about the relationship in general (44).

People do not always distance themselves when hurt in intimate relationships, though. Hurt feelings are only weakly correlated with a tendency to distance oneself from those who hurt one (Vangelisti 2001, 42). When someone overrides her readiness to distance, what enables her to do so? According to Vangelisti, one factor is the perceived unintentionality of the person who hurt her. I think another factor is the perception of trustworthiness in the other, along with a belief that the other will try to work through the hurtful interaction while maintaining connection.

Miller says that as long as people see a possibility of connecting—of positive engagement with the other person in thoughts and feelings—they can grapple with oppositions, hurts, conflicts, and misunderstandings (Miller 1986, 10). Jordan adds:

Questions we might ask when we observe disconnections are: Is it noticed by both people (or all people involved since these observations are not just limited to two-person situations)? Does it matter to both people? Will both people try to change it? Will both people work to sustain the connection? And will they work to understand the disconnection? Will both people attempt to understand and look at what is current? Can both people "hold" responsibility for the effect of disconnections on the relationship? (Jordan 1995, 3)

Being trustworthy through disconnection is difficult when we are the one who has caused the hurt. Sometimes we blame ourselves or the other, sometimes we rush to accommodate. Most often, we feel conflicting desires to soothe the other's hurt, on the one hand, and to protect ourselves from recognizing and facing the hurt we have caused, on the other hand. But it is crucial to sustaining trust and connection that we witness the hurt we have caused, take responsibility for the part we played in causing it, and express sorrow about it (Jordan 1995, 4).

Neither Sue nor Stacy seemed able to do these things after the initial fracture in their friendship occurred. Talking about the hurt didn't help them mend their disconnection. Instead, it entrenched their hurt and further alienated them from one another. I can imagine things going differently, but in order for this imaginary healing to have occurred, they would seem to have needed a stronger commitment to the friendship and to mutuality. But those commitments—which are so central to sustaining connection through difficulties—were not strong enough to override the onslaught of distrust that arose, and each person's trustworthiness in the eyes of the other was not secure enough to override the wavering on implicit commitments when each friend's attributions and accusations began to circulate.

When Stacy felt insulted and betrayed by Sue's Halloween costuming, Stacy revealed her feelings through retaliation—an insult in kind—rather than through anger (or hurt) that Sue might be more likely to receive. This approach is not conducive to connection. Did Stacy act too quickly in expressing her anger, so it came out in an inflammatory way? Or did she need a sign from Sue that Sue could be trusted with her anger? We don't know enough about the situation and the dynamics of their relationship to pinpoint exactly what each person might have done differently, but we do know that Sue's trustworthiness with respect to the racial differences between them was called into question and that that betrayal was felt deeply by Stacy. Stacy attributed racist motives to Sue's costuming because the larger culture in which their friendship exists is infused with racialism where the meaning of "blackface" has a history of deep insult. Stacy's attribution most likely did get in the way of their attempts to address their disconnection, but it is understandable in the context of their partially shared experience as women on the receiving end of racial oppression. Perhaps one of the things Stacy had entrusted to Sue and believed to be mutual was the care of their shared vulnerability regarding racialism, and perhaps that trust was now broken. Although Sue most likely hurt her friend unintentionally, and Stacy most likely construed the hurt in that way, Sue nevertheless did hurt her friend and bore the burden of responsibility for healing the hurt.

When we take responsibility for having done harm to someone we love, we feel vulnerable, especially having to witness the pain we have caused. And it is very difficult to reveal feelings of vulnerability about our responsibility and our remorse when we are uncertain about the trustworthiness of the hurt person. Will the hurt friend be forgiving? Will she accept my remorse? Or will she use it against me? Is her anger at my betrayal too big for me to make myself vulnerable here and now? Of course, other things besides distrust of the hurt one can prevent us from taking responsibility for wrongdoing. We may, for instance, be unwilling to admit to ourselves that we have made a mistake. We may equate even unintentional hurting of others with evil and defend against a negative self-conception by refusing to admit a mistake. We don't know Sue's thinking at this point, but we can surmise that Stacy's retaliatory remarks put Sue on the defensive, exacerbating their disconnection and fueling distrust.

Sue, confronted with the possibility of having made a mistake and having hurt her friend, became accusing rather than reflective. Stacy was fearful that Sue carried unreflective racist attitudes, and Sue's defensiveness led Stacy to decide Sue was likely to repeat this hurt. Thus, although Stacy probably construed Sue's act as unintentional, she also had reasons to believe that Sue was not to be trusted when it came to taking responsibility for hurting her friend. Sue, too, probably began to see Stacy as punitive and angry, untrustworthy when it came to differences that, to Sue, were mere matters of taste.

In Sue and Stacy's friendship, mutual blame replaced mutual trust. Blame, whether directed toward oneself or an intimate other, threatens disconnection. Blame typically casts aspersions on another's judgment or character, temporarily doing damage to the other's ability to flourish. Chronic blame thwarts development and, if it persists within a relationship, diminishes all participants. Blame is antithetical to mutuality, as well: the power to accuse and hold guilty can quickly disrupt efforts to foster just, right relations. To be trustworthy with respect to hurting in a relationship, then, one must not turn discussions of accountability into ones of accusation.

Taking responsibility for harms done is too easy for some, too difficult for others. In a close relationship, we must accept responsibility for our pettiness, small meannesses, insensitivities, and inadvertent mistakes. Sometimes, an indication that one has taken responsibility for hurting another is that one understands that one's trustworthiness is called into question and that one has to earn trust back. Sometimes, one can indicate having taken responsibility by witnessing the pain one has caused and by not running away. For the part of the person hurt, an indication of ongoing trustworthiness in spite of hurt is that one forgives the wrongdoing. Forgiveness is clearly a virtue, and no intimate relationship is likely to fare well without it. But as a virtue, it has a mean, and one can be too forgiving about things too serious to be forgiven (Potter 2001).

CONCLUSION

Baier argues that untrustworthiness usually shows some other fault in the untrustworthy person, such as cruelty or exaggeration. "In order to safeguard ourselves against such possible wounds, we should try to have friends whose general character is such that the chances of their inflicting such wounds are slight enough not to be worth adverting to" (Baier 1989, 276).

This is worthy advice and gives weight to the claim that the trustworthy person also has other virtues. In addition, I stress the point that trustworthiness isn't something that exists independent of social practices and institutional structures, and intimacy does not occur in isolation from those practices and institutions. Returning to the idea of relational awareness, I draw upon Jordan, who urges us to pay attention to the larger context in which relationships exist. What we recognize, honor, and value is highly affected by what cultural meanings are given to different actions, skills, emotions, and so on. "We do not live within a culture that provides a full relational context" (Miller 1986, 10).

Strikwerda and May (1992) have persuasively argued that male friendships are impoverished by cultural taboos prohibiting emotional intimacy between men, and many authors have written about the ways masculinity is constructed away from intimacy through activities such as sports. To the extent that emotional intimacy between men is discouraged, it is a loss. Men who want to be trustworthy intimates to one another, then, must resist an ideology of masculinity (and, often, their internalization of that ideology) that inhibits connection. But again, whether or not particular relationships count as intimate ones will depend partly on the criteria for intimacy we are using. Putting too much emphasis on "intimate talk" over-determines the conclusion that male friendships are impoverished. I do think an important kind of closeness can occur as a result of sharing an activity together regularly (whether the participants are male or female), and I want to honor those kinds of connections as well. In other words, I see the varieties of intimacy as more like

Wittgensteinian family resemblances than as levels of completeness, and I resist the hierarchical normativity of intimate relationships. Connection comes in many forms and doesn't have to be complete or all-encompassing to count as deep closeness. But, for a relationship to count as intimate, connection cannot occur only sporadically, and it needs to be genuine and meaningful to the participants. That cultural norms make such connection difficult to sustain—and make those difficulties different for different groups—is a central part of what each of us has to keep in mind when becoming trustworthy intimates.[7]

As potential intimate others, we must resist romanticized and privatizing conceptions of closeness that derail development and empowerment. But a vision of the possibilities of mutual passionate friendships—including those between variously subjugated people across their differences—is absolutely vital both to personal and institutional transformation. "It is not possible for women to be free, nor to be realistic about the state of female existence in a man-made world, nor to struggle against those forces that are waged against us all, nor to win, if we do not have a vision of female friendship" (Raymond 1986, 207). A belief in the possibilities for connection, mutuality, and intimacy is vital to all those committed to a liberatory politics and ethics. But in order to sustain such a vision, we not only need to seek out trustworthy others and sustain connection with already-intimate others; we need social contexts in which passionate attachments can flourish. Our trustworthiness and our closest relationships are threatened to the extent that our practices and institutions are corrupt. For this reason, trustworthiness with respect to intimate others is always integrally bound up with other aspects of trustworthiness that we call upon as workers, citizens, supplicants, and resistors.

NOTES

1. According to the Oxford English Dictionary, the origin of the term "intimate" is relatively recent, coming from the late Latin word *intimus* of Fifteenth-century origins.

2. This is not to say that we can't help the way we are, but that there are sometimes physiological factors or long-standing traits that are so deep that they seem "natural."

3. This "connection between" is what Miller calls relationship but ordinary language use of "relationship" doesn't carry the normative weight of connection, so I am not using her term here.

4. I think this is generally true even when it is necessary for one's continuing flourishing to detach or even to exit a relationship.

5. How they get unpacked will depend on each person's political commitments, matters of taste, and so on. An example of how the two central commitments can get filled out in sexual ethics can be found in chapter 7 of Heyward's *Touching Our Strength* (1989).

6. This is consistent with Baier's view on honest speech that I discussed in chapter

2. Baier says that 'it is impossible to put into language all of our beliefs and so speech always involves a selection process.

7. An overemphasis on "intimate talk" as a solution to cultural taboos against male friendships tends to obscure the possibilities for connection that men do seize, sometimes in contexts where disconnection seems far more likely. I have in mind some war-time friendships as characterized by writers such as Tim O'Brien and Steward O'Nan. Larry, a Vietnam war veteran in O'Nan's novel *The Names of the Dead* (1996), experiences a kind of intimacy that comes from having to trust in virtual strangers while knowing little of others' history and background. Living together in close quarters under extreme stress and mutual dependence gives rise to closeness through shared experiences and mutual vulnerability that bind the men to one another and exclude non-veterans. Strikwerda and May argue that wartime friendships are more like comradeship than intimate friendship and that in combat, comrades see one another in abstract rather than personal terms. To the extent that this claim is correct, it impedes the ability to develop and sustain the deep closeness involved in intimate friendship. But the authors also recognize that friends in combat share not only mutual vulnerability but their feelings about that vulnerability; they come to depend on one another in substantial ways, and the bonds formed from their experiences together can last a lifetime (Strikwerda and May 1992, 98). Seeing another as a generalized other does reduce the likelihood of genuine intimacy. But I am not convinced that wartime friendships are necessarily, or even typically, abstract relations. Larry, for example, had deep and strong feelings about each platoon member based on that person's quirks, needs, habits, and experiences and on the developing interwoven narrative of their lives over time. When a friend died (and most of them did), he mourned the loss of each person as a person—although the mourning did not come until much later. The conditions of war would seem to render interactions filled with zest and vitality and contributing to the affirmation of each person's worth nearly impossible. Nevertheless, amidst the trauma of combat and the dissociation necessary for psychological survival, some men also sustain connection with one another. That men are able to make and sustain connection in the face of continual terror, loss, and uncertainty is remarkable.

6

Giving Uptake and Its Relation to Trustworthiness

In previous chapters, I discussed features that the trustworthy person would have, and my analyses of case studies illustrate in more detail why these features are so central to trustworthiness and how those features would be exhibited. For example, I emphasized the point that one cannot be fully trustworthy without having the rights sorts of institutions. Institutional structures can promote or impede our trustworthiness, and attention to exploitation and vulnerability in terms of socially situated, particular persons can lead to the recognition for the need to reform or radically alter social institutions. Part of becoming trustworthy, then, includes that we work to create that fully virtuous state.

Another feature of full trustworthiness is a developing sensitivity to the particularities of others. The mean for trustworthiness, I argue, cannot be found without grasping what it is, *from the trusting person's view*, one is caring for; this involves an interactive and imaginative process of gaining some understanding of what the world is like from the perspective of that particular person. Whether one is in an institutional role such as teacher, physician, religious leader, or politician; or a worker who is caught between competing claims of trust; or a friend or lover; or a citizen or refugee, being trustworthy involves reasoning informed by feeling and practical wisdom. This practical reasoning involves a mediated objectivity that is particularized without being narrowly partial. Being trustworthy requires (among other things) that we be committed to a certain picture of justice, and it requires that we see others in their particularity, not just as instantiations of a class or as members of a group. These two features of trustworthiness often work together. In this chapter, I fill out this claim in detail by introducing what I suggest is a related virtue—that of "being the sort of person who gives uptake rightly." This virtue facilitates understanding of what others care about, an understanding that is crucial to trust relations. It allows us to explore one another's expectations, a process that helps avoid misunderstandings that lead to some failures of trust and feelings of betrayal. It affirms one's good will and desire to engage in democratic processes and, in closer relations, to sustain connection. It allows for contestations of power, a feature I argued is central to democratic relations at every level of social relations.

I take the position that trustworthiness is part of a family of virtues that promote social and civic flourishing and that it is nearly always the case that individual virtues work together to produce a fuller expression of virtue. That being my view, I could reasonably select any number of virtues to pair up with trustworthiness. I focus on the virtue of uptake first, because it is a crucial link between trustworthiness and justice, and second, because uptake (unlike justice) has not been discussed from the perspective of virtue ethics.

In this chapter, then, I link up the earlier argument that being trustworthy requires that one attend to injustices and work toward creating a more just society with the claim that being trustworthy requires that one pay attention to others in their particularity. I do this by concentrating on discourse—where "discourse" includes not only speech acts but silences. Discourse is a central way we tell stories, navigate differences, adjudicate wrongs, and initiate change. Habermas argues that we need a discourse ethics for democratic processes; I shift the angle on discourse from abstract public spheres to concrete problems while retaining the democratic vision. I argue that, in order to be trustworthy, we need to cultivate the appropriate attentiveness and orientation to others' speech acts and silences. Giving uptake is a vital component of discursive practices and, in particular, to citizens' ability to make claims against others. Uptake occurs in the context of a speech convention but, I argue, it also reflects and reinforces social conventions about who merits being taken seriously and who holds an authorial place in a society. Expanding on Austin's idea of "uptake" as part of a linguistic act, and following Frye's reasoning that the failure to give uptake often lines up with systems of oppression, I set out an understanding of uptake as a virtue, with a mean and extremes. An analysis of uptake will both enhance our exercising of the virtue of trustworthiness and will move us along toward more just and more peaceful relations.

WHAT UPTAKE IS

When Black civil rights activists finally got desegregation laws passed after insistent claims that their rights were being violated, they were being given uptake about their claims against racial injustice. When the Mille Lacs band of the Chippewa tribe won the right to spearfish on Mille Lacs Lake, their claims to long-standing treaty rights were given uptake. And when the United States Supreme Court agreed to hear Michael H.'s appeal of the California decision that Gerald D. is conclusively presumed father of his wife's daughter—although blood tests showed a high degree of probability that Michael H. is the biological father—the Supreme Court was giving uptake to Michael H.'s claim to legal paternity.[1]

Introduced by J. L. Austin, uptake is a potentially very rich concept but one which Austin applies to relatively unproblematic discursive practices. He seems to assume a speaker/hearer relation where the parties are, for the most part, familiar with and comfortable with normal speech conventions and where the sorts of relevant power differences are fairly simple versions of verdictive and exercitive authority (the authority to render verdicts and issue official commands.) It is my view that uptake is a very fruitful concept to broaden and enrich and thus this chapter extends and expands upon Austinian uptake in a way that takes into consideration our embeddedness in oppressive discursive institutions and practices. My argument is that being the sort of person who gives others uptake is not just a vital aspect of good linguistic practice but that it is part of what is required to be a trustworthy person.[2, 3]

This broader way of framing uptake is situated in virtue theory. As a virtue, it contributes to the flourishing of individuals and society and, as such, is important to understand more fully. The reasons for this will involve understanding how failure to give others uptake affects people individually and collectively and thus can become a vice. As a virtue, giving uptake is a responsibility that is not equally and always binding upon us. Whether or not one is obligated to give uptake to another depends on each party's relation to power, to each other, to the content of speech, and so on. But being trustworthy so often involves knowing how and when to give uptake that these two virtues might be said to go together. Indeed, it is difficult to imagine a person who is fully trustworthy yet lacks the virtue of being able to give uptake rightly. I will say more about the connection later, but first I provide a detailed analysis of uptake.

J. L. Austin, in *How to Do Things With Words* (1975), argues that when we use words we are, in fact, performing actions. As Rae Langton puts it, "Speech acts are a subset of actions in general, so there will always be some description under which a speech act is intentionally performed" (Langton 1993, 301). Austin points out that, although philosophers attend to the content of an utterance (the locutionary act) and the effects of an utterance (the perlocutionary act), we often overlook the action that is constituted by the utterance itself (the illocutionary act). Actions like warning and promising are illocutionary, and illocutionary acts have to produce certain effects on the listener[4] in order to count as successful.

For example, one cannot be said to have warned an audience unless that audience hears what one says and takes what one says in a certain sense, say as an alarm, an alert, or a threat (Austin 1975, 571). When the listener receives another's speech act—especially an illocutionary act—with the conventional understanding, the listener has given the speaker uptake. Another example is that of promising: my promise to you can be said to be successful when you understand my speech act as one in which I place myself under obligation to you. Austin adds that sometimes conventions of language require that you demonstrate uptake through a second speech act, as when someone offers you something and expects you to accept or refuse his offer.

But not just any response will do. Suppose you ask your boss for more responsibility, and he responds by deliberately piling up so much work on your desk that you can't possibly accomplish it all. In Austin's narrow sense of uptake, the crucial issue is whether or not the request was a genuine one and whether the boss recognized this speech act as a request. Since the worker's intention was genuine, and the boss understood it as a request, the worker has secured uptake. That is, Austin's concept of uptake would require us to view the speaker as having secured uptake, but that conclusion seems to miss something important that is going on in the example. The boss's response is an intentional defiance of the worker's locution, even though the speech act of requesting is prima facie responded to according to convention. In the broader sense, then, having a disposition to give uptake rightly does not just involve having an understanding of what illocutionary act was performed and what the superficially interpreted intention of the speaker was; it also involves taking up another's speech act in the spirit in which it is expressed. (And being the sort of person who gives uptake rightly involves not responding in ways that would close off protests by pointing at the intention and the speech act and saying, "But you said such-and-such and I responded to you, so what's the problem?") Sensitivity to the spirit of another's communication to you and working to keep open lines of communication and understanding—even through sharp disagreement or painful criticism—is vital to the sustaining of trusting relations and thus to your trustworthiness.

I am broadening the notion of uptake in another way as well. Austin is using a narrow conception of uptake which doesn't seem to be something we can choose to give or not give. This kind of uptake, since it involves kinds of linguistic conventions, doesn't involve the intentions of the listener to understand the meaning of the speaker's speech. That is, if I hear what you say, and if I know the conventions concerning that particular speech act, I "cannot help" but give you uptake. Clearly, if this was all there were to uptake—if it were something entirely outside our control—then we could not be held responsible when we failed to give it. But there is more to uptake than this sense of it. The kind I discuss goes beyond Austin's idea. I believe that some of our understandings of linguistic conventions are within our control and, furthermore, that some of the conventions themselves are bound up with social conventions and power relations that it is imperative to challenge. In keeping with my vision of trustworthiness as nonexploitative and nondominating, I suggest that part of being trustworthy involves an ongoing commitment to attend to—and sometimes subvert—linguistic conventions that threaten to impede short-range understanding and long-term justice and equality.

Marilyn Frye, expanding on Austin's idea, discusses uptake in terms of anger. "Being angry at someone," she writes, "is somewhat like a speech act in that it has a certain conventional force whereby it sets people up in a certain sort of orientation to each other; and like a speech act, it cannot 'come off' if it does not get uptake" (Frye 1983, 88). Uptake, then, occurs when the second party, listening to my speech act, reorients herself to me and the relation between us "comes off" with an appropriate response. A proper response is one that conveys an empathetic attitude toward me or an earnest attempt to understand things from my point of view. The listener's message, then, is something like "I get it" or "I hear you" or "I can see that"—not expressed glibly but sincerely. Expressions of anger are (usually, but not always) acts of claiming that call for conventional responses to a person's claim that she has been wronged; giving uptake to anger[5] requires that the audience acknowledges not only that a claim is being made that possibly is warranted but also that that claim is asserting the speaker's worth. "To get angry is to claim implicitly that one is a certain sort of being, a being which can...stand in a certain relation and position *a propos* the being one is angry at. One claims that one is in certain ways and dimensions *respectable*. One makes claims upon respect" (90: emphasis in original).

Frye argues that women's justified anger at moral injustices done to them do not get taken seriously and respectfully; instead, women's anger is minimized, trivialized, pathologized, mocked, and ignored by men. "Deprived of uptake, the woman's anger is left as just a burst of expression of individual feeling. As a social act, an act of communication, it just doesn't happen" (Frye 1983, 89).

What Frye is describing in her account of not giving uptake could be the willful misunderstanding of another's speech act, or it could be a convention of its own. In either case, the audience fails to take seriously both the specific claim of the speaker and the worth of the speaker making that claim. In a broader sense, giving uptake to another person involves not twisting, distorting, minimizing, or mocking her words, feelings, and perceptions—even when we disagree, or we are frightened, or we don't understand. In this way, a degree of trust between parties can be sustained.

To give uptake is not necessarily to agree with a speaker; one can take another seriously and yet disagree. In the beginning of this section, for example, I stated that the U.S. Supreme Court can be said to give uptake to petitioners when it considers an appeal, regardless of the outcome of the hearing (and in the case of *Michael H. v. Gerald D.*, Michael ultimately lost the case on appeal). But if one is taking another seriously, one is also taking seriously the reasons that person gives for holding her beliefs or values. Taking seriously another's beliefs or values cannot be superficial. When one genuinely is trying to understand another's reasons for her or his beliefs or values, one is trying to grasp what the world looks like from the other's point of view. As I say, one can do all of this and yet turn out still to disagree. But the sort of perspective-taking and imagination required to grasp another's point of view is often difficult for us to do. And current sociopolitical relations exacerbate this difficulty when it comes to grasping the world-view of those who are marked as different. Hegemonic institutions give rise to conventions of language that render suspicious the consistent intersection of disagreement with subordination. That is, even understood as a convention, uptake is not merely an isolated event occurring at a discrete moment in time. What I am pointing to here are institutionalized speech patterns that accompany sociopolitical and economic relations of power. I'll say more about this below.

To give uptake rightly, then, it is not enough simply to receive another's speech act with the conventional understanding. One must appreciate and respond to the spirit in which something is expressed, and one must take seriously what the speaker is trying to say and the speaker's reasons for saying it. One must have the appropriate emotional and intellectual responses, engaging one's whole heart. Furthermore, one must recognize the responsibility attending social and political privilege. Indeed, giving uptake properly is partly constitutive of the kind of person one is—it requires cultivation of a certain kind of character.

Cultivating a disposition to give uptake rightly is necessary for the full flourishing of individuals and of society, as it provides the means for genuine communication in a variety of kinds of social settings. It facilitates democratic practices, as it enhances the possibilities of understanding what justice is and when we have gotten it wrong. We can see how the facilitation and enhancement of democratic and just practices is the case if we think about this virtue as a corrective. There isn't a virtue of self-love, because we are typically quite naturally attached to the pursuit of our own good—we don't need a corrective virtue to prompt us in this area (Foot 1978, 13). But with respect to open, democratic communicative exchanges, most of us are rather flawed.

People can be dogmatic, close-minded, and overly confident about our own beliefs, values, and interpretations. We can become entrenched in our own world-views and display a tendency to dig in our heels, confident that we are right and others wrong. John Stuart Mill devotes a significant part of his treatise on liberty to arguments urging us to take other points of view seriously so as to foster freedom of thought and speech and increase truth. Mill characterizes this dialogical problem as a tendency in people to be unwilling to entertain opposing points of view. But the creation of a state that makes legally possible the civil freedoms of thought and speech is not, in itself, sufficient to counter people's tendencies toward dogmatism and close-mindedness. This is where virtue comes in. A character trait to give uptake rightly, then, can serve as a corrective, as for people who view others with an arrogant eye (see Frye 1983b) or whose feelings of certainty lead them to discount the views of others.

As with most virtues, uptake has a mean and two extremes. Giving uptake can be done deficiently or it can be done in excess—although Ross reminds us that the intermediate state does not always lie equidistant between two possible extremes (Ross 1980, ix). The mean and the extremes, for this virtue as for others, is relative to us and to the situation at hand. The extremes may be only accidentally or occasionally expressed, in which case they might simply be "out of character" for us. But when they are expressions of our character, they comprise the vices of failure to give uptake and giving uptake excessively. (I discuss the vices below, highlighting the deficiency.) But there is an intermediate condition: to be the sort of person who gives uptake "at the right times, about the right things, toward the right people, for the right end, and in the right way."

Casting a disposition to give uptake rightly as a virtue marks it as analytically distinct from other possible virtues such as respecting, attending, and empathizing. Many of the virtues have a scope by which they can be identified and differentiated from other virtues. Thus, the scope of bravery is feelings of fear and confidence about frightening things; the scope of temperance is bodily pleasures and pains of touch and taste; the scope of mildness is responses to insult and injury. The scope of the virtue I'm calling "the disposition to give uptake rightly" is dialogical responsiveness and openness in the context of plurality and power relations. The scope of respectfulness might be something like attitudes about the worth of others. But I am not convinced that respectfulness is a virtue, if by "respect" is meant granting others an intrinsic moral worth or value. Respect, then, would be something we should always grant others—in which case it wouldn't admit of an excess. Having a respectful attitude might still be necessary to the full expression of the virtue of being the sort of person who gives uptake rightly. But one may be respectful and, say, detached and disengaged in ways that leave the other feeling not quite heard or understood. So (however we classify respectfulness) a disposition to be respectful and a disposition to give uptake are distinct sorts of things.

Perhaps attentiveness could be a virtue, with its scope as perception of particulars and universals, or of details and unity.[6] A deficiency of attentiveness would manifest itself in a tendency not to notice important details or to overlook the particulars of situations, whereas an excess of attentiveness would manifest itself in a tendency toward slavishness when it comes to details or an obsession with pinning down the particulars of a case at the expense of moving on to action—or something like that. I don't know whether or not attentiveness qualifies as a virtue. But if I am right about the scope of attentiveness, that scope is different from the scope of our virtue. And one can be attentive and yet miss the mark when it comes to giving uptake: people who tend to be good at one or the other are not necessarily concerned with the same things. Recall the example of the boss who overloads the worker after she requests more responsibility: it's not attentiveness that is missing from the interaction but something else.

Empathy does seem like a likely candidate for being a virtue (although I will not argue for it here).[7] Furthermore, it seems clear that, in order to cultivate a disposition to give uptake rightly, we must sometimes be empathetic, in that we must try to understand how the other person sees things and experiences things from her point of view. But just because we must sometimes call upon one virtue in order to rightly exhibit another, it doesn't follow that those virtues ultimately collapse into one. The scope of empathy is distinctly different from that of the disposition to give uptake rightly. The virtue of empathy is concerned with cognitive and emotional perspective-taking of others as a response to another's distress, while the virtue of being the sort of person who gives uptake rightly is concerned with dialogic interactions in a pluralistic and unequal society.

While a full treatment of the separateness of uptake from other virtues and dispositional attitudes is beyond the scope of this chapter, I should also say that I am not worried if there is some overlap. Trustworthiness is related to hope, expectation, faith, confidence, predictability, and so on, and this makes for a somewhat messy and difficult conceptual analysis. This doesn't mean that trustworthiness is just hope or expectation but that in pointing to one character trait we frequently invoke another. My aim is not so much to identify necessary and sufficient conditions for what I am calling "uptake" but to illuminate some ways in which being the sort of person who gives uptake rightly is a virtue. At any rate, I believe that much of the distinctiveness of the virtue of having a disposition to give uptake rightly will become clearer as this chapter unfolds.

There are, however, virtues that Aristotle himself identifies that are interesting to consider in light of the virtue of having a disposition to give uptake rightly. Virtues such as friendliness and mildness share a family resemblance with being the sort of person who gives uptake rightly, even though they are all analytically distinct. Without the disposition to give uptake rightly, it's not clear how other virtues could be exhibited well either. Being the sort of person who gives uptake rightly enhances justice, friendship, trustworthiness, and other social virtues—indeed, justice in the absence of people whose characters are constituted such that they give uptake rightly and are trustworthy seems to stand as a rather empty concept. Justice in a democratic society depends, in part, on our ability as citizens to develop sensitivities to others, to respond appropriately to claims against violated rights, and to be trustworthy. As Aristotle says, "our well-being is relational."[8] While we may not need one another for our basic needs, we will still need each other to create jointly a life of virtue (Sherman 1989, 130). Justice, friendship, and trustworthiness, then, depend on the reciprocity of meaningful, responsive presence in dialogic interactions.

The social virtues require vigilance; it is not enough to do what is just or trustworthy, or to give uptake, once or twice or occasionally. The sensitivities involved must become part of character. Another way in which I am conceptualizing uptake within a framework of virtue theory, then, is that I see the giving of uptake as dispositional. When we have a disposition to give uptake rightly, we are acting out of a settled state and are giving uptake in the way a virtuous person would do so.

I am broadening the Austinian view of speech acts as isolated events that occur at a discrete moment in time, by pointing to the need to broaden the context of speech. But I am also highlighting the way in which giving or not giving uptake is connected to our positionality, our ways of seeing the world, and our commitments, values, and interests—in a word, our character. Giving uptake, then, like doing just acts, is not merely a matter of understanding the convention of a particular speech act and responding appropriately but a matter of the sort of persons we are over time, whom we have a tendency to take seriously, treat with dignity, and so on. Giving uptake engages the whole self. As Nancy Sherman says, "others must directly feel our presence, *know* our reactions through the direct communication of emotion and bodily response...At stake is the (emotional) impact we have on others" (Sherman 1989, 49).

This point leads me to another way in which a framework of virtue theory applies to being the sort of person who gives uptake rightly. To find the mean in giving uptake, we need practical wisdom—we need to develop skills at communication that go beyond a mere understanding of linguistic conventions. More than that, we need to acquire a rich understanding of power relations and how they play themselves out in speech and silencing. We have to learn how to make good judgments about where, to whom, when, about what, and in what way uptake is called for. To do so well may require a character change.

A disposition to give uptake rightly can be understood as requiring that we learn to see with the whole heart.

> Without emotions, we do not fully register the facts or record them with the sort of resonance and importance that only emotional involvement can sustain. It is as if our perceptions were strung together in our minds but not fully understood or embraced...the failure to feel is really a failure to record with the whole self what one sees. So, for example, when I fail to help another when I know I can and should, it may be that I see the other's distress, but see it without the proper acknowledgement and sympathy. (Sherman 1989, 47)

Being the sort of person who gives uptake rightly requires that we engage with others not only intellectually but also emotionally. Perception, or attentiveness, is a necessary aspect of developing and appropriately expressing this and other virtues, but perception or attentiveness alone will usually fall short of hitting the mark when uptake is called for.

In summary, then, being the sort of person who gives uptake to others rightly is good. Having a disposition to give uptake rightly tells the speaker something about us and about how we perceive her. By giving uptake, I say: you can count on me to take you seriously according to your idea of seriousness and not mine alone; you can expect me to treat your picture of the world, or your claims against me, or your cries of pain and anger, with respect—but more than that: it's an emotional presence. And by taking the voices, needs, concerns, and emotions of another seriously, we grant that person dignity, thus indicating that we recognize her full humanity. It may also be a way we, at the same time, exhibit trustworthiness. Giving uptake rightly doesn't, by itself, indicate the fuller kind of trustworthiness I've been arguing for; one might be very good at giving people uptake but lousy at being trustworthy with respect to keeping appointments or defending friends against false rumors, for example. But giving uptake indicates that one can be counted on to be trustworthy with regard to others' communicative efforts. And being trustworthy in the more general sense requires that we also have the virtue of uptake, so when we experience the consistent absence of uptake, we should consider broader problems with another's trustworthiness.

THE VICE OF DEFICIENCY

To see why we should consider a deficiency in giving uptake as a potential vice, let's examine what happens when one is not given uptake (keeping in mind that one or two deficient actions do not a vice make, any more than repeated acts of appropriately giving uptake guarantee that a virtue is being expressed). The general idea I will argue for is that the failure to give uptake undermines trust and diminishes flourishing, although I will also discuss a way that people attempt to adapt and flourish even while living in contexts where crucial experiences of uptake are largely absent.

The first point is that a society in which individuals can flourish is one where claiming of rights is possible, and receiving uptake is necessary to claiming. That is to say, I am likening claiming to warning, promising, and marrying: claiming is an illocutionary act that doesn't come off unless there is uptake. Another way of putting the point is this: claiming cannot come off unless the audience is trustworthy with respect to the kind of listening and responsiveness that claiming requires.

One mark of powerlessness is an inability to perform speech acts that one might want to perform (Langton 1993, 314). One way this might happen is at the level of locution itself, where one is unable to make utterances. Another way is when one speaks but doesn't get the desired results; Langton calls this perlocutionary frustration. The third way is through "illocutionary disablement," where one utters words but doesn't get the desired result and it isn't recognized as the action one performed. This is a kind of silencing that occurs when an utterance is prevented from counting as the act it was intended to be.

A community or society that doesn't give uptake to claims thwarts the well-being of (at least some) members of that community and opens the door to other detrimental effects to the overall citizenry as well. Joel Feinberg shows by asking readers to imagine a world called Nowheresville that does not have the concept of rights that "the activity of claiming, as much as any other thing, makes for self-respect and respect for others, gives sense to the notion of personal dignity, and distinguishes this otherwise morally flawed world from the even worse world of Nowheresville" (Feinberg 1970). And when a community or society fails to give sufficient weight to values of mutual respect and dignity, the social trust that holds groups together is undermined.

To fill out this idea, I return to Frye's argument that (most) men are socialized to respond to women's anger with dismissal. Refusing, on the basis of gender, to take seriously a woman's claims that an injustice has been done or a right violated is to reduce her status to membership in a class and then to use that classification to justify ignoring those claims. But the act of claiming ought not be dealt with in this manner. To ignore someone's claims against another on the basis of group membership is both morally and legally objectionable: it is the nature of claiming that each person is entitled to have her or his claims acknowledged at least to the degree that it is determined whether there is a legitimate claim to be investigated.

To affirm or deny that a right has been violated, it first must be acknowledged that a claim has been made. A claim may, in fact, turn out to rest on a mistake. But in some cases, the hearer refuses to acknowledge that an act of claiming has even occurred. The hearer fails to recognize the act, and the claiming is not given uptake. From the perspective of the hearer, nothing is claimed. And if nothing is acknowledged as having been claimed, then the question of whether or not a right has been violated simply doesn't get raised. The fact that claiming requires uptake in order for it to count as a speech act suggests that, in societies with systematic injustices encoded by linguistic conventions and discourses of power, many individuals' rights are likely to be threatened.

This is not to propound a simple equation of claims with rights. Feinberg notes that there is a prima facie sense of "claim" that consists in acknowledging that one is entitled to a fair hearing and consideration—that the audience grants minimum plausibility that the speaker has a right to x without yet establishing that one has a right to x. But Feinberg also says that "having a claim consists in being in a position to claim"—which position is not always recognized even when minimum plausibility ought, objectively speaking, to be granted.

That is, structural injustices sometimes impede members of nondominant groups from being recognized as meeting *prima facie* conditions for claiming. Deciding whether or not to give uptake to a person's claims on the basis of membership of subjugated groups is both a symptom of oppression and an act of oppression.

> The ability to perform speech acts of certain kinds can be a mark of political power. To put the point crudely: powerful people can generally do more, say more, and have their speech count for more than can the powerless. If you are powerful, there are more things you can do with your words…If you are powerful, you sometimes have the ability to silence the speech of the powerless…But there is another, less dramatic but equally effective, way. Let them speak. Let them say whatever they like to whomever they like, but stop that speech from counting as an action. More precisely, stop it from counting as the action it was intended to be. (Langton 1993, 298-99)

Even if the dispositional failure to give uptake is apparently independent of systems of oppression, consistently not giving uptake may be wrong because not to give at least prima facie credence to another's utterance is to treat that person as less than fully human: it is to say that, where that person is concerned, I don't have to consider his or her needs, views, claims, or emotions. Trust is diminished when an act of claiming is ignored as an action to be grappled with, because a refusal to acknowledge the act as one of claiming calls into question the good will of the other to care for things the speaker values.

The link between this cluster of concepts—uptake, rights, and humanity—comes in with the concept of dignity. Dignity, as Bernard Boxill explains, is "the sense that one's manifest humanity makes one manifestly worthy of one's human rights" (Boxill 1992, 197). Dignity functions here as a moral concept that is at once individual and communal. Robin Dillon states that "as various declarations of human rights affirm, the equality of human dignity is taken to be the basis of the equal moral rights that all persons have as persons, independently of social law, custom, convention, and agreement" (Dillon 1995, 22). Failure to give uptake, then (for example, when someone's speech act is that of claiming that a right has been violated), can be an assault on the speaker's dignity.

Presumably we can recover from the occasional assault on our dignity. But power relations render it more likely that the actual distribution of assaults on dignity fall regularly and consistently to the disempowered. A social climate where a group of people come to expect a lack of uptake on claims, coupled with assaults on one's dignity when one attempts to get uptake, eventually can undermine even the most resilient of people. An environment like that is clearly not one for flourishing. Both the individuals themselves and society overall are diminished when dignity is threatened or lost. Furthermore, a society where claiming and giving uptake are activities that fall along power lines is less likely to progress toward the virtue of justice: to create and sustain a just society, claiming and giving uptake must be an ongoing practice in which a plurality of voices can and do participate. Finally, both localized and societal trust is impeded and distrust fueled when linguistic conventions lead to lack of uptake.

Failure to give uptake can also be seen to be a potential vice if we consider not just an assault on one's dignity but on one's deepest psychological self. An example of this is found in Lawrence Langer's *Holocaust Testimonies* (although the focus here isn't on claiming). Langer, in his analysis of interviews with Holocaust survivors, argues that their selves and their memories are fragmented as a result of their wartime experiences (Langer 1991). Interviewers were ostensibly (and probably earnestly) seeking understanding of those experiences.

Recall that giving uptake rightly is not simply a matter of receiving another's speech act with the conventional understanding. The hearer must appreciate and respond to the spirit in which something is expressed and must take seriously the speaker's experiences and point of view from the speaker's perspective. One must have the appropriate emotional and intellectual responses, engaging one's whole heart—which may require the hearer to do more than merely rely on his or her own imagined or remembered responses in a similar situation. The hearer tries to see and understand what the world looks like *from the speaker's position.*

Langer, in carefully going through the interviews with Holocaust survivors, finds that central aspects of their narratives are not given uptake—that the interviewers impose their own language of heroism and moral virtue on the speakers and explicitly discount the interpretations given by the speaker telling the story. The consequence of this deficiency is that it forces deep memory of horrible events, and of survivors' now-fragmented selves, further away from the common memory that can be more comfortably shared. This suggests that the failure to give uptake does further harm to already harmed victims of violence. (This can also be said of political prisoners whose reports of torture are not believed or rape victims whose reports of assault are doubted.) The initial harm done to a victim of violence is exacerbated when the audience fails to give uptake to the victim's experiences.

In asking to whom we can entrust the public memory of the Holocaust, Langer suggests that those looking to understand this history are primarily "witnesses to memory rather than rememberers themselves," searching for what Blanchot calls the "impossible real." As Langer explains it, these witnesses to memory

> have an 'unstory' to tell, that which, according to Blanchot, "escapes quotation and which memory does not recall—forgetfulness as thought. That which, in other words, cannot be forgotten because it has always already fallen outside memory." Blanchot's style may appear cryptic but, in fact, duplicates the frustrated efforts of language to enclose irreducibly intractable material. The oxymoron of an impossible reality is a small knothole piercing the obstacles.
>
> The impossibility, however, lies not in the reality but in our difficulty in perceiving it as reality. (Langer 1991, 39-40)

The survivors are mining their common and deep memory about their experiences, thoughts, and feelings. But the interviewers have no cognitive or moral space to accept as real the things they are being told.

The difficulty the interviewers have in hearing what the survivors are actually saying and in accepting as real their experiences of the Holocaust leads the interviewers, tragically, to fail to give uptake. As a result, survivors learn to view interviewers and other listeners as untrustworthy with respect to the holding of Holocaust memories. As Langer's work implies, we have no conventions to lead us through this discourse in a way that preserves the integrity of the witnesses to memory. And without conventions to map our way that are appropriate to the discourse, most hearers fall back on familiar conventions rather than chart new territory.

The absence of uptake and experiences of others' untrustworthiness can give rise to rage in the speaker. It makes most people frustrated and angry to be ignored or misunderstood, or to have their words trivialized or exaggerated. And rage can lead to violence: consider how the failure of the legal system to give uptake to Black males' reports of police brutality eventually led to collective outrage at injustice, voiced through rioting in cities across the nation after the Rodney King verdict. When individual speech acts are not given uptake (for example, when individual claims against the police force are ignored), collective activity is more likely to be emphatic, even violent, in increasing attempts to obtain that uptake. It seems clear that it would be better (in terms of constructive efforts toward a just society) for court systems and police departments to have given uptake earlier on. That is to say, one reason that not giving uptake should be a cause for concern is that it is one of the causes of the increase of violence in society, which, in turn, diminishes the quality of life for citizens.

Another reason to think that the failure to give uptake undermines trust and is detrimental to flourishing and, hence, is a potential vice is that it may silence the speaker. Uptake is not just a matter of receiving public recognition of various speech acts; part of the problem of institutionalized speech is that persons in nondominant groups do not have equal access to institutionalized speech. This next section, then, focuses on the relationship between uptake and silencing.

SPEECH AND SILENCING

I have argued that the scope of the virtue that concerns giving uptake is that of dialogic responsiveness in the context of pluralities and power relations. I have also argued that a failure to give uptake is a deficiency that can, over time, become a bad habit, or a vice. One kind of failure to give uptake is that of silencing. After explaining how silencing works, I will show how silencing and untrustworthiness are connected.

In discussing the convention of uptake, Austin is thinking about datable speech acts—locutionary acts that occur at a given place and time that also are perlocutionary and illocutionary acts. Austin would agree that uptake is best understood as contextual in the sense that we have to know the context of a given speech act in order to assess proper uptake. (For example, is shouting "fire" given as a warning or a joke? The question cannot be answered in the abstract.) But the broader notion of uptake I am using brings in a larger context that includes a greater temporal span. To determine whether or not a particular silencing is a failure to give uptake in the broader sense, we have to examine the history, the context, and the politics of the situation. If we don't consider dialogical encounters in a larger context, we are likely to over-look the significance of relations of power and structural inequalities to the giving or not giving of uptake. Bringing in a larger sociopolitical and tem-poral context means that we might not be able to pinpoint some kinds of si-lencing as discrete events that occur at given moments. What we find has happened, instead, is that we have gradually become attuned to the silencing of some as a climate that has evolved and entrenched itself over time.

Many of the institutionalized methods available for not giving uptake are more sophisticated means of silencing than overt physical actions of silenc-ing or explicit censorship. Silencing others by such methods as torture are viewed as morally wrong, so the silenced become recognized victims whose rights have been violated. In contrast, by allowing speech to occur, we create the impression that communication is possible. When one doesn't get uptake, then, it may be much less clear who is to blame. But whether or not it is phys-ically possible to make *a* speech act at a given time, silencing may occur. The legal protection of civil liberties isn't sufficient to bring about freedom of speech if the society's majority are dominating discursive practices and sup-pressing, through judgment and exclusion, unpopular views (Mill 1978). The cultural climate, then, may serve to silence members of minority groups even though those minority members have the legal right to engage in dialogue and exercise that right.

Following Langton, I mentioned three ways in which those with relatively less power can be silenced. These ways of silencing parallel the three com-ponents of speech acts that Austin discusses (although I remind readers again that the dialogical interactions that involve responses like giving uptake or si-lencing are not limited to specific actions or events, so this discussion is not meant as a strict parallel): when one cannot utter speech at all, when one speaks but doesn't get the intended effects, and when one speaks but doesn't get the desired effect or get one's action acknowledged as a speech act. The latter we are calling (again, following Langton) illocutionary disablement. I will discuss these kinds of silencing one at a time.

1. Locutionary silencing. In her poem "Cartographies of silence," Rich distinguishes between silence and absence.

The technology of silence
The rituals, etiquette
the blurring of terms

silence not absence
of words or music or even
raw sounds

Silence can be a plan rigorously executed
the blueprint to a life
It is a presence
it has a history a form

Do not confuse it with any kind of absence. (Rich 1978)

Silencing occurs about women's history and about women in history. As Rich says in her introduction to *On Lies, Secrets and Silence*, women's struggle for self-determination has been largely muffled in silence; women's history has been obscured, so each feminist voice sounds idiosyncratic, odd, "orphaned of any tradition of its own" (Rich 1979, 11). But the silencing itself is a presence that can be felt in our various historical constructs.

Rich attributes this silencing to a cultural climate that simultaneously manipulates passivity and nourishes violence against women. This culture, Rich says, "has every stake in opposing women actively laying claim to our own lives" (Rich 1979, 14). Even speaking out, then—for example, by attempting to get uptake through engaging in conversation—amounts to a kind of silencing in which women are, in complex ways, both victimized and complicit. This kind of silencing, then, might take the form of either perlocutionary or illocutionary silencing.

2. Perlocutionary silencing. In this kind of silencing, as Langton explains, "one argues, but no one is persuaded; one invites, but nobody attends the party; one votes, hoping to oust the government, but one is outnumbered. Such frustration can have a political dimension when the effects achieved depend on the speaker's membership in a particular social class" (Langton 1993, 315). Langton gives, as an example of this kind of silencing, a woman whose "no" to sexual advances is spoken and heard but disregarded: the male persists in raping her. In the narrow sense of uptake, then, uptake is secured because she does perform the locution "no" and he recognizes the action as a refusal. But her perlocutionary act was frustrated.

In the broader sense of uptake that I am arguing for, he has failed to give it. I am not suggesting that this counts as a failure of uptake on the grounds that there is an abstract relation between refusals and uptake. It is a failure to give uptake given our understanding of virtue and the intermediate condition. Following an Aristotelian framework of virtue, what is good and right is determined in relation to the situation, context, parties involved, and the goals aimed at. And some ends that people aim at will never be fine, as Aristotle sees it, such as murdering a family member. Actions that have bad ends should never be aimed at: they should be refused, and the refusal should be given uptake.[9] It is reasonable to infer that to proceed in a sexual encounter where one party has said "no" to a sexual advance is to aim at an end that is never fine—nonconsensual sex—and hence such sexual encounters would count as a kind of situation where refusals always require uptake.

Another example might be found in Linda Carty's description of being a Black female student in an English class where Conrad's *Heart of Darkness* and *The Secret Sharer* were discussed.

> When I dared to suggest that we look at Conrad's notion of "darkness" because, despite his seemingly progressive ideas, Conrad's reference to the Congo as the "heart of darkness" is clearly indicative of his own racialist views of Africa and its people, the professor calmly glanced in my direction and informed me that to read such meaning into the work is to miss the sophistication of Conrad's analysis and besides, "Africa with all its strange rituals and primitive cultures is understandably referred to as dark and not only by Conrad." (Carty 1991, 14)

This, then, is silencing through bullying, ridiculing, mystifying, and intimidating. The silenced may indeed speak, even superficially be listened to, but the institutionalized context of the conversation, and the rules of the language-game, do not facilitate genuine dialogue. This is because the language-game, in this case, is structured by power relations that include not only the teacher/student relation, but each party's relation to the text. In the Conrad example above, the racial contract—to borrow a term from Charles Mills' book *The Racial Contract* (1997)—is built into the linguistic exchange in such a way that Carty cannot, as things stand, get uptake about the racist meaning of the phrase "heart of darkness."

3. Illocutionary silencing. Langton clarifies the difference between perlocutionary silencing and this latter form by returning to the example of the woman who refuses a man's sexual advances. When her perlocutionary act is frustrated, her "no" is simply overridden.[10] But when a woman's illocutionary act is not given uptake, her "no" doesn't even register as a "no." It's not that he has heard her refusal and decided to proceed anyway—he didn't hear a "no," or he didn't hear it as a "real no." He heard a "yes." "No," in the gender conventions of heterosexual sexual encounters, means "yes." Her speech act of refusal did not occur, even though the woman did speak.

Langton is pointing to illocutionary silencing where the conventions require the hearer to follow the rules of the language-games. But there is another aspect to illocutionary silencing, as well: conventions require the speaker too to follow the rules of the language-games. That is, silencing also can occur when there are social conventions concerning what cannot be named for what it is (for example, sexual violence such as rape), or that cannot be talked about in certain ways (for example, rape and incest as a problem of male domination), or that cannot be contextualized (for example, abortion rights in the context of the history of women's oppression).

Rich, in the poem on "Cartographies of Silence," is calling our attention to the bind many people find themselves in: silence could be imposed upon them, but it can also be something they are attempting to break through. A central problem, though, is that to break through externally imposed silences often requires that the silenced use terms, conceptual frameworks, and value systems that are not of their own choosing and that distort or falsify those attempts to communicate. This problem can give rise to a different kind of silencing.

In the next sections, I will discuss that kind of silencing and one other kind, neither of which seems to fit quite as neatly into the Austinian framework. Nevertheless, I believe they merit consideration in that they are within the scope of the virtue concerned with dialogical responsiveness under pluralism and power relations. The fourth kind I will call mother-tongue silencing.

4. Mother-tongue silencing. This kind of silence is a result of differences in language where a dominant language is institutionalized. Lugones identifies a problem in the construction of the self where one inhabits different "worlds" more or less comfortably and where one is taken up in these various worlds in ways one may not recognize or understand (Lugones 1997, 152). A "world," she suggests, is an actual or constructed, incomplete or partial, society inhabited by some flesh and blood people (as well as perhaps imaginary ones; 153). We can be at ease in a "world" in different ways, such as being normatively happy, being humanly bonded, and having a shared history. Another determinant of the extent to which one is able to be at ease in a world, Lugones says, is our relationship to the language in that world. "The first way of being at ease in a particular 'world' is by being a fluent speaker in that 'world.' I know all the norms that there are to be followed. I know all the words that there are to be spoken. I know all the moves. I am confident" (153).

In the fourth kind of silencing, one's most familiar language is stifled, and one is confined to moves in language-games that are uncomfortable, odd, and lacking fit. It's not necessarily that speech is ineffective or not recognized as acts, but more that the 'world' one is constructing through the dominant language is a 'world' in which the speaker is far less likely to be able to locate herself as the self she knows in her more familiar 'world.' Lugones' mother-tongue is Spanish, and although she is fluent in English, she isn't at ease in that language: her participation in dialogue is bounded by and made contingent upon her willingness to play the language-games of the dominant

(English-speaking) 'world.' Not only can this kind of experience be destabilizing and disorienting, but it can distort the 'world' of the speaker and twist truths.

But it is also the case that, when one is not fluent in the dominant language of the institutions of society, one is excluded from more than just ease or comfort: one's ability to make claims about injustices, for example, will be seriously impeded. I am reminded of language difficulties experienced among Hmong women in Minnesota who sought legal intervention for domestic violence. Minnesota has a significant Asian population concentrated mostly in the Twin Cities area, and many people are refugees who speak little or no English and do not know their way around the American legal system. One of the features of this system is that those in need of guidance and advice through the legal process can obtain a legal advocate who works in the client's broader legal and social interest. English-speaking plaintiffs, too, often need advocacy when it comes to historically contested legal rights such as the right to be protected from domestic assault. But ten years ago, very few legal advocates even spoke Hmong, and the few who did had trouble adequately translating between Hmong and English for the court. Over time, it was discovered that translators were not really translating after all; instead, they were "conveying the gist of things" and adding their own comments when they were uncertain about Hmong terms. When this practice came to light, many Hmong women were discouraged from continuing in the legal process, and distrust of the American legal system spread through the Hmong community of women.

The kind of silencing I am identifying here is not just a matter of whether or not one can participate in the dominant language when one needs to. It creates a conversation of exclusion.

> We [Hispanas] and you [whites] do not talk the same language. When we talk to you we use your language: the language of your experience and of your theories. We try to use it to communicate our world of experience. But since your language and your theories are inadequate in expressing our experiences, we only succeed in communicating our experience of exclusion. We cannot talk to you in our language because you do not understand it. So the brute facts that we understand your language and that the place where most theorizing about women is taking place is your place, both combine to require that we either use your language and distort our experience not just in the speaking about it, but in the living of it, or that we remain silent. Complaining about exclusion [if the only way to do so is in your language, on your terms, and in a way you'll understand it] is a way of remaining silent. (Lugones and Spelman 1986, 23)

The existence of a dominant language, then, creates a culture of exclusion, and exclusion is a way of silencing people. But Lugones doesn't advocate merely speaking out against exclusion, either. As I understand it, the point Lugones is making—that speech acts that call attention to exclusion don't necessarily address problems in communication—resonates with a theme in Rich's writing: that in having to speak, not in one's mother tongue but in the language of the dominators or the language of the fathers, one is coerced into modes of communication that exist primarily to serve dominant groups and function to maintain the status quo. The conceptual framework, the meaning-making, and the experiences of a people are bound up in the language of that group. To use another group's language, when the linguistic relation mirrors relations of domination and subordination, is to make oneself an outsider to the conceptual framework, meaning-making, and experiences of one's own culture.

Lugones points out that, while members of marginalized groups have to do "world-traveling" as a matter of survival, those whose mother tongue is the dominant language need not do so and so are not likely to experience "outsider" status. While there are situations in which being an outsider is not silencing (for example, an invited public speaker often is an outsider to the community she is asked to address), not to be able to communicate with one's own language—to have to draw upon a conceptual framework and meaning-making that is not only not one's own but has been forced upon one through the violence of domination—is silencing even when a member of a nondominant group has facility with the dominant language. It is silencing because it is an institutionalized and asymmetrical way of impeding communication across difference, and it is silencing because it results in distorted communication while not leaving open other alternatives to using the dominator's language.

To put it another way, exclusion through language difference is institutionalized. And silencing through linguistic exclusion works on another level as well. In the United States, differences in language function as markers of deeper "differences" between those who are worthy or not, deservedly subordinate or not. That is, linguistic markers point to nonlinguistic markers of difference that serve to justify differential and unjust treatment. In today's climate of suspicion toward immigrants and "foreigners," those for whom English is a second language are routinely refused uptake. The fact of language differences, then, can be used as an excuse for exclusion, a reason not to give uptake, based on the existence of a language barrier. And the burden of responsibility for bridging any barriers is arrogantly assumed to be that of the marginalized group.

Linguistic barriers occur, however, even when the speakers speak the same generic language. Dialects, class differences, and educational differences often make it difficult for us to understand one another. More than that, they reflect and reinforce social and economic hierarchies. Rich, in an essay on teaching, identifies this as a tension between empowerment and mystification. Although she expresses confidence in the power of language to enable people to free themselves through the written word, she also recognizes that both the canon and the accepted ways of teaching it can serve to entrench, rather than undermine, relations of domination and subordination. Language and literature, she finds, is often used against students to keep them in their place, to mystify them, to bully them, and to make them feel powerless (Rich 1979, 63).

5. Imitation-uptake silencing. There is another way one can fail to give uptake that is related to silencing as well. I have in mind situations in which someone who seems quite progressive can appear to have a disposition to give others uptake rightly but isn't actually doing so. Can one imitate uptake? I believe so: consider the movement toward so-called politically correct language. One can be careful as a language-user not to use terms marked as offensive or denigrating to others and yet not take seriously the reasons why one ought to be doing so; one's motivation might be to avoid professional or legal problems. The fact that a superficial kind of uptake can occur that can have little to do with taking seriously another's claims or treating him or her with dignity points to the sense in which genuinely giving uptake and giving it properly requires the right motives and intentions and not merely the right behavior. And having a disposition to give uptake properly requires that one be moved by the right motives and intentions not only occasionally but from a settled state.

John Stoltenberg, for instance, in an essay addressing men who claim to be sympathetic to feminism, criticizes them for putting more energy into declaring themselves supporters of feminist concerns than into actually working to change the world. He cynically offers several predictions, one of which is the following:

> Many men of conscience will turn out for one feminist demonstration every twelve months. They will raise their voices in shout. They will shout louder, in fact, than all the women combined. They will even get into a scuffle with some other men, any other men, hostile bystanders, the police: They will make a noble scene; they will stage a cockfight. Then they will go home and try to get in touch with their feelings for another year. (Stoltenberg 1989, 192)

Stoltenberg reminds us of the myriad of ways we can communicate that we "get it" or can say "I hear you" while missing the richness of what is required to genuinely and properly give another uptake. Feminists who work with men like those Stoltenberg describes may not feel utterly silenced by them, but they are likely to feel that they haven't been given uptake. But it's hard to get uptake on the claim that one hasn't been given uptake, when the party being criticized is loudly and publicly proclaiming its sensitivity and loyalty. Ironically, participation in a demonstration can function as a signifier to silence claims that the activist sympathizers and supporters are not giving genuine uptake. When feminists try to point to what is missing, the male activist may respond by pointing to what he has done to show he is taking feminist claims seriously. "What more do you want?" the male activist asks. "Will you never be satisfied?" A similar dynamic can be identified between people of color and white anti-racist activists when whites are criticized for continuing to perpetuate racial hierarchies. "I've included writers of color in the course. How can you still say that this course perpetuates racist ideology?") This kind of exchange ultimately is silencing, in that it shuts down communication from feminists of all colors or activists of color to their proclaimed supporters that they are not getting across their message.

The experience of being silenced, whether discrete or ubiquitous, tells the speaker that some of those things she values are not being cared about by the audience. Central among those valued things are the speaker's dignity and humanity which, regardless of the merit or demerit of her particular views, will be acknowledged by a trustworthy person. Trustworthiness requires that we not silence others and that we pay special attention to the patterned ways in which conventions of language allow us to silence the already marginalized, further exacerbating unequal power relations and rampant distrust. When experiences of being silenced become pervasive, some members of minority groups get discouraged and decide to opt out of dialogue with members of dominant groups altogether. This, then, would be a strategy of silence, and it is to this idea that I now turn.

SILENCE AS AN ACT OF COMMUNICATION THAT REQUIRES UPTAKE

Being silent is different from being silenced because being silenced is an externally imposed silence. Being silent, on the other hand, retains an element of agency. That is, one may be silenced into being silent as a strategic way of circumventing the conventional methods of silencing outlined above. As in the case of silencing, where one can be silenced without that silencing being locutionary, it is also the case in being silent: one can be silent in many ways and for different reasons, only one of which is by opting out of conventional forms of dialogue. (By this I mean that being silent is still a move within a dialogue, but being silent is not overtly dialogical in the sense we usually think of it.) There are many kinds of silence, and their meanings are nuanced: there are "attentive silences, refusal to speak silences, tongue cut out silences, provocative silences, refusal to listen silences, intimate silences" (Lugones1998, 156).

Opting out of conventional dialogical moves by being silent is often more of a default strategy; it is a way of being that one would not choose if things were otherwise but which one chooses under the circumstances. It is a way of taking control and, by doing so, making a point that one couldn't get across under silencing conditions.

This kind of silence is like boycotting. It is a refusal to participate in things as they stand. Like the Montgomery bus boycott, being silent can be a way of being in the world that one is driven to in order to have an effect when more usual routes to gain uptake have failed. And, like the Montgomery bus boycott, being silent is an activity: far from being passive, one is communicating through refusing to communicate by conventional linguistic means. If one is not to be co-opted, one might elect to be silent as "a plan rigorously executed." Such silences are not necessarily acoustic ones, although they may be. But even at the most basic level, silence is not simply a "zero." Being silent is often an attempt to communicate (even if what it is communicating is a refusal to engage in speech acts); silencing is often an attempt to hinder or prevent communication.

An example of being silent that consists in more than a mere refusal to engage in speech acts is the fairly common occurrence in women's studies programs of low attendance of faculty of color. I take this phenomenon to be a kind of boycott that expresses anger and frustration at predominantly white women's studies programs and the white faculty who persist in racist practices. This kind of silence happens, not because women of color are unwilling to be direct about racist issues in women's studies but because they have been direct and have not been given uptake. Although not the preferred method of communication, silence by absence does tell attentive and trustworthy others that something is seriously amiss. In other words, being silent in this manner, although not a conventional speech act, is a move in a dialogue that calls for uptake. Thus again we are reminded that there is more to uptake than the overt speech act of giving uptake.

But not all silences are refusals to speak or to listen. We are also silent as a way of being attentive. We may be silent in intimacy. Our silence may be provocative. These ways of being silent seem to be different from the "boycotting" kind, in that they imply hope in the ability to communicate. Default silence, in contrast, comes about because one has lost hope or become discouraged about other communicative processes.

A central point of this section is that being the sort of person who gives uptake rightly involves more than just understanding speech acts; it also involves having a disposition to try to understand the various ways that silence works in our society and to attend to the ways we need to give uptake to silences. But it is not always easy to tell what kind of silence one is hearing. Is it one of having been silenced by others? Is it an attentive silence that the person willingly engages in? Is it a boycotting silence? What is the silence telling us? What it means to give uptake to silence will depend on what kind of silence it is, what the domain of the silence is, who the audience is, and so on. And determining the answers to those things takes practical wisdom as well as imagination and empathy; it takes cultivation of character.

THE EXCESSIVE UPTAKER

The responsibility to give uptake should not be understood as a requirement on demand: as with trustworthiness, although I am morally bound to exhibit it, there is a right time, a right place, a right way, and so on. Since giving uptake is a move in a dialogue, and participants in dialogue have different social positions, histories, perspectives, and relationships of their own, no set rule can be established that can be applied across the board. And our responsibility to give uptake has to be balanced with other commitments, time constraints, and so on. For another thing, there may be encounters in our lives in which it would be downright dangerous to give uptake to an utterance (for instance, if I am walking home alone late at night and a stranger tries to make conversation with me.)

But someone may, over time, develop a disposition to give uptake excessively. What would this look like? I can imagine two ways in which such a character trait would show up.

First let's return to the idea that the virtue we are considering—that of being the sort of person who gives uptake rightly—requires that one give uptake toward the right people, at the right time, in the right way, and so on. Now, one might, instead, develop a tendency always to give uptake to certain people such as authority figures or to an important person in one's life. When the excessive uptaker is faced with decisions or asked to voice opinions, she not only consults those others for advice—she takes their point of view to be the correct point of view without trying to differentiate her own beliefs from theirs or assessing ideas autonomously. As a disposition, this would be a deficiency because the person would not be in the habit of thinking for herself, and this habit would undermine her ability to be a good practical reasoner. Instead, she would listen so carefully to others and take seriously their views to the detriment of discerning for herself what is good and fine and pleasurable. Listening to others' advice and views to the exclusion of the development of one's own voice also calls one's trustworthiness in more general matters into question. How can others be confident that we can be counted on to take care of what is valuable to them if we are easily influenced by others' arguments and desires?

A second way that the excessive uptaker might be seen to develop a bad character trait over time is when she is so committed to giving others uptake that she puts off decision-making. Thinking that she must hear "everyone" out before taking action, she judiciously weighs each speaker evenly and fairly and avoids the rush-to-judgment, unfortunately, too long. Part of getting it right about any virtue is that there is a right time to decide and to act, and the excessive uptaker, in the interest of being inclusive, may miss the moment again and again. Being trustworthy is more than an orientation toward others; it is something we exhibit in action and feeling. And it means that sometimes we must make choices to come down on one side or another, as in the case of Patty in chapter 3.

THE RESPONSIBILITY TO GIVE UPTAKE

The social organization of the United States is founded on structural inequalities. This means that many, if not most, of our social, institutional, and interpersonal relationships may be infused with power imbalances. When it comes to the uptake given various speech acts, we are not on a level playing field. Given the sociopolitical and material reality of our lives, how are we to understand our responsibility to give uptake? Those who are in a position of institutional or structural power relative to another bear more of the responsibility to give uptake to the disenfranchised. Part of being trustworthy involves being willing to take prima facie responsibility for the distrust of those to whom one stands in a relation of relative power. And to extend the point, I suggest that the responsibility to give uptake similarly lines up along dimensions of power.

People who are members of nondominant groups are much more likely not to have their part in dialogue given uptake. This is partly because this is the way power operates: those in a position to choose whom to give or not give uptake to *can* decide to ignore, twist, mock, or deny the voices of the marginalized, whereas members of nondominant groups learn to give uptake to dominant voices as a matter of survival, socialization, and internalized oppression. Social conventions converge with linguistic ones to shape our responses to others in terms of power relations. Furthermore, those in dominant groups do not recognize that there is a prima facie moral responsibility to give uptake to the disenfranchised; we are not aware of it, we do not think it applies to us, or we reject it as a moral responsibility altogether.

The lack of reciprocity in giving uptake—the asymmetry—is a common phenomenon embedded in systems of oppression. Those with relatively more power and privilege have a prima facie responsibility to give uptake to the claims of the disenfranchised that accompanies their position of power. This moral (and in some cases, legal) responsibility is weightier for those with more power in order that inequalities and injustices can be appropriately and fairly addressed. Such a responsibility does not require that we always agree with claims of the disenfranchised, but I do think the more powerful must be on guard against the tendency to be dismissive of those claims. Those in relative positions of power, then, will take a somewhat suspicious attitude toward their own convictions about rights and harms.

So how do we enter into meaningful dialogue with others, given the complexity of uptake and silence? Lugones provides a beginning to the answer by emphasizing a kind of dialogical openness:

Una conversacion: a word, a look, a gesture, directed out, anticipating a response that anticipates a response in turn without closing out meaning not already contained in the expectations; without pulling by the roots tongues that break the circle of expectations. Our creativity lies in our putting out gestures, words, looks that break closed cycles of meaning en un desafio erotico. (Lugones 1998, 156)

Conventions can close meaning. They can create meaning that is static and, as I argued, riddled with the social conventions expressing domination and subordination. Langer says of those listening to Holocaust survivors that "we should not come to the encounter unprepared…We cannot listen to what we are about to hear with normal ears" (Langer 1991, 20). Being the sort of person who gives uptake rightly, then, requires that we learn to listen and converse differently. And learning to do that requires that we change not only speech patterns but also our ways of seeing and being in the world.

CONCLUSION

Given that dialogue between members of conflicting and disagreeing parties is part of what is involved in order to *reveal* possible shared goods, it turns out that some development of the virtues of trustworthiness and giving uptake are crucial to the project of identifying, refining, and challenging common goods, creating a more inclusive list of contemporary virtues, developing the right sorts of institutions and practices, and so on. Without the virtue of trustworthiness, in conjunction with the virtue of giving uptake, it is difficult to see how that space for dialogue between and among members of diverse and conflicting communities can be created. If we commit ourselves to the cultivation of virtues such as trustworthiness, uptake, and honesty, we will be in a better position to listen across differences and to be in relation through conflict. Being trustworthy will always involve some degree of navigating through rough and unmarked terrain, but since relations of trust are so central both to the development of subjectivity and to the sustaining of communities and societies, efforts to be trustworthy in ways I suggest will enhance and express democratic values of justice and equality in nonviolent ways.

The theory of trustworthiness that I presented situates virtue within relations of power. I began with two premises. The first premise, emerging from an analysis of the concept of trust, was that trust carries with it both the inherent vulnerability of trusting and some degree of discretionary power granted to the one trusted: trusting another alters the power relation between the parties involved. The second premise, an empirical one, was that, as socially situated and historically constructed selves, our relations are framed by institutionally sanctioned imbalances in benefits and burdens. These imbalances give rise to interpersonal and institutional relationships that are infused with the dynamics of privilege and injustice, opportunity and exploitation, recognition and marginality. Differences in social, economic, legal, and political standing, therefore, are entwined in our relationships in ways that affect the extent to which we can and should trust one another. Theorizing about the virtue of trustworthiness in light of trust and failures of trust in an unjust and imperfect world, then, contributes to moral inquiry in two ways. First, it helps clarify what it is we need to look for in others when we find ourselves in a position to trust, and second, it indicates what sort of persons we need to be in order to be worthy of the trust of others—both of these things in the context of relations of power as they are socially constructed and as they form in the trusting relationship.

Trustworthy people, I have argued, have the following dispositional features:

1. They can be counted on, as a matter of the sort of persons they are, to take care of those things that others entrust them with and their ways of caring are neither excessive nor deficient.
2. They care for that which others value "at the right times, about the right things, toward the right people, for the right end, and in the right way."
3. They reason well, exhibiting intellectual virtue.
4. They are willing to take prima facie responsibility for the distrust of those to whom they stand in relations of power.
5. They give signs and assurances of their trustworthiness.

6. They take their epistemic responsibilities seriously.
7. They are sensitive to the particularities of others.
8. They respond properly to broken trust, making reparations or at least attempting to restore broken trust when appropriate.
9. They recognize the importance of being trustworthy to the disenfranchised and oppressed.
10. They are committed to mutuality in intimate as well as in civic relationships.
11. They work to sustain connection and transform disconnection in intimate relationships, while neither privatizing nor endangering mutual flourishing.
12. They deal with hurt in relationships—both the hurt they inflict on others and the hurt they experience from others—in ways that sustain connection.
13. They exhibit the virtue of giving uptake.
14. They have other virtues such as compassion, beneficence, courage, and justice.

Finally, the extent to which we are trustworthy can be limited or enhanced by our institutions and practices. I argued that

15. full trustworthiness in individuals requires that our institutions be virtuous.

The claim that becoming trustworthy is not solely an individual task but requires a transformation of our institutions and practices could lead to a cynical view of the possibility for any of us to really be fully trustworthy—and, hence, a cynical view toward a theory which holds that it is crucial to virtue for our institutions and practices to be virtuous and then points to the corruptions of our institutions and practices. In other words, it may seem that this project suggests that, given current social and material injustices, full trustworthiness cannot be achieved but only aspired to. In a way, this is true: unless and until institutions and practices transform, full trustworthiness will be more of a vision than a reality. Writing this chapter in the aftermath of the September 11 attacks in the United States, I have sometimes found it difficult to resurrect my optimism that large-scale positive social change is possible.

On the other hand, it is clearer to me than ever before that becoming trustworthy requires a social and cultural climate in which individuals can sustain one other in their efforts to bring about justice, peace, and equality without encountering legal, economic, political, and psychological barriers and threats. Unless and until we as moral agents commit ourselves to developing full trustworthiness, institutions and practices are unlikely to be transformed.

Here, again, an Aristotelian sort of circularity emerges, not unlike that which I discussed in the first chapter. But it is not a worrisome one. People learn to become virtuous by doing virtuous actions. Although imitating virtue is not sufficient for virtue, it is a viable start. For those in a position to effect changes in the structure of institutions and practices, part of being trustworthy may involve a re-examination of the ways in which those institutions and practices rest on exploitation and oppression, and it may require resistance to them. Once we commit ourselves to cultivating this virtue, we commit ourselves to living our lives differently not just as private individuals but as persons whose lives connect with the lives of others in intersecting and overlapping ways, providing us with continuous opportunities to exhibit the features of trustworthiness and to stretch ourselves both to become that to which we aspire and to transform institutions and practices.

Being trustworthy is sometimes difficult. The intersection of power, privilege, and multiple oppressions shapes our social, historical, political, and psychological selves in ways that make relations of trust particularly difficult. Our interests often clash, and it may appear that there are many and varied conceptions of the good and no way to arbitrate or to find common ground. When conflicts arise, domination by the more powerful may serve to protect the interests of dominant groups, thus simultaneously reenacting and perpetuating domination.

In examining trust between persons of unequal power, Baier argues that the best reason for having confidence that another will care well for what you care about is that it is a common good, and "the best reason for thinking that one's own good is also a common good is being loved" (Baier 1986, 243). Of course, even if love were to provide a common good—the good of the beloved—love would be just a starting point for trusting relations. Even those who love us may get it wrong about how best to take care of what is entrusted to them. My love for Karen may make me more aware of Karen's needs, it may make me more attentive, and it may make me more eager to care well. But love, by itself, does not help me determine how best to care for Karen's valued and entrusted goods; for that, I need both moral and intellectual virtue with practical reason as a guide. Furthermore, loving and being loved by *particular* others (and sharing a desire for the good of the loved ones) doesn't give us reasons to trust or to care about being trusted by the many with whom love is not the binding emotion. That is, loving and being loved may sometimes, though not necessarily, provide the common ground that makes it most reasonable to trust, but many of our relationships are not founded on love.

The responsibility to cultivate relations of trust, then, by developing trustworthiness in ourselves and in institutions and practices, can be seen not only to concern our intimate personal relationships but to include institutional relationships as well as more impersonal relations (such as a scientist might have to "the public"). A flourishing life should be possible for each of us to partake in, and the virtuous person will not impede the flourishing of others' lives but, instead, enhance mutual flourishing in a spirit of *philia*.

Carter Heyward, in writing that she is accountable to those who are committed to justice for all, describes her people as those with whom she both shares values, commitments, and projects and to whom she is mutually accountable. They are "friends, *compañeras*, sisters and brothers, known and unknown" who are struggling together against unjust power relations.

> My people keep me growing and expect me to be relationally aware. They ask me to be honest with them about what I am doing, what I yearn for, what my commitments are, what I delight in, what I am willing to suffer, if need be die for—and what I am trying, therefore, to live for. My people ask me to realize and celebrate ways in which my accountability is reliable, trustworthy, and empowering to them as well as to me, which it is not consistently or always. (Heyward 1989, 98)

Because we do sometimes fail to be trustworthy, because we "hurt each other in ways particular to who we are, ways neither of us knows fully," as Heyward writes, we need to be forgiving. Forgiveness, she says, "is in the possibility of our reconnecting" from woundedness, alienation, and nonmutual power relations (Heyward 1989, 145). Even Aristotle reminds us that we needn't be perfect, making a point about how much we can ask of ourselves and others. We cannot demand perfection, if perfection is understood as always finding and expressing virtue precisely in each and every particular situation. We need to show proper forgiveness, then, while we hold one another and ourselves accountable in our *becoming* trustworthy, as a virtue we are committed to developing but do not yet have in its fullness.

Two final comments are called for. My objective in theorizing about trustworthiness has been to provide a conceptual account which generates practical considerations for the enhancement of trusting relationships by attending to the ways in which social and political institutions and practices intersect with the virtue of trustworthiness. I selected cases and contexts in which important issues in trust, failures of trust, and trustworthiness arise in order to draw out some central features of trustworthiness and to provide practical knowledge about how to become trustworthy. In drawing attention to neglected areas in moral philosophy and providing a lens through which we can examine them, my work helps us see what moral reasoning might be required in new cases. But although these case studies illuminate what I take to be some of the important considerations for a theory of trustworthiness as a virtue, they are not meant to be sufficient to fill out the theory. Because the mean is always relative to particulars, no theory will be able to cover every single case in advance. But while the particulars will vary, by closely examining selected cases, we have come to see what sorts of questions might need to be considered—questions that might not have arisen without a careful analysis of earlier ones. This makes it possible for us to come to new cases wiser: we know more about what to pay attention to and what sorts of questions to ask. This is one reason why it is so important to develop intellectual virtue: so we can acquire the skills of good perception and practical reasoning needed to find the mean in a given case. Other voices are needed, too, because the questions I take to be important may not encompass others' concerns. This project is but a beginning: "for, presumably, the outline must come first, to be filled in later. If the sketch is good, then anyone, it seems can advance and articulate it, and in such cases time is a good discoverer or [at least] a good co-worker" (Aristotle 1985, 1098a24).

The second comment is that this is a theory that will not—indeed, cannot—give us precise rules by which to live. (Aristotle, for instance, warns that we cannot expect precise rules for virtue to be discovered [1985, 1104a].) What it does provide, though, is a rich description of the trustworthy person in a variety of contexts and a vision of where we need to direct our attention and energy in order to become trustworthy ourselves. People in different communities and other cultures will identify other features of trustworthiness, refine or transform the ideas presented here, and situate problems in trust such that new ways of looking at trustworthiness emerge.

In war and revolution, for example, how would a theory of trustworthiness make a difference? It's daunting to contemplate these questions in the face of the United States' war on Afghanistan, or the past hundred years of violence in Ireland, or civil war in apartheid South Africa. Trustworthiness isn't all that's needed to solve problems of mass human rights violations and institutionalized brutality. Yet breakdowns of trust are surely one of the contributors to overt violence, and we can hardly go wrong in coming together to ask of ourselves and each other what trustworthiness, in this or that situation, would look like. Nonexploitative, nondominating engagement with one another in democratic processes, giving and receiving uptake, mending wounds, repairing broken trust—and with a healthy dose of forgiveness—these activities shift us away from violence and toward justice and peace.

NOTES

1. California's statute says that a husband is presumed father of his wife's child (unless he was away at all relevant times or is proven sterile, neither of which was the case here), and California courts upheld the constitutionality of its statute. The

Supreme Court upheld the California decision on appeal. *Michael H. v. Gerald D.*, 491 U.S. 110 (1989).

2. Giving uptake is important epistemologically as well, but I discuss this sort of thing in "Loopholes, Gaps, and What is Held Fast: Democratic Epistemology and Claims to Recovered Memories" (Potter 1996).

3. I focus primarily on speech acts that involve claiming, but I also examine the relation of speech to silences.

4. This is the case most of the time but, as I understand it, there are exceptions. For example, an order given by a commanding officer counts as successful even if the soldiers do not acknowledge the order. The subsequent court-martial indicates that the order was successful as a speech act.

5. The examples in the beginning of this paper are not meant to suggest that being the sort of person who gives uptake appropriately entails agreeing with him or accepting his claims.

6. I'm thinking especially of Iris Murdoch's discussion of attention in *The Sovereignty of Good* (1985).

7. For a discussion of empathy as a virtue and the role of moral education in learning how to be empathetic, see Potter, "Can Prisoners Learn Victim Empathy? An Analysis of a Relapse Prevention Program in the Kentucky State Reformatory for Men," forthcoming.

8. See Sherman 1989, 128, citing Aristotle's *Eudemian Ethics*, 1245b18-19.

9. Aristotle 1969, 1110a27.

10. As Langton notes, what we're really talking about in this case is the crime of rape—and an academic concept called "perlocutionary frustration" doesn't capture the act or meaning of rape.

Bibliography

Achebe, Chinua. 1991. "Postscript: James Baldwin." In *Critical Fictions: The Politics of Imaginative Writing*. Edited by Philomena Mariani. Seattle: Bay Press.

Alexie, Sherman. 1993. "The Approximate Size of My Favorite Tumor." In *The Lone Ranger and Tonto Fistfight in Heaven*. New York: Atlantic Monthly Press.

Aristotle. 1985. *Nicomachean Ethics*. Translated by Terence Irwin. Indianapolis: Hackett Publishing Co.

Aristotle. 1984. *The Complete Works of Aristotle: The Revised Translation. Vol. 2*. Edited and translated by Benjamin Jowett and revised by J. Barnes. Bollingen Series. Princeton, N.J.: Princeton University Press.

Aristotle. 1969. *Nicomachean Ethics*. Translated by Sir David Ross. London: Oxford University Press.

Armstrong, Louise. 1990. "Making an Issue of Incest." In *The Sexual Liberals and the Attack on Feminism*. Edited by Dorchen Leidholdt and Janice Raymond. New York: Pergamon Press.

Austin, J. L. 1975. *How to Do Things with Words*. Edited by J. O. Urmson and Marina Sbisa. Cambridge: Harvard University Press.

Baier, Annette. 1995. *Moral Prejudices*. Cambridge: Harvard University Press.

Baier, Annette. 1990. "Why Honesty is a Hard Virtue." In *Identity, Character, and Morality: Essays in Moral Psychology*. Edited by Owen Flanagan and Amelie Rorty. Cambridge: MIT Press.

Baier, Annette. 1989. "Trusting Ex-Intimates." In *Person to Person*. Edited by George Graham and Hugh LaFollette. Philadelphia: Temple University Press.

Baier, Annette. 1986. "Trust and Antitrust." *Ethics* 96 (3): 231-60.

Baier, Annette. 1985. *Postures of the Mind: Essays on Mind and Morals*. Minneapolis: University of Minnesota Press.

Belenky, Mary, Blythe Clinchy, Nancy Goldberger, and Jill Tarule. 1986. *Women's Ways of Knowing*. New York: Basic Books, Inc.

Blum, Lawrence. 1980. *Friendship, Altruism, and Morality*. Boston: Routledge & Kegan Paul.

———. 1987. "Compassion." In *The Virtues: Contemporary Essays on Moral Character*. Edited by Robert B. Kruschwitz and Robert C. Roberts. Belmont, Calif.: Wadsworth Publishing Company.

Bok, Sissela. 1987. *Lying*. New York: Random House.

Boxill, Bernard. 1992. *Blacks and Social Justice*. Lanham, Md.: Rowman & Littlefield.

Boxill, Bernard. 1976. "Self-respect and Protest." *Philosophy and Public Affairs* 6: 58-69.

Brock, Debi. 1993. "Talkin' 'Bout a Revelation: Feminist Popular Discourse on Sexual Abuse." In *And Still We Rise: Feminist Political Mobilizing in Contemporary Canada*. Edited by Linda Carty. Toronto: Women's Press.

Brody, Howard. 1992. *The Healer's Power*. New Haven, Conn.: Yale University Press.

Cahoone, Lawrence. 1992. "Limits of the Social and Relational Self." In *Selves, People, and Persons: What Does It Mean to Be a Self?* Edited by Leroy Rouner. Notre Dame, Ind.: University of Notre Dame Press.

Card, Claudia. 1990. "Gender and Moral Luck." In *Identity, Character, and Morality: Essays in Moral Psychology*. Edited by Owen Flanagan and Amelie Rorty. Cambridge: MIT Press.

Carty, Linda. 1991. "Black Women in Academia: A Statement from the Periphery." In *Unsettling Relations: The University as a Site of Feminist Struggles*. By Himani Bannerji, Linda Carty, Kari Dehli, Susan Heald, and Kate McKenna. Toronto: Women's Press.

Clarke, Cheryl. 1981. "Lesbianism: An Act of Resistance." In *This Bridge Called My Back: Writings by Radical Women of Color*. Edited by Cherrie Moraga and Gloria Anzaldua. New York: Kitchen Table: Women of Color Press.

Churchill, Ward and Jim Vander Wall. 1988. *Agents of Repression: The FBI's Secret Wars Against the Black Panther Party and the American Indian Movement*. Boston: South End Press.

Code, Lorraine. 1991. *What Can She Know? Feminist Theory and the Construction of Knowledge*. Ithaca, N.Y.: Cornell University Press.

Code, Lorraine. 1987. *Epistemic Responsibility*. Hanover, N.H.: University Press of New England.

Cohen, Jean. 1999. "Trust, Voluntary Association and Workable Democracy: The Contemporary American Discourse of Civil Society." In *Democracy and Trust*. Edited by Mark Warren. Cambridge: Cambridge University Press.

Cook, Karen, ed. 2001. *Trust in Society*. New York: Russel Sage Foundation.

Courtois, Christine. 1988. *Healing the Incest Wound: Adult Survivors in Therapy*. New York: W. W. Norton and Company.

Crisp, Roger, ed. 1996. *How Should One Live? Essays on the Virtues*. Oxford: Oxford University Press.

Davis, Angela. 1975. "The Nature of Freedom." In *Ethics In Perspective*. Edited by Karsten J. Struhl and Paula Rothenberg Struhl. New York: Random House.

————. 1981. "Rape, Racism, and the Myth of the Black Rapist." In *Women, Race, and Class.* New York: Vintage Books.

Dillon, Robin. 1995. Introduction to *Dignity, Character, and Self-Respect.* Edited by Robin Dillon. New York: Routledge.

Dworkin, Andrea. 1990. *Mercy.* New York: Four Walls Eight Windows.

Dodd, Susan. 1998. *The Mourner's Bench.* New York: William Morrow and Company.

Erdrich, Louise. 1984. *Love Medicine.* New York: Holt, Rinehart, and Winston.

Feinberg, Joel. 1970. "The Nature and Value of Rights." *Journal of Value Inquiry,* 4 (4).

Foot, Philippa. 1978. *Virtues and Vices.* Los Angeles: University of California Press.

Fornes, Marie Irene. 1980. "Fefu and Her Friends." In *Word Plays.* New York: Performing Arts Journal Publications.

Fraser, Sylvia. 1987. *My Father's House: A Memoir of Incest and of Healing.* New York: Harper and Row.

Freire, Paulo. 1992. *Pedagogy of the Oppressed.* Translated by Myra Bergman Ramos. New York: Continuum Publishing Company.

Fried, Charles. 1970. *An Anatomy of Values: Problems of Personal and Social Choice.* Cambridge: Harvard University Press.

Frye, Marilyn. 1983. "A Note on Anger." *The Politics of Reality: Essays in Feminist Theory.* Freedom, Calif.: Crossing Press.

————. 1983b. "In and Out of Harm's Way: Arrogance and Love." In *Politics of Reality.* Freedom, Calif.: Crossing Press.

Geiger, Susan and Jacqueline Zita. 1985. "White Traders: The Caveat Emptor of Women's Studies." *Journal of Thought* 20 (3): 106-21.

Gilligan, Carol. 1982. *In A Different Voice.* Cambridge: Harvard University Press.

Good, David. 1988. "Individuals, Interpersonal Relations, and Trust." *Trust: Making and Breaking Cooperative Relations.* Edited by Diego Gambetta. New York: Basil Blackwell Ltd.

Govier, Trudy. 1991. "Trust, Distrust, and Feminist Theory." *Hypatia* 7 (winter): 16-33.

————. 1994. "Is It a Jungle Out There? Trust, Distrust, and the Construction of Social Reality." *Dialogue* 33: 237-52.

————. 1998. *Dilemmas of Trust.* Montreal: McGill-Queen's University Press.

Hardie, W. F. R. 1980. *Aristotle's Ethical Theory.* 2nd ed. Oxford: Clarendon Press. Hardie's citation of the *Nicomachean Ethics* is from *Works of Aristotle*: Oxford Translation, ed. J.A. Smith and W.D. Ross.

Harre, Rom. 1999. "Trust and Its Surrogates: Psychological Foundations of Political Process." In *Democracy and Trust.* Edited by Mark Warren. Cambridge: Cambridge University Press.

Herman, Judith Lewis. 1992. *Trauma and Recovery.* New York: Basic Books.

Heyward, Carter. 1989. *Touching Our Strength: The Erotic as Power and the Love of God.* New York: Harper Collins.

Hill, Thomas. 1987. "Servility and Self-Respect." In *The Virtues: Contemporary Essays on Moral Character.* Edited by Robert B. Kruschwitz and Robert C. Roberts.

Belmont, Calif.: Wadsworth.

Hoagland, Sarah. 1990. *Lesbian Ethics: Toward New Value*. Palo Alto, Calif.: Institute of Lesbian Studies.

Horsburgh, H. J. N. 1960. "The Ethics of Trust." *Philosophical Quarterly,* 10 (October), 343-354.

Jackson, Jennifer. 2001. *Truth, Trust, and Medicine*. London and New York: Routledge.

Jordan, Judith. 1991. "The Meaning of Mutuality." In *Women's Growth in Connection: Writings from the Stone Center*. Judith Jordan, Alexandra Kaplan, Jean Baker Miller, Irene Stiver, and Janet Surrey. New York: Guilford Press.

———. 1995. "Relational Awareness: Transforming Disconnection." In *Work in Progress*. Wellesley, Mass.: Stone Center Publications.

Josselson, Ruthellen. 2000. "Relationship as a Path to Integrity, Wisdom, and Meaning." In *The Psychology of Mature Spirituality: Integrity, Wisdom, Transcendence*. Edited by Polly Young-Eisendrath and Melvin E. Miller. Philadelphia: Routledge.

Kant, Immanuel. 1993. *Grounding for the Metaphysics of Morals*. Translated by James W. Ellington. Indianapolis: Hackett Publishing Company, Inc.

Kraut, Richard. 1989. *Aristotle on the Human Good*. Princeton, N.J.: Princeton University Press.

Langer, Lawrence. 1991. *Holocaust Testimonies: The Ruins of Memory*. New Haven, Conn.: Yale University Press.

Langton, Rae. 1993. "Speech Acts and Unspeakable Acts." *Philosophy and Public Affairs*, 293-330.

Le Carre, John. 1986. *The Perfect Spy*. New York: Knopf.

Lorde, Audre. 1984. "Uses of the Erotic: The Erotic as Power." In *Sister Outsider*. Freedom, Calif.: Crossing Press.

Lugones, María. 1997. "Playfulness, 'World'-traveling, and Loving Perception." In *Feminist Social Thought: A Reader*. Edited by Diana Meyers. New York: Routledge.

———. 1998. "El Pasar Discontinuo de la Chacapera/Tortillera del Barrio a la Barra al Movimiento" (The discontinuous passing of the cachapera/tortillera from the barrio to the bar to the movement). In *Daring to be Good: Essays in Feminist Ethico-Politics*. Edited by Bat-Ami Bar On and Ann Ferguson. New York: Routledge.

Lugones, María and Elizabeth Spelman. 1986. "Have We Got a Theory For You! Feminist Theory, Cultural Imperialism, and the Demand for 'The Woman's Voice.'" In *Women and Values: Readings in Recent Feminist Philosophy*. Edited by Marilyn Pearsall. Belmont, Calif.: Wadsworth.

Luhmann, Niklas. 1979. *Trust and Power*. Chichester: John Wiley and Sons Ltd.

MacIntyre, Alasdair. 1984. *After Virtue*. Notre Dame, Ind.: University of Notre Dame Press.

Martin, Biddy and Chandra Talpade Mohanty. 1986. "Feminist Politics: What's Home Got to Do With It?" In *Feminist Studies/Critical Studies*. Edited by Teresa deLauretis. Bloomington, Ind.: Indiana University Press.

Martin, Mike. 1993. "Honesty in Love." *Journal of Value Inquiry* 27 (3-4): 497-507.

Matthiessen, Peter. 1991. *In the Spirit of Crazy Horse*. New York: Penguin Books.

McFall, Lynn. 1987. "Integrity." *Ethics* 98 (October).

Miles, Steven H. and Allison August. 1990. "Courts, Gender and 'The Right to Die'." *Law, Medicine & Health Care* 18 (1-2): 85-95.

Mill, J. S. 1978. *On Liberty*. Edited by Elizabeth Rapaport. Indianapolis: Hackett Publishing Co.

Mills, Charles. 1997. *The Racial Contract*. Ithaca, N.Y.: Cornell University Press.

Miller, Jean Baker. 1986. "What Do We Mean by Relationships?" In *Stone Center Work in Progress*. Wellesley, Mass.: Wellesley College.

Murdoch, Iris. 1961. *A Severed Head*. Toronto: Penguin Books.

———. 1985. *The Sovereignty of Good*. New York: Schocken Books.

Nagel, Thomas. 1979. *Mortal Questions*. Cambridge: Cambridge University Press.

Nyberg, David. 1993. *The Varnished Truth: Truth Telling and Deceiving in Ordinary Life*. Chicago: University of Chicago Press.

Okin, Susan Moller. 1989. *Justice, Gender, and the Family*. New York: Basic Books.

O'Nan, Stewart. 1996. *The Names of the Dead*. New York: Doubleday.

Oliver, Harold. 1992. "The Relational Self." In *Selves, People, and Persons: What Does It Mean to Be a Self?* Edited by Leroy Rouner. Notre Dame, Ind.: University of Notre Dame Press.

Oliverio, Annamarie. 1998. *The State of Terror*. Albany, N.Y.: State University of New York Press.

Paul, Ellen Frankel, Fred Miller, and Jeffrey Paul, eds. 1998. *Virtue and Vice*. Cambridge: Cambridge University Press.

Pellegrini, Ann. 1992. "S(h)ifting the Terms of Hetero/Sexism: Gender, Power, Homophobias." In *Homophobia: How We All Pay the Price*. Edited by Warren J. Blumenfeld. Boston: Beacon Press.

Pharr, Suzanne. 1988. *Homphobia: A Weapon of Sexism*. Little Rock, Ark.: Chardon Press.

Potter, Nancy. 1996. "Loopholes, Gaps, and What is Held Fast: Democratic Epistemology and Claims to Recovered Memories." *Philosophy, Psychiatry, and Psychology*. (3:4): 237-54.

———. 2001. "Is Being Unforgiving a Vice?" In *Feminists Doing Ethics*. Edited by Peggy DesAutels and Joanne Waugh. New York: Rowman & Littlefield.

———. Forthcoming. "Can Prisoners Learn Victim Empathy? An Analysis of a Relapse Prevention Program in the Kentucky State Reformatory for Men." In *Putting Peace into Practice: Evaluating Policy at the Local and Global Levels*. Rodopi Press.

Rachels, James. 1975. "Why Privacy is Important." *Philosophy and Public Affairs* 4 (4): 295-333.

Rawls, John. 1971. *A Theory of Justice*. Cambridge: Harvard University Press.

Raymond, Janice. 1986. *A Passion for Friends: Toward a Philosophy of Female Friendship*. Boston: Beacon Press.

Reagon, Bernice Johnson. 1992. "Coalition Politics: Turning the Century." In *Race, Class, and Gender: An Anthology*. Edited by Margaret Anderson and Patricia Hill Collins. Belmont, Calif.: Wadsworth Publishing Company.

Reiman, Jeffrey. 1976. "Privacy, Intimacy, and Personhood." *Philosophy and Public Affairs* 6: 26-44.

Rich, Adrienne. 1978. "Cartographies of Silence." In *The Dream of a Common Language: Poems 1974-1977*. New York: W. W. Norton and Company.

———. 1979. "Disloyal to Civilization: Feminism, Racism, Gynephobia." In *On Lies, Secrets, and Silence*. New York: W. W. Norton and Co.

———. 1979. "Women and Honor: Some Notes on Lying." In *On Lies, Secrets, and Silence*. New York: W. W. Norton & Company.

———.1980. "Compulsory Heterosexuality and Lesbian Existence." *Signs: Journal of Women in Culture and Society* 5 (4): 631-60.

Ross, W. D. and J. A. Smith, eds. *Works of Aristotle*. Oxford Translation. Oxford: Clarendon Press.

Ruddick, Sara. 1989. *Maternal Thinking: Towards a Politics of Peace*. Boston: Beacon Press.

Scheffler, Samuel. 1982. *The Rejection of Consequentialism: A Philosophical Investigation of the Considerations Underlying Rival Moral Conceptions*. Oxford: Clarendon Press.

Schneider, Carl. 1998. *The Practice of Autonomy: Patients, Doctors, and Medical Decisions*. Oxford: Oxford University Press.

Seligman, Adam. 1997. *The Problem of Trust*. Princeton, N.J.: Princeton University Press.

Sherman, Nancy. 1989. *The Fabric of Character*. Oxford: Clarendon Press.

Slote, Michael. 2001. *Morals From Motives*. Oxford: Oxford University Press.

Smart, J. J. C. and Bernard Williams. 1973. *Utilitarianism For and Against*. Cambridge: Cambridge University Press.

Stoltenberg, John. 1989. "Feminist Activism and Male Sexual Identity." In *Refusing to be a Man: Essays on Sex and Justice*. New York: Penguin Books.

Strikwerda, Robert and Larry May. 1992. "Male Friendship and Intimacy." In *Rethinking Masculinity: Philosophical Explorations in Light of Feminism*. Edited by Larry May and Robert Strikwerda. Lanham, Md.: Rowman & Littlefield.

Sztompka, Piotr. 1999. *Trust: A Sociological Theory*. Cambridge: Cambridge University Press.

Ta hsueh. 1943. *The Great Learning and the Mean-in-Action*. Translated by E. R. Hughes. New York: Dutton and Co.

Terr, Lenore. 1990. *Too Scared to Cry: Psychic Trauma in Childhood*. New York: Basic Books.

Thomson, Rupert. 1996. *The Insult*. New York: Alfred A. Knopf.

Trianosky, Greg. 1990. "What Is Virtue Ethics All About?" *American Philosophical Quarterly*, 335-44.

Tronto, Joan. 1993. *Moral Boundaries: A Political Argument for an Ethic of Care*. New York: Routledge.

Urmson, J. O. 1980. "Aristotle's Doctrine of the Mean." In *Essays on Aristotle's Ethics*. Edited by Amelie Rorty. Los Angeles: University of California Press.

Vangelisti, Anita. 2001. "Making Sense of Hurtful Interactions in Close Relationships: When Hurt Feelings Create Distance." In *Attribution, Communication Be-*

havior, and Close Relationships. Cambridge: Cambridge University Press.

Walker, Maureen. 1999. "Race, Self, and Society: Relational Challenges in a Culture of Disconnection." In *Work in Progress*. Wellesley, Mass.: Stone Center Publications.

Warren, Mark, ed. 1999. *Democracy and Trust*. Cambridge: Cambridge University Press.

Wasserman, Cathy. 1992. "FMS: The Backlash Against Survivors." *Sojourner: The Woman's Forum* 18 (3).

Watson, Gary. 1990. "On the Primacy of Character." In *Identity, Character, and Morality: Essays in Moral Psychology*. Edited by Owen Flanagan and Amelie Oksenberg Rorty. Cambridge: MIT Press.

Weiler, Kathleen. 1988. *Women Teaching for Change: Gender, Class & Power*. New York: Bergin & Garvey Publishers.

Whitbeck, Caroline. 1989. "A Different Reality: Feminist Ontology." In *Women, Knowledge, and Reality*. Edited by Ann Garry and Marilyn Pearsall. New York: Routledge.

Williams, Bernard. 1973. *Problems of the Self*. Cambridge: Cambridge University Press.

———. 1988. "Ethical Consistency." In *Essays on Moral Realism*. Edited by Geoffrey Sayre-McCord. Ithaca, N.Y.: Cornell University Press.

——— 1988. "Formal Structures and Social Reality." In *Trust: Making and Breaking Cooperative Relations*. Edited by Diego Gambetta. New York: Basil Blackwell Ltd.

Williams, Patricia J. 1991. *The Alchemy of Race and Rights*. Cambridge: Harvard University Press.

Wilson, Barbara. *The Dog-Collar Murders*. Seattle: Seal Press.

Wittgenstein, Ludwig. 1969. *On Certainty*. Edited by G. E. M. Anscombe and G. H. von Wright. Translated by Denis Paul and G. E. M. Anscombe. New York: Harper and Row.

Young, Iris Marion. 1990. *Justice and the Politics of Difference*. Princeton, N.J.: Princeton University Press.

Index

About the Author

Nancy Nyquist Potter is an Associate Professor of Philosophy at the University of Louisville. She has published articles in feminist ethics, philosophy of psychiatry, and philosophies of peace, and is currently editing an anthology called *Putting Peace Into Practice: Evaluating Policy on Local and Global Levels* that will be published by Rodopi Press. She is a board member of the Association for the Advancement of Philosophy and Psychiatry and a board member of International Philosophers for Peace.